PHRASE AND SUBJECT
STUDIES IN LITERATURE AND MUSIC

LEGENDA

LEGENDA, founded in 1995 by the European Humanities Research Centre of the University of Oxford, is now a joint imprint of the Modern Humanities Research Association and Maney Publishing. Titles range from medieval texts to contemporary cinema and form a widely comparative view of the modern humanities, including works on Arabic, Catalan, English, French, German, Greek, Italian, Portuguese, Russian, Spanish, and Yiddish literature. An Editorial Board of distinguished academic specialists works in collaboration with leading scholarly bodies such as the Society for French Studies and the British Comparative Literature Association.

MHRA

The Modern Humanities Research Association (MHRA) encourages and promotes advanced study and research in the field of the modern humanities, especially modern European languages and literature, including English, and also cinema. It also aims to break down the barriers between scholars working in different disciplines and to maintain the unity of humanistic scholarship in the face of increasing specialization. The Association fulfils this purpose primarily through the publication of journals, bibliographies, monographs and other aids to research.

Maney Publishing is one of the few remaining independent British academic publishers. Founded in 1900 the company has offices both in the UK, in Leeds and London, and in North America, in Boston. Since 1945 Maney Publishing has worked closely with learned societies, their editors, authors, and members, in publishing academic books and journals to the highest traditional standards of materials and production.

A Musical Story by Chopin (1879), by Andrew Carrick Gow (1848–1920)
British, oil on canvas (698mm × 902mm): by kind permission of the Tate Collection UK
Picture research by Robert Samuels

Phrase and Subject

Studies in Literature and Music

EDITED BY DELIA DA SOUSA CORREA

LEGENDA

Modern Humanities Research Association and Maney Publishing
2006

Published by the
Modern Humanities Research Association and Maney Publishing
1 Carlton House Terrace
London SW1Y 5DB
United Kingdom

LEGENDA is an imprint of the
Modern Humanities Research Association and Maney Publishing

Maney Publishing is the trading name of W. S. Maney & Son Ltd,
whose registered office is at Hudson Road, Leeds LS9 7DL, UK

ISBN 1 904713 07 6 / 978-1-904713-07-4

First published 2006

Printed in Great Britain

Cover: 875 Design

Copy-Editor: Michael Wood

CONTENTS

ACKNOWLEDGEMENTS

This volume emerges from a project undertaken jointly with Robert Samuels of The Open University's Music Department. His vision and enthusiasm were vital to the book's inception, and he played a major part in planning the structure and content of the collection to which he is also a contributor. The Arts Faculty of The Open University provided a supportive context for us to develop our combined interests in literature and music, and it generously funded two conferences, from which half of the present essays originate. The enthusiastic response to the initial call for conference papers alerted us to the extent and calibre of research currently being undertaken into liaisons between literature and music, and was the inspiration behind this book. Those who contributed to the conferences and who wrote the chapters that follow have helped to foster the shared research culture that is the the book's *raison d'être*.

The Modern Humanities Research Association generously provided subvention funding to make publication of this book possible and the Arts Faculty of The Open University made a substantial grant to cover the cost of illustrations and indexing. Thanks are due to the Tate Picture Library and to M. Christian Ducasse for permission to reproduce images from their collections. I should like to thank Graham Nelson and Michael Wood at Legenda for their commitment to producing fine scholarly books. Remaining errors in this one are my responsibility. Thanks also go to Peter Dayan for help in procuring the cover image for this volume, to Margaret Christie for compiling the index, and to Anne Ford and Yvonne Reynolds at The Open University for administrative support. I am especially grateful to my family, above all to my daughter Rosamund, to whom this book is dedicated, for accommodating my work on the collection so early in her existence.

Delia da Sousa Correa
Literature Department
The Open University

ABOUT THE CONTRIBUTORS

Daniel Albright is Ernest Bernbaum Professor of Literature at the University of Harvard. His books include *Representation and the Imagination: Beckett, Kafka, Nabokov, and Schoenberg* (1981) and *Untwisting the Serpent: Modernism in Music, Literature, and Other Arts* (2000).

Sue Asbee lectured at Queen Mary College, University of London before joining The Open University as Staff Tutor in Literature. She has written on Kate Chopin for an Open University series on *The Nineteenth Century Novel* (2001), and has published on Flann O'Brien, Virginia Woolf, and T. S. Eliot, among others.

Rosamund Bartlett lectures in Russian and music at the University of Durham. Her books include *Wagner and Russia* (1995), and *Chekhov: Scenes from a Life* (2004). She has published several articles on sonata form in Chekhov, and her latest project is a cultural history of opera in Russia for Yale University Press.

Guillaume Bordry is Professeur agrégé des lettres modernes at the Université de Nancy II, teaching French language and history. He is currently completing a doctoral thesis at the Sorbonne nouvelle (Paris III) and the Conservatoire national supérieur de musique, Paris, on the topic of musical ekphrasis and the verbal description of music.

Mark Byron was awarded his PhD at the University of Cambridge in 2001. His dissertation examines the composition and transmission of exilic modernist texts, specifically Ezra Pound's *Pisan Cantos* and Samuel Beckett's *Watt*, and the consequences for theories of textuality and text editing. He has published on Renaissance Tragedy and the treatment of technology in Heidegger and Beckett, and has contributed to the Ezra Pound Encyclopedia (forthcoming).

Federico Celestini is coordinator of the musicological team in the research project *Moderne — Wien und Zentraleuropa um 1900* at the Karl-Franzens-Universität, Graz. He has published on medieval music and instrumental music of the eighteenth century, as well as on theoretical and methodical questions in musicology. He is currently preparing a book about the Grotesque in Viennese modernism.

Tom Cooper studied at the Guildhall School of Music and the Royal College of Music in London before obtaining a PhD at the University of Liverpool. He is an Associate Lecturer on various arts courses at The Open University, and is currently writing on nineteenth-century French opera for a book on French music after Berlioz.

David Crilly is Director of Research and Senior Lecturer in Music at Anglia Ruskin University, Cambridge, and since 1988 has been Artistic Director of the annual Cambridge Shakespeare Festival. He has published on music aesthetics and analysis, semiotic theory, and the music of Debussy and Charlie Parker. His research interests include intertextuality in twentieth-century music, especially in Britten and Tippett, and the lute music of John Dowland.

Tili Boon Cuillé is Assistant Professor of French in the Department of Romance Languages and Literatures at Washington University in St Louis. Her research focuses on French eighteenth-century literature, aesthetics, and the performing arts. She is the author of *Narrative Interludes: Musical Tableaux in Eighteenth-Century French Texts* (2006) and is currently working on the Enlightenment irrational.

Delia da Sousa Correa is a lecturer in Literature at The Open University. Her research focuses on connections between literature, music, science, and other aspects of nineteenth-century culture. She is the author of *George Eliot, Music and Victorian Culture* (2002) and editor of *The Nineteenth-Century Novel: Realisms* (2000). She is currently working on Katherine Mansfield.

Peter Dayan is Reader in French at the University of Edinburgh. After writing books on Mallarmé, Nerval, Lautréamont, and Sand, he produced a series of essays on the necessity of music to the concept of literature, and vice versa, from Sand to Derrida via Debussy; he is now working on a book on that subject, *Music Writing Literature*.

Tina Frühauf is an editor for the Répertoire international de littérature musicale (RILM), City University of New York. Her research interests include synagogue music, music and identity, music and emigration, and Jewish music in the Balkans. Her published work includes 'The Destruction of a Cultural Tradition in Germany: Organs and Organ Music in the Synagogue' (2001).

Anthony Gritten is Head of Postgraduate Studies and Research at the Royal Northern College of Music, Manchester. Co-editor of *Music and Gesture* (2006), his research interests include Igor Stravinsky, French musical and intellectual culture, performance studies, philosophy and aesthetics of music, and theory and analysis of twentieth-century music.

Regula Hohl Trillini studied the piano in Basel and London, qualifying as a teacher and chamber music player. She teaches English and piano at the Grammar School in Olten, Switzerland, and lectures in English at the University of Basel, where she has recently completed her PhD on fictional representations of domestic music making.

Lawrence Kramer is Professor of English and Music at Fordham University, New York, and co-editor of *19th-Century Music*. His books include *Music as Cultural Practice, 1800–1900* (1990), *Classical Music and Postmodern Knowledge* (1995), and *Musical Meaning* (2001).

Robert Samuels is a lecturer in Music at The Open University. His work on nineteenth- and twentieth-century music is principally concerned with analytical theory, aesthetics, and relationships between music and other art forms, especially literature. He has written on Schubert, Schumann, Mahler (*Mahler's Sixth Symphony: A Study in Musical Semiotics*, 1995), and Birtwistle, and is currently writing on the nineteenth-century symphony and the novel.

Lawrence Woof is a full-time composer and performer. He previously worked for six years at Lancaster University as a Research Fellow in the departments of Music and English, often in collaboration with the Computing Department. He has research interests in eighteenth- and nineteenth-century culture, humanities, computing, and composition.

INTRODUCTION

Delia da Sousa Correa

The confluence between literature and music — long hymned as sister arts — is recently established as a dynamic field of critical inquiry. Criticism of both arts has begun to employ the innovative comparative and interdisciplinary approaches that characterize the present collection of essays. As the combined literary and musical resonances of the title indicate, this book works between literature and music, investigating their mutual influence and their common historical ground. It is a timely enterprise in the context both of present-day literary criticism, and of what has come to be termed the 'new musicology'.

Until the mid-1980s critical approaches that brought together literature and music, rather than literature and the visual arts, were rare.[1] Since then, increasing attention has been paid to aesthetic and cultural interactions between literature and music. As the field of literary studies progressively embraces interdisciplinarity, there have been signs of a burgeoning interest in the role played by music within literary culture. This has frequently been accompanied by a desire to understand how these interactions have engaged with other cultural developments such as ideologies of gender (the subject of several essays in this collection).

Critical attention to the interaction of literature and music might be seen, in part, as an attempt to recover, as well as account for, the aesthetic that led nineteenth-century composers to style themselves as *Tondichter*, or 'sound-poets', and writers to bemoan their self-perceived failings as composers — a line stretching at least from Rousseau to Anthony Burgess. This aesthetic has also impinged upon those keen to assert oppositions rather than correspondences between the two arts. Paradoxically, an understanding of music in literary terms and of literature in musical terms has been fundamental to our efforts to apprehend the distinctive qualities of each art.

The diversity of contemporary critical theory has opened up new ways of conceptualizing the connections between literature and music. These often emerge from a reconfiguration of the relationship between music and language that has been a source of fascination since ancient times. Fundamental contrasts between the clear, referential attributes of verbal language and the fluid, indefinable nature of musical expression seem harder to sustain than they once did. In her 1942 study *Philosophy in a New Key* Susanne Langer contrasted the 'fixed connotation[s]' of verbal language with the indefinite nature of musical expression, the latter, in her view, being an advantage since music, unlike language, has the power to express contradictory emotions.[2] Current theorists of language and literature do not share Langer's confidence in the stable referentiality of language, and this skepticism has reopened and enriched long-standing debates about analogies between music and language.[3]

The representational power of both language and the visual arts once made them natural companions. Now, language is valued for the referential uncertainty that was previously music's preserve, and music, arguably, offers a richer fund of analogy for literature and new modes of understanding language itself — a possibility explored below in the chapters by Daniel Albright and Peter Dayan. Albright calls our attention to Wittgenstein's insight that 'understanding a sentence is much more akin to understanding a theme in music than one may think',[4] whilst Dayan finds that music maintains an insistent relevance within deconstructive theory.

With language beginning to look more like music, the challenge for music criticism has been to come to terms with the loss of music's 'privileged access to the ineffable'.[5] As Lawrence Kramer sees it, 'the resistance to signification once embodied by music now seems to be an inextricable part of signification itself'; it follows that music may itself 'be understood as part of a general signifying process, and network of cultural practices'.[6] Music's 'meaning' can now be discussed in terms of these processes and networks in a way not previously encouraged by the formal practices of musicology.

Since the 1990s important attempts have been made to apply a diversity of critical theories to musical texts.[7] This has been Kramer's major project,[8] and is exemplified here in his essay on the cultural contexts and significance of Beethoven's 'Ghost' Trio. Anthony Gritten's essay also probes some of the theoretical implications of a situation in which music has come to look more like literature. Work in this field is driven by a diversity of contending theoretical commitments; yet, underpinning this variety is a determination to move beyond discipline boundaries. Whilst relationships between literature and music are central to this book, the essays involve approaches that are interdisciplinary rather than simply comparative: bringing literary and musical criticism together produces not so much a mutual accommodation as a shared revision of critical practice. Indeed, music itself provides a powerful metaphor for the kind of interdisciplinary scrutiny that emphasizes the vertical or 'homophonic' relationships between art works in different media, rather than viewing them horizontally or 'polyphonically', with only intermittent attention to moments of harmonious coincidence.[9]

Phrase and Subject draws together an international group of authors from a wide variety of different academic disciplines and backgrounds. The contributor biographies indicate that the field of study in question encourages the mixture of scholarly and practitioner involvement to which many interdisciplinary endeavours aspire, attracting authors not only in academic teaching posts, but also performers, directors, and composers. Earlier versions of eight of the essays were given as papers at conferences held under the auspices of The Open University (UK) in 2001 and 2002. Further contributions were invited so that the final collection would offer both an introduction to the interdisciplinary study of music and literature, and exemplary studies of the interactions between specific works. The book groups together chapters devoted predominantly to theoretical, critical, and historical inquiry. This structure helps to define the scope of the field, but by no means represents a system of fixed categories: many of the essays would have been equally at home within different groupings. The variety on offer here gives some indication of the increasingly serious attention that intersections between music and literature have received in recent years.

The first section, 'Theoretical Issues', presents a series of reflections on the relationship between music and language. The contributions consider both the consequences for theories of language of analogies with music, and the challenge posed to music by its apparent assimilation by literary theory. The second section, 'Generic Alliances', groups together chapters dealing with allusions to music within literary texts and to literature within musical works. Music is scrutinized as an agent of cultural value in essays that consider music's use in promoting realism within the eighteenth-century novel, the role of narrative in containing the potency of the nineteenth-century musical sublime, and music as an illuminating analogue for literary modernism. The third section, 'The Gendered Text', features works in which connections between music and literature are especially germane to the interrogation of gender — an important dimension of recent research on literature and music. The essays discuss Germaine de Staël's riposte to Rousseau's view of female musicality, the depiction of female musicianship in Victorian poetry, the gendered narratives of two of Schumann's song cycles, and the role of musical analogy in Kate Chopin's protest against the gender stereotypes of late nineteenth-century Louisiana. The final section, 'Narrative Modes', investigates literary and musical works that are structured on close formal comparisons between the arts. Essays considering literary works in which music is an analogy for literary composition are complemented by others that examine musical works whose structure is informed by literary models. There are analyses of Dostoevsky's affinities with Bach and Wagner, Berlioz's construction of imagined literary analogues, Mahler's intermedial exploitation of works of literature and visual arts, and Britten's literary subversions of the Requiem genre.

The challenges and advantages involved in finding a language for this interdisciplinary field of study are concerns that underpin many of the chapters in this collection. These concerns go hand in hand with the ever-teasing issue of how the relationship between music and language is to be understood. In the opening chapter Daniel Albright scrutinizes several common approaches to the question of music's 'linguistic' status. He examines definitions of music as a 'complete' language, or as something intrinsically opposed to language. In the view of music as a complete language, music and speech are so closely identified that they can replace one another — as implied in E. M. Forster's account of the 'dialogue between orchestra and piano' in Beethoven's Fourth Piano Concerto. Albright also surveys attempts to describe music in terms of a 'defective' language, as, for example, the speculations about music's potential as a language without nouns in early music writers such as Johann Mattheson and Benedetto Marcello. Having queried the validity of attempts to impose linguistic models on music, Albright considers the views of theorists such as Hanslick and Stravinsky, who saw music as quite unconnected with the semantic structures of language, and he discusses examples of compositions that apparently support this view. However, it is doubtful whether so complete an opposition between music and language can be sustained, for our tendency to verbalize musical experience appears inescapable. In *Untwisting the Serpent* (2000) and earlier works, music is central to Albright's consideration of the obdurate mutuality of abstraction and representation in art. In the present essay he savours the paradox whereby 'the more we try to understand music as language, the more strongly it resists that understanding; and the more we try to understand music as the opposite of language, the more sweetly, strongly, plainly it speaks to the ear'.

In the second chapter Anthony Gritten continues some of the lines of inquiry established by Albright. His essay poses and discusses a number of questions from a musicologist's viewpoint. What is the 'gap' between the musical and the textual? What can theories of performance predicated on notions of music as a linguistic or literary object tell us about what performers do and think they do? Indeed, can music be understood without 'reading' it? Are there ways of phrasing what music and performers do that work best prior to the interventions of literary models and methods into critical activity? Drawing on Mikhail Bakhtin's notion of 'eventness', Gritten suggests that, for ethical reasons, the critical interpretation of musical performance is — ought to be — irreducible to the purely textual or literary.

Tina Frühauf, in her essay on Nietzsche, considers the role of music in *Human, All Too Human* (1876). This work marks a shift from Nietzsche's specific focus on music in *The Birth of Tragedy*, and is concerned chiefly with his observations on psychology, social relationships, politics, and religion. Nonetheless, Nietzsche's ongoing evaluation of music can be found dispersed throughout his analysis of society and culture. Frühauf investigates Nietzsche's complex and contradictory reflections on the symbolic content of music and its relationship to literature — concerns that are central to many of the writers and composers discussed in this volume.

Peter Dayan, concluding the first section, scrutinizes the intransigent correlations between language and music, with specific reference to Jacques Derrida and deconstructive theory. He points out that deconstruction, as a critical practice, would at first seem unsuited to the study of music, since music, for Derrida, symbolizes the abstract in art, and so marks the limit of the discourse that deconstruction apparently exists to analyse. However, whilst this may explain why Derrida does not write directly about music, Dayan proposes that music nevertheless plays an important role in his theorization of textuality. Artistic abstraction, although it threatens to silence deconstruction, is also necessary to its analysis of the origin of meaning. Dayan suggests that music emerges as the perfect metaphor for Derrida's conception of the original unknowable 'trace'. His essay also investigates how in *La Carte postale*, for example, Derrida deals with the individuality of musical works by a composer such as Monteverdi.

The second section, dealing with 'Generic Alliances' between literature and music, begins with a consideration of musical realism. Lawrence Woof's essay on 'Samuel Richardson, Italian Opera and English Oratorio' explores the reason for music's prominence in *Clarissa* and *Sir Charles Grandison*, and the author looks for answers to these questions in the links between music and the novel that are rooted in the cultural and economic life of eighteenth-century Britain. In particular, Woof examines the classical concept of 'luxury', and its points of overlap with the emerging discourse of 'sensibility', to cast light on the relationship between eighteenth-century literature and music.

Far-reaching cultural contexts are fundamental to Lawrence Kramer's essay on 'Beethoven's "Ghost" Trio and the Wheel of History'. Kramer's influential research has rapidly advanced his advocacy of the important modes of understanding music that are offered by critical theory. His work frequently allows us to see musical compositions as 'shaping forces in the culture of their era rather than as mere reflections of it'.[10] In the present chapter Kramer examines one of the paradoxes of music history: that European instrumental music in the first half of the nineteenth century developed a strong tendency to affiliate itself with literary forms, especially narrative, at the same time that its apparent autonomy was valorized and increasingly advocated as the model for art in general. Kramer suggests potential explanations for this apparent contradiction. Perhaps 'music was simply recovering the narrative connections' shed during its 'progressive "emancipation" from language', a dissociation epitomized by Beethoven's status as a composer of 'pure' instrumental music. Alternatively, narrative constructs may have helped to contain the avowed transcendent powers of instrumental music, regarded as 'both magnificent and dangerous'. The 'ordinary' is, paradoxically, a somewhat novel focus of aesthetic and cultural attention, but Kramer employs it to suggest that narrative may have offered an accommodation between the ordinary and this extreme sublimity of music. Kramer's essay examines Beethoven's 1807 'Ghost' Trio (Piano Trio in D Major, op. 70, no. 1), one of the earliest compositions to raise these issues, and discusses it in relation to Shakespeare's *Macbeth* and E. T. A. Hoffmann's famous review 'Beethoven's Instrumental Music'. Hoffmann, the acknowledged master of the grotesque and uncanny in literature, seems an especially apt subject for Kramer's elucidation of the ordinary; the German *unheimlich* is, after all, a word that contains both the unfamiliar and the ordinary within it — indeed, distinctions between the meanings of its component parts have segued so far that *heimlich*, literally 'homely' (or 'ordinary'), is sometimes a synonym for the *Unheimliche*, or 'uncanny'.[11]

If music was a more central feature of nineteenth-century culture than has sometimes been acknowledged, it was, in different ways, equally crucial to the Modern period, when artists consciously working amidst the echoes of Pater's famous dictum that 'all art constantly aspires to the condition of music', were influenced by the philosophy of Bergson and a multiplicity of other theories about rhythmical correspondences between the arts. Mark Byron's essay investigates the cultural and historical contexts in which literary modernism intersects with music, displaying the same fascination with the musical presences within modernist literature that has impelled much of Daniel Albright's research. Rather than treat the interchange of music and literature as an entirely thematic or rhetorical device, Byron observes a fertile collaboration. He singles out two cases where musical notation actually occurs within a literary text: the violin line of Clément Janequin's *Le Chant des oiseaux* in Canto LXXV of Ezra Pound's *Pisan Cantos*, and the threnes and choruses in Samuel Beckett's *Watt*. For Pound and Beckett, steeped as they were in theories of correlation between different art forms, music 'served as an exemplary field for meditation upon the status and purpose of literary production'. The presence of music within their texts challenges the reader to share in this meditation and to find new modes of interpretation.

The group of essays on 'The Gendered Text' represents a significant dimension of the recent study of connections between music and literature in the eighteenth and nineteenth centuries.[12] Tili Boon Cuillé, in the first essay of this section, considers the response of Germaine de Staël to Rousseau's writings on music. Referring to Staël's novel *Corinne*, Cuillé reads the author's use of musical allusion and her representations of female musical performance as a particularly subversive appropriation of musical ideals communicated in Rousseau's *Lettre sur la musique française*, the *Essai sur l'origine des langues*, and his novel *Julie*. Cuillé's essay is a contribution to the recent scholarly re-examination of long-standing assumptions that Staël was largely uncritical of Rousseau's writings on women. Cuillé notes how Staël exploits specific aspects of Rousseau's discourse on music in order to contest his view of female creativity; she demonstrates that Staël used Rousseau's terminology to lend authority to Corinne's conversation and to enhance the descriptions of her musical sensibility and improvisatory performances. By appropriating Rousseau's musical ideal on behalf of a woman, Staël freed her heroine from the 'stigma of sensuality' with which her sex was traditionally marked, and granted her — and, by extension, women in general — access to a creative realm from which she had previously been excluded.

The next chapter moves on to examine a once copious sub-genre of British poetry, namely, that featuring women at the pianoforte. Regula Hohl Trillini investigates the operation within Victorian and Edwardian poetry of particular feminine and musical tropes more readily associated with realist prose. Her essay explores the ambiguous status of both music and women, and the challenges faced by writers wishing to invoke the domestic piano in conventional poetic terms. She investigates the particularly drastic 'genre-specific' measure adopted in most of these works: the pianist is killed off and is thereby safely and romantically consigned to 'the dear dead past'. The evocation in these poems of memory, loss, and nostalgia colours their representation of the same dangerous erotic power that attaches to female musicianship in prose fiction of the Victorian period.

Conscious revulsion at Victorian stereotypes is a feature of the novel that forms the subject of the chapter jointly authored by Sue Asbee and Tom Cooper. Their essay on Kate Chopin's *The Awakening* reflects on the importance of music within a novel that has become an important text for feminist literary criticism. In particular, they discuss Kate Chopin's allusions to the compositions of her musical namesake Fryderyk Chopin. They compare the reception history of the composer and writer to support their reading of such references in the novel as signalling a subversive sensuality. They also consider the way in which music is invoked to convey emotion otherwise unarticulated by the novel's heroine, and explore a number of formal analogies between the work of both artists. Kate Chopin's method of composing her brief novel via a series of suggestive episodes linked by varied and repeated images that operate as 'incremental refrains' is seen both as a departure from the detailed inclusivity of the Victorian novel, and as closely allied to techniques of musical composition.

Robert Samuels's chapter 'Two Schumann Song Cycles: Narratives of Masculinity and Femininity' also focuses closely on analogies between music and literary texts, drawing in the concerns about the relationship between music and narrative that re-emerge throughout this collection. The sort of narrative that should be read from the organized sequence of texts constituting a song cycle is not self-evident. Some cycles present a relatively 'legible' story, approaching opera in the sequence of events and characters (such as Schubert's *Die schöne Müllerin*), whilst others leave the narrative to be inferred by the listener. Samuels's chapter contrasts the approach taken by Schumann in the two cycles *Frauenliebe und Leben* and *Dichterliebe*, each dating from 1840. In both cases the narrative of the cycle is created not only by the text of the poetry but equally by musical form. This is particularly true of *Dichterliebe*, where Schumann has selected sixteen of Heine's poems from a collection of well over a hundred, so that the narrative of courtship, betrayal, and loss is one that is as much his creation as the poet's. But in both cases a distinctive form of narrative arises from the combination of music and word, a narrative that cannot be described adequately either as literary or as musical. It is, genuinely, both. The richness of aesthetic experience brought out by the contrasts between these works accounts, in part, for their continuing popularity long after the passing (or diminution) of the social assumptions they embody; they also represent a unique form of storytelling from perhaps the most innovative age of musico-literary experiment.

The final group of chapters looks at the operation of 'Narrative Modes' within specific works of music and literature, beginning with Guillaume Bordry's essay analysing a particularly rich example of literary–musical cross-fertilization in the work of Hector Berlioz. Bordry focuses on Berlioz's verbal reconstructions of different forms of music in his accounts of concerts, and proposes that the literary analogues suggested by the programme for the *Symphonie fantastique* comes close to making this piece appear to be a musical paraphrase of a pre-existing literary text. Whilst Berlioz's absolutist aesthetic, as articulated in his essay 'On Musical Imitation' (1837), defined music as expressive rather than imitative, three of his most celebrated works present themselves as musical adaptations of works by Shakespeare, Byron, and Goethe. Peter Dayan's chapter earlier in the collection considers the verbal text as requiring the support of music, despite its dangerous powers of abstraction. Here, Bordry's analysis of the role of narrative in Berlioz's work represents music's declared supremacy over the other arts as being none the less dependent on its affinity with the structures of literary narrative.

Federico Celestini's chapter focuses on the third movement of Gustav Mahler's First Symphony. Celestini sees the work's engagement with literary narrative as rather different from the programmatic procedures of Berlioz's *Symphonie fantastique*; and he argues that the extramusical references in the *Trauermarsch in Callots Manier* — Mahler's title for his third movement — connect music and literature in a manner that abolishes the traditional division between programme music and absolute music. The movement is woven from a surprising concentration of intermedial references, including to the visual art of Callot and the writings of Hoffmann and Jean Paul. Celestini describes how Mahler consciously blends tragic and trivial allusions to literary and pictorial media with intimations of childhood experience of the kind that formed the basis of his psychological discussions with Freud. Literary or pictorial sources are implicated in his compositional process on the basis of their worth as psychological experience and memory — 'as a kind of *déjà-vu*'. In Celestini's view the *Trauermarsch* offers a radical intermediality through which internal subjectivity and allusions to external objects fuse in the memory, connecting different media so as to undermine any sense of the objective or independent existence of works of art.

Formal analogies between the works of J. S. Bach, Wagner and Russian literature are the subject of Rosamund Bartlett's chapter on Dostoevsky's *The Brothers Karamazov*. It has become a commonplace of Dostoevsky criticism to discuss his novels in terms of their 'polyphony' and 'counterpoint'. However, Bartlett argues that there is more to Dostoevskian musicality than a multiplicity of competing narrative voices and styles. While the religiously inspired formal design of Dostoevsky's novels has something in common with the music of Bach, the writer's innovative use of myth, leitmotif, and symbol in his novels, coupled with the intensely dramatic qualities of his writing, suggests parallels with Wagnerian music drama. Although 'largely uninterested in each other's existence', Bartlett comments, 'the creative careers of Wagner and Dostoevsky were coterminous, and it is perhaps not surprising to find points of contact between the œuvres of these two great nineteenth-century artistic revolutionaries'. Her chapter explores *The Brothers Karamazov* through the prism of Wagnerian music drama, to reveal structural and thematic parallels with works such as *Der Ring des Nibelungen* and *Parsifal*.

In the final chapter of the volume David Crilly looks at the intermingling of music and literature in Britten's *War Requiem*. This is a work whose historical and cultural significance has provoked debate over whether this resonance has insured its continuing popularity rather than the intrinsic qualities of Britten's music and the texts that he set. Many of the essays collected here query the possibility of dissociating either music or literature from their cultural contexts, and Crilly adopts the notion of intertextuality from literary criticism to show that Britten can be seen as operating in a way that is both formally and culturally subversive. By taking Britten's setting of a variety of texts for mere imitation of past styles, critics miss a rhetoric that productively distorts the conventions of Requiem setting. In the *War Requiem* Britten interpolates nine of Wilfred Owen's anti-war poems with the Requiem text. The juxtaposition of ancient and modern, sacred and secular, has struck some critics as spurious. However, in Crilly's view the *War Requiem* creates a dialogue between the Requiem text and the poems and also between the Requiem and other genres, in particular the medieval planctus and baroque Passion. Britten's intertextual subversions reinterpret the verbal texts, and the listener, hearing juxtapositions of apparently unlike materials, confers new significance upon them.

The contents of this collection involve a number of unexpected conjunctions and new insights. Together, the essays provide a range of vantage points onto the intersection of literary and musical 'phrase and subject'. They are contributions to an expanding, shared research culture at a point when connections between literature, music, and other arts are beginning to occupy a significant place within the interdisciplinary study of the humanities at large. A sense of music's having 'arrived' within the broader sphere of interdisciplinary studies was palpable at a 2003 conference on 'In(ter)disciplines' held at the new Centre for Research in the Arts, Social Sciences and Humanities in Cambridge. The conference featured a substantial number of papers on musical topics, and in her concluding comments the cultural theorist Mieke Bal exclaimed that she would never have expected to have had such fun at a conference that included so much music! We hope that what follows will be enjoyed both by those already working in the field and those to whom it is as yet unfamiliar.

Notes to Introduction

I am grateful to Robert Samuels for his helpful comments on a draft of this introduction.

1. Despite the pioneering nature of Calvin S. Brown's *Music and Literature: A Comparison of the Arts* (Athens, GA: University of Georgia Press, 1948), Lawrence Kramer's comparative study *Music and Poetry: The Nineteenth-Century and after* (Berkeley: University of California Press, 1984) was still part of too fledgling a field to be recognised as a distinct area of study. Daniel Albright included music in his *Representation and the Imagination: Beckett, Kafka, Nabokov, and Schoenberg* (Chicago: University of Chicago Press, 1981), a study of the relationship of abstraction and realism in modernist art. Others who had looked at literature and music in parallel include Joseph Kerman, whose 1957 *Opera as Drama* (London: Cambridge University Press, 1957 [c. 1956]) uses the Wagnerian conception of 'music drama' to reflect on the relationship between music and drama in post-Wagnerian opera. Subsequently, Peter Conrad, in *Romantic Opera and Literary Form* (Berkeley: University of California Press, 1977), proposed that the proper literary analogue for opera was not the outward action of drama, but the more subjective, interiorizing form of the novel; and Robert K. Wallace's *Emily Bronte and Beethoven: Romantic Equilibrium in Fiction and Music* (Athens, GA, and London: University of Georgia Press, 1986) looks at the work of these two artists in parallel.

2. Susanne K. Langer, *Philosophy in a New Key: A Study in the Symbolism of Reason, Rite and Art* (Cambridge, MA: Harvard University Press, 1942), pp. 228, 233, 243.

3. This theoretical fascination is exemplified in *The Sign in Music and Literature*, ed. by Wendy Steiner (Austin: University of Texas Press, 1981).

4. Ludwig Wittgenstein, *Philosophical Investigations* (1953), trans. by G. E. M. Anscombe (Oxford: Basil Blackwell, 1972), p. 143.

5. Christopher Morris, 'Songs of the Living Dead', Review article, *19th-Century Music*, 27 (2003), 74–93 (p. 86); the quotation is taken from a passage reviewing Carolyn Abbate's *In Search of Opera* (Princeton, NJ: Princeton University Press, 2001).

6. Lawrence Kramer, *Classical Music and Postmodern Knowledge* (Berkeley: University of California Press, 1995), p. xii.

7. In this respect a valuable precursor of the present volume of essays is *Music and Text: Critical Inquiries*, ed. by Steven Paul Scher (Cambridge, Cambridge University Press, 1992), which features a concluding commentary by the historical theorist Haydn White. The international as well as interdisciplinary scope of research in this field is illustrated by Scher's own work, which includes publications on links between literature and music in both English and German.

8. Kramer's *Music as Cultural Practice, 1800–1900* (Berkeley: University of California Press, 1990) pays particular attention to the potential offered to music criticism by poststructural and historicist approaches. This was followed by *Classical Music and Postmodern Knowledge* (Berkeley: University of California Press, 1995), in which Kramer outlines the revised perceptions of music demanded by postmodernist conceptions of knowledge. *After the Lovedeath: Sexual Violence and the Making of Culture* (Berkeley: University of California Press, 1997) extends Kramer's contextual study of music to analyse its role in the construction of gender identity; and in *Franz Schubert: Sexuality, Subjectivity, Song*, Cambridge Studies in Music Theory and Analysis, 13 (Cambridge, Cambridge University Press, 1998) he considers the cultural influence of Schubert's songs. His most recent theoretical exploration is *Musical Meaning: Toward a Critical History* (Berkeley: University of California Press, 2002).

9. This analogy is developed by Daniel Albright in *Untwisting the Serpent: Modernism in Music, Literature, and Other Arts* (Chicago: University of Chicago Press, 2000), p. 5.

10. Kramer, *Franz Schubert*, p. i.

11. In his 1919 essay 'Das Umheimliche' Freud traces evolutions in the meaning of 'heimlich' from 'homely', thus 'private', thus 'hidden', until it denotes its opposite: 'secret' and 'unheimlich'.

See Sigmund Freud, 'The 'Uncanny', in *Art and Literature: Jensen's 'Gravida', Leonardo da Vinci and Other Works*, The Pelican Freud Library, 14, ed. by Albert Dickenson (London: Penguin, 1985), p. 345.

12. For studies that explore the relationships between literature and music in the light of both ideologies of gender and scientific theory, see Phyllis Weliver, *Woman Musicians in Victorian Fiction, 1860–1900: Representations of Music, Science and Gender in the Leisured Home* (Aldershot: Ashgate, 2000), and Delia da Sousa Correa, *George Eliot, Music and Victorian Culture* (Basingstoke: Palgrave, 2002).

PART I

Theoretical Issues

CHAPTER 1

Stances towards Music as a Language

Daniel Albright

One of the chief issues in evaluating the relation between words and music is the status of music as a language. When words and music are combined, does there exist a confluence of two distinct linguistic systems, or a single language-system smacked on top of, or to the side of, a non-linguistic system of sounds? In this essay I attempt to classify and evaluate some of the possible relations of music to language.

It is important to note that for many composers and poets music and language belong together so intimately that they are almost inseparable. Wagner and Ezra Pound did not agree on much, but both thought that, at the origin of culture, speech was song and song was speech. As Wagner put it:

> If we look closer at the evolutionary history of the modern European languages, even today we meet in their so-called word roots a rudiment that plainly shows us how at the first beginning the formation of the mental concept of an object ran almost completely parallel with the subjective feeling of it; and the supposition that the earliest speech of man must have borne a great analogy with song, might not perhaps seem quite ridiculous.[1]

And Pound believed that in antiquity music and poetry had been in alliance, that 'the divorce of the two arts had been to the advantage of neither, and that melodic invention had declined simultaneously and progressively with their divergence'.[2] For composers who felt that music had dwindled into a kind of aphasia through the loss of its archaic oneness with language, the task was to find strategies for recapturing by instrumental means the ease, the referential sureness, the oomph of speech. This conscious re-tonguing of music could be approached intensely, or circumspectly, or humorously, or it could be rejected altogether. I shall take up first the strongest possible case.

Music as a Language

According to this model, music can act as a Pentecostal tongue of fire, for it behaves as a language not learned systematically but understood intuitively and universally. This model is in some ways obviously untenable: how could one say 'The persimmons are mottled but unripe' without recourse to spoken words? But it provides a powerful dream for activating certain potentialities of musical expression, even though it is most pervasive as a trope of comedy, as, for example, when Harpo Marx, in *Duck Soup*, carries on one end of a telephone conversation strictly by means of a bicycle horn. Still, there is a respectable case to be made for the thesis that music can operate as a complete language, since every formal property of speech — formal in the sense of non-denotative — can, I believe, be understood as a formal property of music.

Among the schemes for classifying the formal properties of speech are those based on small units, such as inflection and phoneme construction; those based on middle-sized units, such as syntax; and those based on large units, such as the structures of rational persuasion that we call rhetoric, or the structures of seduction that we call narrative and drama. (The distinction between persuasion addressed to the understanding and seduction addressed to the will goes back to Pascal's essay 'The Art of Persuasion'.) It is not possible here to offer a comprehensive review, but I can suggest how profoundly we understand music as a language. Or, to put it better, how profoundly language understands music as a language, since language tends to understand everything as a language.

The vocabulary of music analysis is amazingly dependent on terms from linguistics, as the words 'phrase' and 'theme' quickly show; and I suspect that the history of music has been strongly shaped by the conscious or subconscious tendency of composers to literalize the vocabulary of music analysis. Consider the term subject: the instant that I denote the main melodic entity in a composition as a 'subject', I have thereby promoted that thing into a little person, or at least into a crucial matter with as-yet-unexplained properties, and I compel a tacit grammatical search for a way of explaining the rest of the composition as a predicate to that subject. The rest of the composition becomes a way of learning about the subject, of teasing out its attributes, of defining its contours, its submissions to new harmonic contexts, its recalcitrances against ill-treatment. The term 'subject' imparts a prestige, a centrality, that the sequence of notes might not otherwise possess. Indeed the term has an implicit push towards narrative, in that the vicissitudes of the subject during the course of the composition start to become heard as adventures. This process is sometimes quite explicit, as in Rimsky-Korsakov's *Sheherazade*, in which the composer uses the same theme to represent the Sultan listening to his new wife's stories, and Sindbad navigating his boat through sea-sickening orchestral swells. Sometimes it is only implicit, but still fairly compelling, as in the famous analysis in Mann's *Doktor Faustus* of the variations movement in Beethoven's Piano Sonata op. 111, in which the hero's music teacher explains in great detail how the simple arietta tune is first damned, then ambiguously redeemed, like Faust himself in some versions of the story.

Large musical structures can recall other sorts of large speech structures. The opening of the slow movement of Beethoven's Fourth Piano Concerto (1807), in which the piano and the orchestra do not speak at the same time but are confined to separate acoustic and emotional domains, impresses most listeners as a drama rather than a narrative or a piece of rhetoric. I once heard a radio broadcast which reported that the pianist Krystian Zimerman thought that the movement represented Christ before Pontius Pilate. The novelist E. M. Forster also heard a drama:

> This famous little movement consists of a dialogue between orchestra and piano, the orchestra rough, the piano plaintive, the orchestra gradually calmer. It is very easy music; it strikes or strokes immediately, and elderly gentlemen before myself

have called it 'Beauty and the Beast'. What about Orpheus and the Furies, though? That is the idea that has slipped into my mind to the detriment of the actual musical sounds, and when the movement begins I always repair to the entrance of Hell and descend under the guidance of Gluck through diminishing opposition to the Elysian Fields. There has been no word-making, to be sure, but there has been a big operatic import [...]. The piano turns into Orpheus and *via* him into Miss Marie Brema, whom I best remember in that rôle, and the strings and wind, waving less and less their snaky locks, sink at last into acquiescence with true love. Then the third movement starts. The parallel breaks, and I am back in a world which seems four-square and self-contained, the world of the opening.[3]

Forster felt sad when the Concerto lost its linguistic character, and disenchanted itself back into 'mere' music — as if Beethoven's imagination had failed him at the instant that the music failed to approximate some sort of speech act. It is slightly disquieting, perhaps contrary to experience, to think that music is less potent — in a sense, less music — if it fails to support clear story outlines.

Sometimes music addresses itself not to the imagination but to the discerning intellect, and attempts to ape the language of oratory. In his 1739 treatise *Der vollkommene Capellmeister* Johann Mattheson understands the art of musical composition as classical rhetoric transposed into a language of tones, cleanly organized into *inventio*, *dispositio* (articulation of the invented idea into parts), *decoratio*, and *pronuntiatio* (delivery); he even plays with forensic models of musical rhetoric, in which a composition is divided into *exordium*, *narratio* (statement of facts), *divisio* (forecast of main points in the speaker's favour), *confirmatio*, *confutatio* (rebuttal), and *peroratio*. Mattheson and other musical rhetoricians also provided tables of figures of speech complete with examples, so that the reader can ponder the musical equivalent of, say, anaphora, repetition, exclamation, ellipsis, and pleonasm. Many of the tropes in the tables pertain to insistence, and it is clear that music is quite handy at repeating, ornamenting, developing, augmenting, or otherwise waxing large upon an idea; in that sense music is much like spoken oratory. On the other hand, a table of figures of speech in spoken discourse looks very different. In speech and writing, most tropes pertain not to insistence but to transposition: here the basic figures are metaphor and simile, which, alas, seem not to exist in the world of music, or to exist only tangentially. How can one sequence of notes take the place of, or allude to, or hover alongside an absent sequence of notes? Furthermore, a central oratorical device is contradiction: not only am I right, but you are wrong. But music, while it may have many parts of speech, seems to lack a privative, an intelligible 'not': a musical event cannot easily be annulled, or vitiated, or dismissed by another musical event. So to evaluate music as a reasonable discourse becomes a frustrating matter. A musical composition may have many discursive aspects, may even, like Charles Ives's Second Quartet, represent a bunch of guys screaming at each other about topics concerning the American Civil War, but finally seems able to go only so far in mapping itself according to oratorical form.

Perhaps the most successful of all strategies for discursifying (if that is a permissible word) music lies on the level of inflection. Here we have not only such stunts as Harpo's bicycle horn, but also the hero's wife in Richard Strauss's *Ein Heldenleben* (1899), who 'speaks' so intelligibly through a violin that it tempts the listener to imagine actual verbal dialogue, wheedling, cajoling, pouting, vituperating, or, as Strauss indicates in one particularly challenging instruction to the violinist, 'hypocritically languishing'; and 'Bacchus at whose orgies is heard the noise of gaggling women's tattling tongues and shouting out of boys', the fourth of Benjamin Britten's *Six Metamorphoses after Ovid* (1951), in which a solo oboe tattles and shouts a language that the listener has never been taught and yet understands quite clearly. By choosing Bacchus as the god of speech music, Britten stresses the Dionysiac character of this art: music seems to be nothing more than speech grown so excited that only the excitement is intelligible, not the words. Britten seems to appeal to old fantasies of an all-compulsive archaic language of sound-gestures. Rousseau, for example, imagined that a modern European only faintly acquainted with Arabic would prostrate himself, abandon his Christian beliefs, and march in the armies of Islam, if he had heard Mohammed preach, burning with the enthusiasm of his prophecy.[4]

And yet, even in these examples where music seems ready to assert itself as a language, as a modality of word inflection in the absence of the word, there are certain counterpressures that threaten to destroy music's linguistic character. Britten's *Six Metamorphoses after Ovid* begins with 'Pan who played upon the reed pipe which was Syrinx, his beloved'; and this nobly poised cantilena makes the Bacchus movement seem by contrast almost submusical, a kind of woodwind gargling. To introduce musical speechifying into a composition usually means that the composer thereby specifies other areas of a composition with higher melodic contour and clearer harmonic articulation — in short, more like music because less like speech. An old but effective example of this tendency can be found in Charpentier's miniature opera *Les Plaisirs de Versailles*, in which La Musique and La Conversation debate whether Louis XIV would be more delighted to hear music or to engage in a lively chat. La Conversation argues in favour of talk, by singing her lines in a *langue frétillante*, a garrulous gabble above a hectoring bass viol; whereas La Musique preens herself in *accords charmants*, singing her lines in a long slow, ravishing legato. Although Charpentier characterizes La Conversation by musical means, music itself seems the exact opposite of talkiness.

Furthermore, there is a notable lack of coordination among the various linguistic models possible to music. Britten's Bacchus movement is extremely talkative on the level of inflection, but not talkative at all on the level of rhetoric or narrative: there is scarcely even the ghost of a story or an argument, just a series of speech gestures. Similarly, the examples of rhetoric that Mattheson cites tend not to have any inflectional force behind them. In Strauss's tone poems one can find several examples of inflectional imitation, but often oddly detached from the story, indeed slowing down the momentum of the story: Strauss's hero's wife is, from the point of view of the narrative, a tedious digression, inhibiting the hero from getting on with his business. Strauss's chatterboxes — the monks in *Don Quixote* (1898), for example — provide comic relief, as if discursivity were a sort of local colour or amusement pasted onto the music, instead of the crucial matter of music. Even the narrative aspect of the tone poem can seem dangerously extrinsic — which is why composers have often been so uneasy about publishing them. Strauss is famous for narrative specificity, but the programme of *Till Eulenspiegel* (1895) remained unpublished: it is known only through a table of twenty-three motifs that exists in the manuscript score, and through some help the composer gave to Wilhelm Mauke when Mauke was writing a guide to the work. Strauss's own programme is revealing — without it most listeners would not guess just how central anti-clericalism was to Strauss's intent; but amidst amazingly precise details ('But the rogue's big toe protrudes beneath the cassock'), there are also episodes of utter vagueness ('On to new pranks'). Every tone poem I know has episodes where a programme is not only superfluous but impossible to construct. Strauss in particular always inserts blurs, patches of indescribable confusion, like the grey blob that disturbs the centre of Manet's painting *Music in the Tuileries Gardens*.

The more closely we examine the hypothesis that music is a language, whether in theory or in practice, the less tenable it appears. After exhaustive study of Mattheson's tables of tropes and of many other old treatises, the musicologist George J. Buelow (to whom I am much indebted) concludes that 'many of the musical figures [...] originated in attempts to explain or justify irregular, if not incorrect, contrapuntal writing'.[5] In other words, the rhetorical aspects of music seem to be concentrated in various areas of deviance from accepted musical practice; so we are left with the uncomfortable dilemma that (1) music is a kind of rhetoric, while (2) music is more rhetorical when it breaks down the rules rather than when it obeys them. I believe that similar paradoxes and aporias result from any attempt to impose a linguistic character on music. Perhaps the finest of all recent students of musical narrative, Carolyn Abbate, has announced, in effect, that the more she studies musical narrative, the less she finds: 'In my own interpretations [...] I will interpret music as narrating only rarely. It is not narrative, but it possesses moments of narration, moments that can be identified by their bizarre and disruptive effect'.[6] Jean-Jacques Nattiez offers a still bleaker view, seeming to deny even those rare moments of narration that Abbate found:

> 'Music has no past tense', as Carolyn Abbate rightly observes. It can evoke the past by means of citations or stylistic borrowings, but it cannot narrate, cannot speak what *took place* in time past [...]. Literary narrative is an invention, a lie. Music cannot lie. The responsibility for joining character-phantoms with action-shadows lies with me, the listener, since it does not lie within *music's* semiological capacities to join subject and predicate.[7]

A musical narrative, then, is a confabulation of the listener, or of the composer, who is evidently merely another listener with no special mythopoeic credentials. It seems that music behaves linguistically only in a spasmodic, haphazard, and irregular manner. The search for music's tongue seems to render music completely mute.

Furthermore, from the beginning of theoretical discourse about music, there are strong hints that something is desperately wrong with the attempt to understand music as a language. For example, there exists a curious manual of advice for writing a bad opera, *Il teatro alla moda* (c. 1720), in which Benedetto Marcello informs the apprentice hack how to organize his arias:

> Let [the composer] see to it that the arias, to the very end of the opera, are alternatively a lively one and a pathetic one, without regard to the words, the modes, or the proprieties of the scene. If substantive nouns, e.g., *padre*, *impero* [empire] *amore*, *arena*, *beltà* [beauty], *lena* [vigor], *core* [heart], etc. [...] should occur

in the arias, the modern composer should base upon them a long passage; e.g., *pa ... impeeee ... amoooo ... areeee ... reeee ... beltàaaaa ... lenaaaaa* [...]. The object is to get away from the ancient style, which did not use passages on substantive nouns or on adverbs, but only on words signifying some passion or movement; e.g., *tormento, affanno* [breathlessness], *canto, volar* [to fly], *cader* [to fall], etc.[8]

Marcello is profoundly suspicious of nouns: he would like to banish solid objects from serious attention by musicians. This makes sense, in that the denotative functions of language have always seemed the least likely to translate into music. On the other hand, what hope is there for creating a language without nouns? Jorge Luis Borges once imagined a language (in 'Tlön, Uqbar, Orbis Tertius', 1947) consisting entirely of impersonal verbs: 'there is no word corresponding to 'moon', but there is a verb that in English would be 'to moon' or 'to moonate'. 'The moon rose above the river' is *hlör u fang axaxaxas mlö*, or, literally, 'upward behind the on-streaming it mooned'.[9] To understand the behaviour of the ocean in Debussy's *La Mer* in similar terms — 'onwards beneath the up-diamonding it surged' — has a certain attraction; and it could be argued that it would be easier to comprehend the interactions of Wagner's leitmotifs if we named them as gerunds, rather than as nouns: instead of speaking of 'spear', we might better speak of 'down-smiting'. And yet, to accept music as a defective language is merely to call increasing attention to its defectiveness rather than its power.

Music as a Non-Language

If music slips through our grasp when we try to understand it as a language, the next step is to attempt to put together a non-linguistic theory of music. On this side of the divide there are distinguished historical precedents: Pythagoras, who heard music as a sort of celestial arithmetic, a sound-map of the starry sky; and Eduard Hanslick, the Viennese music critic and champion of Brahms, who defined music as *tönend bewegte Form* — a term that might be translated literally as 'soundingly moved form', or, less literally, as 'dynamic sound-form', or 'form set into motion through sound', or, perhaps best of all, 'motion-form perceptible through the ear'. It is no wonder that Hanslick and Wagner detested one another — Wagner even toyed with the idea of using the name Hanslick for the ignorant carping critic in *Die Meistersinger* — for Hanslick's asemantic theory of music is exactly opposed to Wagner's semantic, overcharged notions of music. For Hanslick, music is to the ear what Alexander Calder's mobiles, in the next century, would be to the eye: a shifting series of acoustic cross-sections. To listen to a musical compositions is not to hear a displacement of speech, but to attend to shapes opening through modulatory space and then closing up at cadences.

In the twentieth century such non-linguistic models would continue to attract certain composers. Erik Satie wrote a piece of *musique d'ameublement* — 'furniture music' — which he entitled 'Wallpaper in forged iron'; George Antheil considered his works to be paintings on a time canvas; and Stravinsky audibly pieced together such works as *Renard* by the method of collage, pasting together short snippets into repetitive chains — the scissors and the gluepot have replaced the rhetoric book as a means of organization. Stravinsky's famous distaste for expression — 'I consider that music is, by its very nature, essentially powerless to *express* anything at all, whether a feeling, an attitude of mind, a psychological mood, a phenomenon of nature, etc'[10] — has, of course, strong anti-linguistic tendencies. What Pythagoras, Hanslick, Satie, Antheil, and Stravinsky have in common is that by refusing the idea that music is a language, they embrace the idea that music is a species of visual art realized in sound. When discourse seems to evaporate, pictures fly in to occupy the empty space, for theory, like nature, abhors a vacuum.

And yet, it is not clear that the opposition between discourse and the visual arts can be sustained. From Apelles to Jackson Pollock and beyond, pictures have seemed pregnant with stories, and have been understood through rhetorical models. It is possible that music's attempt to flee from language through reliance on pictorial methods will only lead back to language by means of an oblique route: we are all so thickly imprisoned in verbal constructions of reality that every escape tunnel we dig will turn out to lead us back to the same jail.

Of course, there are some composers whose methods seem to exclude any possibility of contamination by language. John Cage, for example, whose post-1951 reliance on various sorts of aleatory construction and indeterminate performance vitiates any normal notion of the semantic, or the rhetorical, or the grammatical, or the speech inflective. If Cage's compositions are music, then music would seem not only to be non-linguistic, but the antidote to language. But it is precisely here, where music and speech seem to diverge utterly, that they start to swerve together: for Cage treats speech simply as a form of non-sung mouth music, by constructing discourse according to the same aleatory procedures that he used to govern his music. In one well-known example he wrote out a series of random statements and then, during the question–and–answer session following a lecture, simply read the statements one after another, without regard to the actual questions. A more thorough deconstruction can be found in *Solo for Voice 2* (1960), where Cage instructs the performer to write vowels and consonants on a transparent sheet, and then, through certain manipulations of this sheet over a piece of paper inscribed with lines, to devise an array of phonemes that will be the text to be performed.

This sort of anti-language can be dismissed as a special stunt with no relevance to speech as we usually speak it. But the tendency of linguistics from Saussure to Derrida has been to remove physical objects from the domain of language; to understand language as chains of endlessly-deferred signifiers, never terminating in any actual thing. Every attempt to dereferentialize language tends to turn what the TV weatherman says into an occult version of *Solo for Voice 2*, in which the phonic aspects grow increasingly opaque, increasingly an occasion for aesthetic delight in their heard immediacy. Wittgenstein's later philosophy repeatedly stresses the musical aspects of normal speech; as he says in *Philosophical Investigations* 527, 'Understanding a sentence is much more akin to understanding a theme in music than one may think. What I mean is that understanding a sentence lies nearer than one thinks to what is ordinarily called understanding a musical theme'.[11] It fascinates me that these two sentences are, in effect, musical variations of the same sentence, as if Wittgenstein were proving his point in the act of making it. For Wittgenstein, music is not like speech; instead, speech is a special case of music. Some of the things you say to me I understand in the way I understand Mozart; some of them in the way I understand Cage; some in the way I understand the Spice Girls. But in all cases speech is a game with sounds, just as music is a game with sounds; neither strictly possesses meaning, or conviction, but meaning and conviction may glide around either.

Recent rhetoricians also describe a rhetoric that looks musical rather than discursive. Andrzej Warminski has claimed that it is impossible to construct a semantic or grammatical model of a text that is truly reliable; there exists too much excluded, too much for which the model cannot account, too many disruptive aspects. Rhetoric cannot solve the problem of the indeterminacy of language, but can only reaffirm it. No text can be reduced to lucidity through study of its grammar, or reference, or figures of speech.[12] According to Paul de Man, 'every text generates a referent that subverts the grammatical principle to which it owed its constitution ... [there is a] fundamental incompatibility between grammar and meaning'.[13] But if the language is beset by the same problems of jarring and incommensurable, un-unifiable models that beset music, then music and language are in exactly the same uncomfortable situation. Yes, Strauss's tone poem *Till Eulenspiegel* lurches wildly from narrative to speech inflection to exasperating tangles of unconstruables; but a written chronicle of Till's adventures would behave identically. So we are left in paradox: the more we try to understand music as language, the more strongly it resists that understanding; and the more we try to understand music as the opposite of language, the more sweetly, strongly, plainly it speaks to the ear. We understand the siren's song only at the moment when we stop trying to understand it.

Notes to Chapter 1

1. Richard Wagner, *Wagner on Music and Drama*, ed. by Albert Goldman and Evert Sprinchorn, trans. by H. Ashton Ellis (London: Gollancz, 1970), p. 153.
2. R. Murray Schafer, ed., *Ezra Pound and Music: The Complete Criticism* (London: Faber, 1978), pp. 4–5.
3. E. M. Forster, 'Word-Making and Sound-Taking,' *Abinger Harvest* (London: Edward Arnold, 1936), pp. 100–04 (p. 105).
4. Jean-Jacques Rousseau, in *On the Origin of Language*. See Jean-Jacques Rousseau, *On the Origin of Language: Jean-Jacques Rousseau, 'Essay on the Origin of Languages'; Johann Gottfried Herder, 'Essay on the Origin of Language'*, trans. by John H. Moran and Alexander Gode (New York: Ungar, 1966; Chicago, University of Chicago Press, 1986), p. 49.
5. George J. Buelow, 'Rhetoric and Music: Musical Figures', in *The New Grove Dictionary of Music and Musicians*, ed. by Stanley Sadie and John Tyrrell, 29 vols (London: Macmillan, 2001), XXI, p. 236.
6. Carolyn Abbate, *Unsung Voices: Opera and Musical Narrative in the Nineteenth Century* (Princeton, NJ: Princeton University Press, 1991), p. 29.
7. Jean-Jacques Nattiez, *Music and Discourse: Toward a Semiology of Music*, trans. by Carolyn Abbate (Princeton, NJ: Princeton University Press, 1990), p. 128.
8. Benedetto Giacomo Marcello, *Il teatro alla moda, o sia metodo securo, e facile per ben comporre, eseguire l'opera italiane in musica all'uso moderno* (Venice, [1720]) (trans. Albright).
9. Jorge Luis Borges, 'Tlön, Uqbar, Orbis Tertius' (1947), in *Labyrinths: Selected Stories and Other Writings*, ed. by Donald A. Yates and James E. Irby (Harmondsworth: Penguin, 1970), pp. 32–33.
10. Igor Stravinsky, *Igor Stravinsky: An Autobiography* (1936), with an introduction by Eric Walter White (London: Calder and Boyars, 1975), p. 53.
11. Ludwig Wittgenstein, *Philosophical Investigations* 527 (1953), trans. by G. E. M. Anscombe (Oxford: Basil Blackwell, 1972), p. 143.

12. Andrzej Warminski, 'Introduction: Allegories of Reference', in Paul de Man, *Aesthetic Ideology* (Minneapolis: University of Minnesota Press, 1996), pp. 1–33.
13. Paul de Man, *Allegories of Reading: Figural Language in Rousseau, Nietzsche, Rilke and Proust* (New Haven, CT: Yale University Press, 1979), p. 269.

CHAPTER 2

Music before the Literary:
Or, the Eventness of Musical Events

Anthony Gritten

If everything in the world were sensible, nothing would happen. There would be
no events [...] and there must be events.

FYODOR DOSTOEVSKY, *The Brothers Karamazov*

I

In the early 1990s, in the wake of studies like Nicholas Cook's *Music, Imagination,
and Culture*,[1] musicologists became aware of the 'gaps'[2] between what performers do
and what listeners do, and between what they think they do and what they do. The
performativity of musical practice, it was said, needed rethinking. The multi-authored
volume *Rethinking Music* was paradigmatic in this regard.[3] Much of Cook's own
forceful and charismatic work beyond the work ethic has helped to push through at
least four major reconfigurations of common knowledge: listeners and performers
respond to and do different things, things not necessarily related to the activity of
composing; performing is not merely the instantiation, realization, or reading of a
text, but creative; understanding music is itself performative, and scholarship is not
transparent; and we need to be constantly vigilant against lapsing into 'theorism'.[4]
José Bowen's remark that we would benefit from an 'event-centred' history of music
('event' being used here in a broader sense than I shall use below) is similarly apt in
suggesting one of the possible directions open to musicology.[5]

It is surely right that to remain firmly fixed in a conception of performing as
no more than the 'realization of the score' — as a form of 'instantiating the text'
— is, as far as the standard performing tradition (performing 'works') is concerned,
to turn performing into 'a form of genuflection' towards the work.[6] Conceived
thus, performing aspires to nothing more than a correct 'reading' of the text. Even
substituting 'script' for 'text' changes very little other than the grammar of performing,
replacing a literary performance 'of a text' with a dramatic performance 'from a
script'. Another option is to substitute 'musicking' for 'music'.[7] This is laudatory, but
no more than an inversion of the nominal 'opposition' between performing and work,
and a move with more validity for the understanding of collective improvisation and
the social ritual of performance than for the understanding of the performing 'of

musical works', especially solo performing (my concern here). It is important not to essentialize the distinction between performing and work, between process and product, for music partakes of both. This is the third way Cook has staked out in 'Between Process and Product', by far and away the most challenging survey yet of musical performance.[8]

But does this provide an adequate description of the performer's act of performing? Perhaps it satisfies the listener in the audience, who simultaneously chooses to participate in the process and to concentrate upon mentally constructing its product. For the performer, though, should her activity also necessarily end as process rather than as product? That is, should the event of performing subsume the work (however widely conceived), the process its product? Should performing have its own dynamic? I believe that it should, and I shall argue why and how below. Rather than deflate theories of 'performing as reading', theories that, in the broadly Kantian tradition of art as representation, assimilate music to the model of the linguistic (as often as not the literary), and after summarizing the reasoning behind such well-rehearsed deflation, I shall describe, with the help of Mikhail Bakhtin's theory of 'the event', some of the consequences of accepting such deflation and some of the characteristics of what the performer actually confronts: musical events.

II

Why prioritize musical events? There are two main reasons: one large, one small. The small reason is relatively easy to address and concerns the degree of inclusivity that theories of performing — those held by performers and by scholars — maintain with regard to what falls within their purview. Some theories ignore the many forms of 'musical noise'.[9] Others relegate the corporeality of performing — its bodily, physical aspects — to a psychological problem to be overcome, rather than treating it as something that the performer seeks to come to terms with, which would be more realistic. Examples include the way muscular tension is discussed, the treatment of stage fright, the problem of errors and mistakes in live performing, and so on. These theories of performing tend to idealize, and thereby idolize, the event of performing, and in so doing transcribe it into a text for adoration. Of course, there is undoubtedly a sense in which, in some performing traditions and not others, we value the image of the performer as unsullied by the sordid traces of her embodiment — the listener wants to see a furrowed brow, perhaps, or the performer breaking into a (little) sweat. My concern here, however, is with the performer's own relations to the corporeal aspects of her performing: with how she relates to herself and her self-activity in so far as these present themselves to her textually, as, broadly speaking, texts to be performed.

The larger of the two reasons concerns a more serious problem within many theories of performing, theories that, by assimilating music to the model of language and turning it into a text (literary or otherwise), construe performing as the reading of a text and finalize its temporality. Assuming that to understand performing is to show that it is the reading of a text or the representation of a textual object, they accordingly emphasize the power of models that 'map' performing onto parallel symbolic schemes, such as 'duration structures'.[10] No place is left for the performer's creativity and choice, for a 'figural' relation to the text,[11] since even 'creativity' and 'choice' have become options with answers. Such theories leave the temporality of performing closed, which means, inevitably, that the performer does what the laws prescribe (even if they have not yet been prescribed), instantiating, but never going beyond, the laws. The performer is unable to make genuine judgements about her actions and movements, and even to imagine otherwise is futile, since 'imagining otherwise' has already been accounted for. With the loss of choice, her creative potential is reduced to the mechanical discovery of something that is already waiting in the wings, like the solution to a simultaneous equation.

The problem with such theories of 'performing as text reading' is not that they treat music as text or performing as reading. Clearly, in the mainstream performing tradition at least, the performer can neither escape from texts, nor does she need to: performers perform works and works are performed, and there is certainly some kind of relation, if not exactly a middle ground, between these two activities. The problem is, rather, that these theories misconstrue the nature of temporality; in fact, they remove it altogether from the event of performing and from reflective musical judgement.[12] In contrast, consider the following remark: 'Insofar as I have thought of an object, I have entered into a relationship with it that has the character of an ongoing event.'[13] (A context for this remark will emerge below through a discussion of Bakhtin's theory of the event and 'eventness'.)

If we wish to understand the performer's perspective on performing, therefore, a focus on musical events is needed, rather than on musical works and their generalized, often notated, form: texts. Creativity and artistry arise in the midst of musical events, and in the mainstream performing tradition we value precisely this sense (illusory or not) of freedom and spontaneity of action and thought on the part of the performer. We shall find that it is both what the performer does and what she does 'with' what is always already given to her — that which is never originally 'hers' — that characterizes her performing as creative, and precisely as hers. Reading — this essay included — is never just reading; it performs.

III

'Play Birtwistle's *Précis*.'[14] What is the performer to make of this obligation? In its published form the score contains numerous typographical errors, and so as a score 'of the work' is somewhat unreliable. For many years, the only recording, by John Ogden (now unavailable),[15] was of the printed score. Is this a recording of the work? What is the work? Is the oft-cited criterion of authenticity relevant to *Précis*? Should *Précis* be played as it stands, or should performing be unfaithful to the notated score? One way or the other, I shall argue that there comes a point, both temporal and logical, at which the performer should put aside such questions and focus on the performing 'event' in question. The performer obviously knows this pragmatically as she walks on stage ('that's it, here I go!'), but my point is not so much concerned with the sheer volume and accuracy of knowledge about the work and its textuality, which the performer can choose to accumulate prior to walking on stage, as with the nature and role of such knowledge during the actual event of performing. That is, regardless of whether or not such questions about *Précis* are answered and the performer is presented with a correct(ed) score or recording from which to begin, and even in ostensibly more standard cases where (she thinks) she is sure of what the work is and in what internal syntactic and semantic conventions and determinations it consists, another kind of question — about the event of performing — still remains, stubbornly demanding an answer, not before performing (which is called 'practice' for good reason), but at the very moment she begins to play and throughout live performing. This is because during performing there is no such stable thing as 'the musical work'. The musical text is overtaken by the event of its presentation, which demands of the performer that she distinguish, consciously or otherwise, between two simultaneous intonations of 'the musical work'. On the one hand, this phrase refers to the product of performing, to the musical work represented; on the other hand, it refers to the work 'to be done', to the work accomplished during performing as part of the process by which the product comes about. This is more than a grammatical point about the hypostasis by which a verb (action) is said to become a noun (being). These two intonations are presented to the performer not as a pair of choices, but as a predicament, as simultaneous obligations out of which arises an ontology — more accurately, as will be seen below, an ethics — which is different from that encountered by the listener in the audience. For the performer the work to be done is an activity directed towards the work, and as such it is encountered as an event.

This brief account of how the performer attends to the musical work through the work to be done suggests that her activity is, in a broadly Kantian sense, a 'moral' act. The argument seems to be this: the performer's focus during performing is, or (being realistic) should be, on performing, not in order to achieve a conditioned end, but in order to achieve an unconditioned end, which seems to be something like performing on the sole motive of a good musical will (whatever that might be). However, the performer's act is more complex than this, for her activity is Janus-faced;[16] it looks both towards the musical work and towards the event of performing. In so far as the musical work is performed, her activity is aesthetic, concerned with the presentation of the musical work as a readable text. In so far, though, as her activity is also directed towards an actual act of performing, it is at the same time ethical, subject to ethical criteria and evaluation. How can the performer acknowledge these two co-present intonations of her activity?

Here the Kantian account of morality,[17] with its well-known aversion to art (and music in particular), needs revision if morality and ethical experience are to account for and include within their remit artistic activity, such as performing music, in anything like a strong sense.[18] The weak sense has often been described in terms of the contractual obligations that the performer has to the historical text, the notated score, the work, and the audience, often in explicitly Kantian terms.[19] In order to invigorate a strong sense of the phrase 'performing as moral/ethical practice' we need to rethink the concept of responsibility (what Kant calls 'duty') in such a way that its constituent elements of 'singularity' and 'temporality' — essential elements of musical performing as far as the performer is concerned and in so far as she is valued in a musical culture — are pushed further to the fore than in the Kantian model of morality and of what constitutes a moral act. In addition, the sublime moment of the event needs to be given as much emphasis as the beautiful, if not more.[20] In what follows I shall be less concerned with what I have termed the weak sense of responsibility (authenticity-as-fidelity) than with the strong sense.

IV

I begin with an idea that goes hand in hand with theories of how the performer should understand and perform musical texts: respect. When we invoke the desideratum of authenticity, of performing being true to the work, we are ultimately referring the performer and the event of performing, and indeed ourselves, back to the Kantian ideal of respect for the law: something like fear, something like inclination. This, according to Kant, provides the motivation for a properly moral act.[21] Such a referral to the law, however, erases any intimate, personal relation the performer may have had with the musical text, effaces it of any singularity — and hence creativity — it may have had, the referral universalizing the singularity of the performer's presence (her relation to the work) and making it comparable to other cases, both hypothetical and actual. By way of reparation, we need to loosen the universalizing moment — the 'as if' — in such a way that we may nonetheless retain the criterion of comparability, without which the act of performing becomes solipsistic.

This requires rethinking the anthropomorphic leap structuring the performer's relation to the work. If she is to have a properly personal relation to the work she performs, she ought not to think of the work as separate from herself, as something she performs and 'some-thing' she respects, and instead ought to think of it as being implicated within her very identity and subjectivity, in the manner of the everyday musical practices in which we usually refer simply to 'my music',[22] such music being, in the terms appropriate to this metaphor of social consumption, the 'self-effacing [...] ultimate hidden persuader'.[23] This conceptual shift towards an ethics of performing grounded on something more intimate than respect — love — deflates the deontological ethics of music as text in favour of a post-foundationalist ethics of musical performing. The shift helps to distinguish music from language,[24] and musical performing from the reading of a text. Love, after all, is less something I have than something I accomplish in real time, indeed never finish accomplishing. In a loving relationship I do not simply read the text (read: other person): I am also 'exposed' to him (Levinas) and his use of his 'surplus' (Bakhtin). I invest in the loved one in ways that take me out of myself, that question the boundaries between 'me' and 'him', and that are fundamentally open and creative.

Such a shift, then, involves acknowledging that 'subjectivity' is not the central point of performing, even if it is central to the listener's activity. That 'arguments for subjectivity are disguised arguments about reason'[25] is precisely the problem with accounts of musical performing that deal with questions of emergent subjectivity in terms of the primacy of the self, which is to say, in terms of the primacy of the text: they end up in the contradictory position of positing performing as the instantiation of the self-identical. My point is that rethinking performing in terms of the intimacy of love allows for a certain beneficial otherness to present itself within the musical event.

V

Going beyond notions of musical respect and duty, then, requires reconceiving what the performer does in terms kinder towards the intimate personal relation to the work that she undertakes, both before and during performing, to create and maintain. To speak of the performer's relation 'to' the work may already be misleading or partial, and it may be better to speak of her loving relation 'with' the work; at any rate, the point is to realign performer and work more closely, yet maintain their mutual outsideness (the complementary facts that, except metaphorically, the performer is usually not composing the work as she performs it, and the work does not usually perform itself).

The move here is to rethink the 'proximity' of the relation.[26] Proximity is not only a sociological term whereby we might describe performing as a collective dialogue of various participants, as often happens in musicological appropriations of 'the dialogic'. The proximity of the performer's relation to the musical work is a 'participative outsideness' informing her relation to her 'own' physical and cognitive activity. This leads us necessarily to the concept of the 'event'.

There are, of course, many theories of the event, of what constitutes an event, of how they are lived and experienced, from Derrida, Lyotard, and many others.[27] Bakhtin's early writings, concerned more with the world than the word, are centrally concerned with events, and gloss the concept of participation in broadly the manner that I suggested above. Bakhtin describes participation in terms of 'eventness,' which he understands as the sense that time is truly open and that the present is a gateway, a 'threshold' for events.[28] By participation Bakhtin means participation in what he calls 'Being-as-event'. This has certain consequences, since he conceives participation both as a state of being and as a demand, as an obligation. In fact, once participation ends, the event ends, for it 'cannot be determined in the categories of non-participant theoretical consciousness — it can be determined only in the categories of actual communion, i.e., of an actually performed act'.[29] Elsewhere he writes that 'without co-evaluating to some extent, one cannot contemplate an event as an *event* specifically'.[30]

There are four types of event, each configuring the relation between self and other differently: aesthetic, ethical, cognitive, and religious.[31] In his early writings, 'Art and Answerability', *Toward a Philosophy of the Act*, 'Author and Hero in Aesthetic Activity', and the 1929 version of *Problems of Dostoevsky's Poetics*, Bakhtin was concerned with the various relations between these types of event and the types of act through which they come into being. In the Dostoevsky book in particular he was interested in the possibility that aesthetic and ethical events might dissimulate each other, 'non-fused yet undivided'[32] and 'played out at the point of dialogic meeting between two or several consciousnesses';[33] this is the possibility of polyphony. I shall pick this up later when I return to the possibility of reinvigorating the strong senses of the notions of participation and of musical performing as moral practice. In particular, I shall suggest that, in so far as she is both performing a musical work and performing, the performer has the difficult task of managing the intertwining drift of aesthetic and ethical events.

For Bakhtin, an event is both a constituent moment of consciousness and something that happens between consciousnesses in the event of being. 'The *event* of being [...]

presents itself to a living consciousness as an event, and a living consciousness actively orients itself and lives in it as in an event.'[34] The event is characterized by uniqueness and singularity. 'I occupy a place in once-occurrent Being that is unique and never-repeatable, a place that cannot be taken by anyone else and is impenetrable for anyone else. [...] That which can be done by me can never be done by anyone else.' As such, the event cannot be transcribed in theoretical terms, which deal with the general and recurrent. It 'cannot be transcribed in theoretical terms if it is not to lose the very sense of its being an event, that is, precisely that which the performed act knows answerably and with reference to which it orients itself.' Indeed, 'it is an unfortunate misunderstanding (a legacy of rationalism) to think that truth can only be the truth that is composed of universal moments; that the truth of a situation is precisely that which is repeatable and constant in it.'[35]

The event, according to Bakhtin, cannot be contained by the circumstances that occasioned it or by any repeatable transcription of it into a text, even though *qua* event it presupposes the very possibility of such a transcription. This 'excess'[36] or what Bakhtin elsewhere calls a 'surplus'[37] constitutes its singularity, for the concrete event is historically contingent and its temporality is central to its very identity. This means that the musical event is, *qua* event, unrepeatable; it is an 'unrecoverable act'.[38] Its meaning and weight are inextricably linked to the precise moment in which it is performed. Performative decision making turns on the elusive notion of the present, on the epiphanic here and now of the performer's activity, on the eventness without which the present moment loses the qualities that give it special weight and make it 'compellently obligatory'[39] with regard to the future. Concerned precisely with this 'event potential' and the nature of the act that embodies a 'will to the event',[40] Bakhtin notes that 'this unitary and unique truth of the answerably performed act is posited as something to be attained *qua* synthetical'.[41]

The event is therefore constituted by moments that abstract models such as that of 'performing as reading' cannot foretell. The event should produce something genuinely new; indeed, 'the event surprises or else it is not an event; so it is all a matter of knowing what "surprise" is', especially since, paradoxically, 'the decision surprises itself'.[42] If eventness is possible, then neither historical knowledge nor a theory of what it means to be 'true to the work' can reliably predict the future contours of the event. They are necessary but not sufficient conditions for eventness.

VI

Such are events as Bakhtin describes them. While his theory of the event, bound up in issues of intentionality and ethics, is more idealistic than Lyotard's, it has the benefit, being phenomenologically orientated, of describing how it is that the performer lives, not in the absence of the work (an ideology), but with the work, both right now and in general. 'The point is not to escape [logocentrism], but to reckon with it; not to "critique" it, but to deploy it reflectively.'[43] In order to do this we must now focus on what Bakhtin's notion of participation means with regard to performing music. This means returning from a sense of the work to be done — the ethical demand to participate in Being-as-event — back to the issue of the performer's loving 'relation to' or 'contact with' the musical work in so far as the work itself pre-exists her act of performing, as, of course, it usually does.

In order to argue that performing must be considered not only in terms of events but also in terms of a particular kind of participation within such events, I shall show that the relation to the musical work that the performer maintains *within* her participation in the event of performing is not the type of relation presupposed by the model of performing as 'text reading', that is, not the weak notion of 'the dialogic' assumed in many liberal appropriations of Bakhtin whereby the dialogic is unproblematically assumed to enact a metaphysical condition of wholeness and presence rather than an ethical dynamic of 'presentation'.[44] As Bakhtin says, pointing to the importance of eventness, 'it is our relationship that determines an object and its structure, not conversely';[45] and this relationship is, at root, temporal and always fragile.[46] Listening, I shall argue, describes the mode of attention the performer gives to the musical text *qua* music (rather than *qua* sound), and constitutes the sublime moment within which the text leaves itself and becomes for her a musical event.

Bakhtin glosses the term participative outsideness as 'an active (not a duplicating) understanding, a willingness to listen',[47] meaning something more complex than empathy: active love. In order to understand specifically musical events, though, we need to inflect Bakhtin's concept of 'outsideness' with a concept of 'posteriority', since the outsideness of which Bakhtin speaks is primarily a visual economy of the self–other relation. This we can find by interweaving Bakhtin with Levinas' concept of 'passivity', which is slightly more fine-tuned than Bakhtin's.[48] According to Levinas, I am always passive in the face of the other, since the other reaches out to me before I myself come into existence as subject. The other is before me; his temporality brings mine into being in the form of an imperative. Hence, ethics comes before ontology. The invasiveness and 'proximity' of the other,[49] however, do not lead to my mastery over him, my assimilation of the other to the same, since his invasiveness is precisely what Levinas calls his infinite 'exteriority' and his 'destitution',[50] to which I respond because he calls to me. As Levinas writes:

> We call ethical a relationship between terms such as are united neither by a synthesis of the understanding nor by a relationship between subject and object, and yet where the one weighs or concerns or is meaningful to the other, where they are bound by a plot which knowing can neither exhaust nor unravel.[51]

Participative outsideness, then, is a passivity in the face of the musical work and a condition of musical eventness prior to the intention that the performer embodies with regard to the musical work. It is the fact of being positioned by the other on the 'threshold' of temporality.[52] It is the fact that the performer listens.

From this it ought to become clear that listening is not only an act in itself, in the sense that we talk of the 'act of acting', the 'act of composing', the 'act of performing', and the 'act of listening' as practised by the audience. What are confused are two senses of the term 'listening' (like the two senses of 'the musical work' mentioned above): on the one hand, the actual person who is being described, usually in the audience; and, on the other hand, the constituent element of the activity of all members of 'the musically involved'.[53] Listening as participative outsideness underlies performing and composing and listening, and concerns the precise intonation with which each is undertaken. In fact, it is the central element of the event of performing; it is what turns the musical work into the musical event; it is the response to time, the temporal response. A mode of attentiveness, it informs the performer's activity and the direction of her participation in the musical event at a fundamental level,[54] since, because she must act intentionally towards the accomplishing of physical actions, listening becomes the participative outsideness that she maintains with respect to the event of her activity. This notion of listening also provides a useful complement to explications of Bakhtin's ethics, which, tending imperceptibly towards privileging the word over the world, speak of the performer's live judgements as if they were both leisurely thought through and entirely spontaneous, and at the root of creativity and responsibility.[55] Indeed they are, but at their root lies what I have attempted to explicate as passivity or listening.

Listening, then, constitutes the very relation between performer and work in so far as that relation is musical rather than simply sonic.[56] To say that a performer is listening is both to utter a tautology (!) and to say that her relation to the event of performing that subsumes her act is open-ended, open-minded, and responsive to the needs of the musical work: in short, to say (again) that she loves the work.

Of course, the performer is caught in a double bind, having to act physically in the world and to respond cognitively to it. Her schizophrenic activity is aesthetic and ethical. On the one hand, she is '*truly* in time'[57] and lacks the 'technological advantage' of the analyst and indeed the listener;[58] on the other hand, she listens and feels.[59] As Bakhtin remarks aphoristically:

> Thought about the world and thought in the world. Thought striving to embrace the world and thought experiencing itself in the world (as part of it). An event in the world and participation in it. The world as an event (and not as existence in ready-made form).[60]

The performer's double bind is played out in the fact that she cannot restrict actions and movements to those parts of her body that are autonomic and beyond conscious control; she cannot be only a listener. After all, the flipsides of responsiveness and love are single-mindedness and fear; the beautiful and the sublime dissimulate each other. Her actions have to be at some level active and willed (hence performing is often studied in terms of 'generative processes'), and this element of intentionality brings to the event an element of form, yet also a threat of violence concomitant with — indeed, a necessary foundation for — her creative activity with respect to that very aesthetic form that she is presenting. This intertwining of form and creativity, of aesthetic and ethical moments, and, for the performer herself arguably, the inevitable dominance of the ethical moment, is both frightening and exciting, and a source of the pleasure we get from both participating in and watching events of performing — and perhaps, *en passant*, one of Kant's reasons for distrusting music.

VII

I have been arguing that we should consider performing in terms of 'events' rather than in terms of the reading of 'texts' (literary or otherwise). My purpose has been to elucidate the ethical moment (in the strong sense) of musical performing. While a Kantian ethics would have allowed me to construct a sense of the relation the performer has to the musical work *qua* textual object (her respect for it), it would not have provided an adequate framework for also dealing with the eventness of her activity: her act not as a representative token of a class of types but her act *qua* act — her love. I have been interested in glossing the notion that 'if in doing what I have to do, I do not act to actualise myself, neither do I act in order to actualise the universal agent [contrary to what Kant maintained]'.[61] Hence the (Bakhtinian) ethics towards which I have worked emphasizes in a post-Kantian manner the concept of 'eventness'. Since the performer's activity — her participation in the musical event — does not cancel out or conflict with, but in fact subsumes her relation to the work, I have been arguing that we need to talk of eventness both before and after we talk about musical works or texts.

Of course, it might justifiably be said that I have reinvented the wheel. We have been studying musical events all along, especially in the study of music performance. I agree. But I suggest that usually we are concerned more with the kind of listening going on in the audience — the kind of listening concerned ultimately with the synthesis of an experience — than with the different kind of listening (if indeed that is the best word) going on between the performer's ears. One of my motivations has been my belief that our understanding of musical events and specifically our understanding of the relationship between performing events and musical works is often confused. Frequently conflating language and music, as often as not unconsciously and implicitly in our attitudes towards musical works, we have a tendency to confuse the everyday function of language, namely, communication in its broadest sense, with the somewhat less everyday *raison d'être* of musical practice: artistry.[62] The two overlap, but are not the same. As Eric Clarke has acknowledged:

> The essential characteristic of artistic activity (and aesthetic objects) is a radical form of ambiguity and creativity, and while the expressive resources may be outlined, their precise disposition on any occasion can be accounted for only in retrospect, not predicted. Were this not the case, and our curiosity in these ambiguities and possibilities not boundless, we might all have given up going to concerts long ago.[63]

Notes to Chapter 2

1. Nicholas Cook, *Music, Imagination, and Culture* (Oxford: Oxford University Press, 1990).
2. Eric Clarke, 'Mind the Gap: Formal Structures and Psychological Processes in Music', *Contemporary Music Review*, 3 (1989), 1–13.
3. Nicholas Cook and Mark Everist, eds., *Rethinking Music* (Oxford: Oxford University Press, 1999).
4. Nicholas Cook, 'Perception: A Perspective from Music Theory', in *Musical Perceptions*, ed. by Rita Aiello (Oxford: Oxford University Press, 1994), pp. 64–95 (p. 81).
5. José Bowen, 'Finding the Music in Musicology: Performance History and Musical Works', in *Rethinking Music*, ed. Cook and Everist, pp. 424–51 (p. 424 n. 2).
6. Derek Bailey, *Improvisation* (Ashbourne: Moorland, 1980), p. 85.
7. Christopher Small, *Musicking: The Meanings of Performing and Listening* (Hanover, NH: University Press of New England, 1998).
8. Nicholas Cook, 'Between Process and Product: Music and/as Performance', *Music Theory Online*, 7.2 (2001) <http://www.societymusictheory.org/mto/issues/ mto.01.7.2.cook.html> [accessed 19 October 2005]; repr. in condensed form as 'Music as Performance', in *The Cultural Study of Music:*

A Critical Introduction, ed. by Martin Clayton, Trevor Herbert, and Richard Middleton (New York: Routledge, 2003), pp. 204–14.

9. James Hamilton, 'Musical Noise', *British Journal of Aesthetics*, 39 (1999), 350–63.

10. For example, Neill Todd, 'A Model of Expressive Timing in Tonal Music', *Music Perception*, 3 (1985), 33–58.

11. Jean-François Lyotard, *Discours, Figure* (Paris: Klincksieck, 1971).

12. See Andrew Benjamin, ed., *Judging Lyotard* (London: Routledge, 1992); Jean-François Lyotard, *Peregrinations: Law, Form, Event* (New York: Columbia University Press, 1988); Jean-François Lyotard, 'Judiciousness in Dispute, or Kant after Marx', in *The Aims of Representation: Subject / Text / History*, ed. by Murray Krieger (Stanford, CA: Stanford University Press, 1987), pp. 23–67; Geoffrey Bennington, 'Is It Time?', in *Interrupting Derrida* (London: Routledge, 2000), pp 128–40.

13. Mikhail Bakhtin, *Toward a Philosophy of the Act*, trans. by Vadim Liapunov (Austin: University of Texas Press, 1993), p. 33 (cf. p. 32).

14. A work for solo piano dating from 1960.

15. John Ogden, LP HMV ALP 2098 or ASD 645.

16. Lydia Goehr, *The Quest for Voice: Music, Politics, and the Limits of Philosophy* (Oxford: Oxford University Press, 1998), pp. 132–73.

17. Immanuel Kant, *The Moral Law, or Kant's Groundwork of the Metaphysic of Morals*, trans. and ed. by H. J. Paton (London: Hutchinson, 1948; repr. London: Routledge, 1991); Immanuel Kant, *The Metaphysics of Morals*, trans. by Mary Gregor (Cambridge: Cambridge University Press, 1996); cf. Lawrence Pasternak, ed., *Immanuel Kant: 'Groundwork of the Metaphysic of Morals' in Focus* (London: Routledge, 2002).

18. Arden Reed, 'The Debt of Disinterest: Kant's Critique of Music', *Modern Language Notes*, 95 (1980), 563–84.

19. For example, Stephen Davies, 'Authenticity in Musical Performance', *British Journal of Aesthetics*, 27 (1987), 39–50; Stephen Davies, 'Transcription, Authenticity and Performance', *British Journal of Aesthetics*, 28 (1988), 216–27; Lydia Goehr, 'Being True to the Work', *Journal of Aesthetics and Art Criticism*, 47 (1989), 55–67; Morris Grossman, 'Performance and Obligation', in *What is Music? An Introduction to the Philosophy of Music*, ed. by Philip Alperson (New York: Haven, 1987; repr. with updated bibliography, University Park, PA: Pennsylvania State University Press, 1994), pp. 257–81; J. O. Urmson, 'The Ethics of Musical Performance', in *The Interpretation of Music: Philosophical Essays*, ed. by Michael Krausz (Oxford: Clarendon Press, 1993), pp. 157–64.

20. Jean-François Lyotard, *Lessons on the Analytic of the Sublime*, trans. by Elizabeth Rottenberg (Stanford, CA: Stanford University Press, 1994); Jean-François Lyotard, *The Inhuman: Reflections on Time*, trans. by Geoffrey Bennington and Rachel Bowlby (London: Polity, 1991), esp. chaps 6, 7, 9, 11; Hugh Silverman, ed., *Lyotard: Philosophy, Politics, and the Sublime* (New York: Routledge, 2002), pp. 179–229.

21. Immanuel Kant, *Critique of Practical Reason*, trans. by Lewis White Beck (New York: Bobbs-Merrill, 1956), pt I, bk 1, chap. 3.

22. Tia DeNora, *Music in Everyday Life* (London: Routledge, 2000).

23. Nicholas Cook, *Music: A Very Short Introduction* (Oxford: Oxford University Press, 1998), p. 131.

24. Susan Bernstein, *Virtuosity of the Nineteenth Century: Performing Music and Language in Heine, Liszt, and Baudelaire* (Stanford, CA: Stanford University Press, 1998), pp. 36–57.

25. Craig Ayrey, 'Universe of Particulars: Subotnik, Deconstruction, and Chopin', *Music Analysis*, 17 (1998), 339–81 (p. 341).

26. Emmanuel Levinas, *Otherwise than Being or Beyond Essence*, trans. by Alphonso Lingis (Pittsburgh, PA: Duquesne University Press, 1981), pp. 61–97.

27. For example, Jacques Derrida, 'Signature Event Context', in *Limited Inc*, trans. by Samuel Weber and Jeffrey Mehlman (Evanston, IL: Northwestern University Press, 1988), pp. 1–23; Jean-François Lyotard, *The Differend: Phrases in Dispute*, trans. by Georges Van Den Abbeele (Minneapolis: University of Minnesota Press, 1988), esp. pp. 59–85.

28. Mikhail Bakhtin, *Problems of Dostoevsky's Poetics*, trans. by Caryl Emerson (Minneapolis: University of Minnesota Press, 1984), pp. 61–63.

29. Bakhtin, *Toward a Philosophy of the Act*, pp. 12–13.

30. Mikhail Bakhtin, 'The Problem of Content, Material, and Form in Verbal Art', in *Art and*

Answerability: Early Philosophical Essays, trans. by Vadim Liapunov (Austin: University of Texas Press, 1990), pp. 257–325 (pp. 281–82).

31. Mikhail Bakhtin, 'Author and Hero in Aesthetic Activity', in *Art and Answerability*, pp. 4–256 (p. 22).

32. Bakhtin, *Toward a Philosophy of the Act*, p. 41.

33. Bakhtin, *Problems of Dostoevsky's Poetics*, p. 88.

34. Bakhtin, 'Author and Hero', p. 188 n.

35. Bakhtin, *Toward a Philosophy of the Act*, pp. 40, 30–31, 37 (cf. p. 31).

36. Bakhtin, 'Author and Hero', pp. 22–27.

37. Bakhtin, *Problems of Dostoevsky's Poetics*, p. 73.

38. Rose Rosengard Subotnik, Review of *Musical Elaborations* by Edward Said, *Journal of the American Musicological Society*, 46 (1993), 476–85 (p. 477).

39. Bakhtin, *Toward a Philosophy of the Act*, p. 20 (cf. pp. 40–46).

40. Bakhtin, *Problems of Dostoevsky's Poetics*, pp. 81, 21.

41. Bakhtin, *Toward a Philosophy of the Act*, p. 29.

42. Respectively, Jean-Luc Nancy, 'The Surprise of the Event', in *Being Singular Plural*, trans. by Robert Richardson and Anne O'Byrne (Stanford, CA: Stanford University Press, 2000), pp 159–76 (p. 167); Jean-Luc Nancy, *The Experience of Freedom*, trans. by Bridget McDonald (Stanford, CA: Stanford University Press, 1993), p. 142.

43. Lawrence Kramer, 'Analysis Worldly and Unworldly', *Musical Quarterly*, 87 (2004), 119–39 (p. 134).

44. Robert Sokolowski, 'The Issue of Presence', *Journal of Philosophy*, 77 (1980), 631–43.

45. Bakhtin, 'Author and Hero', p. 5.

46. Zali Gurevitch, 'Plurality in Dialogue: A Comment on Bakhtin', *Sociology*, 34 (2000), 243–63.

47. Bakhtin, *Problems of Dostoevsky's Poetics*, p. 299.

48. Bakhtin, *Toward a Philosophy of the Act*, pp. 41–42.

49. Emmanuel Levinas, *Existence and Existents*, trans. by Alphonso Lingis (Dordrecht: Kluwer, 1988), p. 65.

50. Emmanuel Levinas, *Totality and Infinity: An Essay on Exteriority*, trans. by Alphonso Lingis (Pittsburgh, PA: Duquesne University Press, 1969).

51. Emmanuel Levinas, 'Language and Proximity', in *Collected Philosophical Papers*, trans. by Alphonso Lingis (Dordrecht: Kluwer, 1987), pp. 109–26 (p. 116 n. 6).

52. Bakhtin, *Problems of Dostoevsky's Poetics*, pp. 61–63; Levinas, *Existence and Existents*, p. 99.

53. Jerrold Levinson, 'Evaluating Musical Performance', in *Music, Art, and Metaphysics: Essays in Philosophical Aesthetics* (Ithaca, NY: Cornell University Press, 1990), pp. 376–92 (p. 376).

54. David Michael Levin, *The Listening Self: Personal Growth, Social Change and the Closure of Metaphysics* (London: Routledge, 1989), pp. 223–35; F. Joseph Smith, *The Experiencing of Musical Sound: Prelude to a Phenomenology of Music* (New York: Gordon & Breach, 1979), pp. 27–64.

55. Gary Saul Morson and Caryl Emerson, 'Introduction: Rethinking Bakhtin', in *Rethinking Bakhtin: Extensions and Challenges*, ed. by Gary Saul Morson and Caryl Emerson (Evanston, IL: Northwestern University Press, 1989), pp. 1–60 (p. 18); Gary Saul Morson and Caryl Emerson, *Mikhail Bakhtin: Creation of a Prosaics* (Stanford, CA: Stanford University Press, 1990), pp. 123–268.

56. Roger Scruton, 'Understanding Music', in *The Aesthetic Understanding* (Manchester: Carcanet, 1983), pp. 77–100; Roger Scruton, 'Analytical Philosophy and the Meaning of Music', *Journal of Aesthetics and Art Criticism*, 46 (1987), 169–76; Roger Scruton, *The Aesthetics of Music* (Oxford: Oxford University Press, 1997), pp. 19–79, 80–96.

57. Agata Bielik-Robson, 'Bad Timing: The Subject as a Work of Time', *Angelaki*, 5.3 (2000), 71–91 (p. 91 n. 25).

58. Anthony Pople, 'Systems and Strategies: Functions and Limits of Analysis', in *Theory, Analysis, and Meaning in Music*, ed. by Anthony Pople (Cambridge: Cambridge University Press, 1994), pp. 108–23 (p. 114 n. 15).

59. Daniel Putnam, 'Music and the Metaphor of Touch', *Journal of Aesthetics and Art Criticism*, 44 (1985), 59–66.

60. Mikhail Bakhtin, 'Toward a Methodology for the Human Sciences', in *Speech Genres and Other Late Essays*, trans. by Vern McGee (Austin: University of Texas Press, 1986), pp. 159–72 (p. 162).

61. Alphonso Lingis, *The Imperative* (Bloomington: Indiana University Press, 1998), p. 222.

62. Jonathan Dunsby, *Performing Music: Shared Concerns* (Oxford: Oxford University Press, 1995), pp. 29–38.

63. Eric Clarke, 'Generative Principles in Musical Performance', *Generative Processes in Music: The Psychology of Performance, Improvisation, and Composition*, ed. by John Sloboda (Oxford: Oxford University Press, 1988), pp. 1–26 (p. 24); cf. L. Henry Shaffer, 'Cognition and Effect in Musical Performance', *Contemporary Music Review*, 4 (1989), 381–89 (pp. 388–89).

CHAPTER 3

Music in the Philosophical Imagination: Deconstructing Friedrich Nietzsche's *Human, All Too Human*

Tina Frühauf

In July 1876 Friedrich Nietzsche began working on a manuscript of aphorisms, later published in 1878 as the first part of *Human, All Too Human*; the other two parts, *Opinions and Maxims* and *The Wanderer and his Shadow*, appeared in 1879 and 1880, respectively, and Nietzsche published all three parts together in 1886 as *Human, All Too Human: A Book for Free Spirits*.[1] Written just after he had given up his post as professor at the University of Basel, the work marks a complete break with Nietzsche's previous philosophical thinking and direction. Having now lost the shackles of youth and employment, he was indeed at his most free-spirited.

Human, All Too Human was Nietzsche's next major work after *The Birth of Tragedy out of the Spirit of Music*, which was published in November 1871. His thinking about music before *Human, All Too Human* was influenced by his present idols Richard Wagner, to whom the *The Birth of Tragedy* is dedicated, and Schopenhauer, whose writings he had discovered in 1865. In *The Birth of Tragedy* music is seen as a thing-in-itself, an object as it is (or would be), independent of our awareness of it. Music thus represents the metaphysical world directly, whereas the non-musical arts represent it, at best, only indirectly. Nietzsche further believed that the relationship between music and language was questionable, as language can never convey the symbolism of music adequately. The combination of a Schopenhauerean metaphysical interpretation of music and a defence of Wagnerian opera does not, however, lead to a coherent representation of the relationship of music and language.[2] In this respect Nietzsche's writing in *The Birth of Tragedy* and beyond bears on the shifting relations between music and literature during the nineteenth century.

As Nietzsche clearly states in the preface, his intention in *Human, All Too Human* was to deny allegiance both to Schopenhauer and (after the 1876 Bayreuth Festival) to Wagner.[3] Distancing himself aesthetically from Wagner, philosophically from Schopenhauer, and stylistically from German Romanticism, by writing short, dry, and witty aphorisms, he no longer focuses on metaphysics but concentrates on a historical philosophy bound to science. Previously, under the Schopenhauer–Wagner influence, he had avoided the subjects of history and science, which he considered inimical to the individuality he wished to establish.[4] Now, he aimed to forge his own path by means of his unaided intellect, aspiring to become a truly free spirit. This freedom can be read literally: he endeavours to strike out on his own intellectually-assertive path, trying to be independent of Schopenhauer and Wagner and liberated from the voice of German nationalism.

In *Human, All Too Human* Nietzsche attacks society's imposition of rules of behaviour and ways of thinking. He investigates the role of habits, rights, morality, and tradition within collectivism,[5] and he examines family, society, politics, and religious upbringing. At first sight the discussion of music and literature seems secondary and, unlike in *The Birth of Tragedy*, no more than a subdivision of aesthetics. He does address topics such as the connections between art and science, as he does matters of literature, poetry, and music, but these subjects are scattered throughout almost every section of *Human, All Too Human*. The following reflections and aphorisms, for instance, deal with music: PREFACE, §8; Section III: RELIGIOUS LIFE, §131; Section IV: FROM THE SOULS OF ARTISTS AND WRITERS, §152; Section VII: WOMAN AND CHILD, §397; Section IX: MAN ALONE WITH HIMSELF, §§599 and 626. Thoughts on literature and poetry can be found in Section II: ON THE HISTORY OF THE MORAL SENSATIONS, §61; Section IV: FROM THE SOULS OF ARTISTS AND WRITERS, §§148, 152, 154, and 155; Section VI: MAN IN SOCIETY, §344; Section IX: MAN ALONE WITH HIMSELF, §610.[6]

Since the themes of music and literature are present in sections other than FROM THE SOULS OF ARTISTS AND WRITERS, the question arises: How are music and literature represented in *Human, All Too Human*? How do Nietzsche's concepts of music and literature contribute to the world that he constructs? More specifically: What is the function of music and literature in Nietzsche's construction of society and culture? His approach to these matters is multidimensional.

The Connotations of Music and Literature

Whilst music in earlier writings had a more fundamental role than literature, Nietzsche's perspective changes with *Human, All Too Human*, where the themes of literature and language become more significant. Now Nietzsche focuses his analysis of language on the guiding or controlling elements that are prior to, and operational within, language. These he calls grammar, logic, reason, knowledge, but also race, atavism, instinct, or, simply, the physiological conditions of the human being. Nietzsche approaches language from two basic perspectives: (1) as a science, and (2) as an idealized medium with perfect means of designation and communication:

> The significance of language for the evolution of culture lies in this, that mankind set up in language a separate world beside the other world, a place it took to be so firmly set that, standing upon it, it could lift the rest of the world off its hinges and make itself master of it. To the extent that man has for long ages believed in the concepts and names of things as in *aeternae veritates* he has appropriated to himself that pride by which he raised himself above the animal: he really thought that in language he possessed knowledge of the world. (PREFACE, §11)

There are three separable assertions in Nietzsche's statement: (*a*) that language mediates humanity's relation to the world; (*b*) that in so doing it alters the world; and (*c*) that its alteration takes priority over any immediacy of the world. Nietzsche stipulates that man has an impulse to define or to represent the world through language, and he theorizes language as itself a second world standing against and outside the real world. Thus language appears as a putative science, the tool for shaping the evolution of culture.

Another function of language appears when language is connected to music. In the reflection 'Music' (IV, §215) Nietzsche starts with the doctrinaire sentence: 'Music is, of and in itself, not so significant for our inner world, nor so profoundly exciting, that it can be said to count as the *immediate* language of feeling'. He rationalizes music and dissociates it from the metaphysical position it had in *The Birth of Tragedy*. Its deep inner meaning is not the nature of music, but is superimposed by the human intellect. Consequently, music is not a direct language or expression of feeling; it is not considered a language of emotion; it is, rather, a projection and an object of our emotions. Because of music's strong connection to literature throughout history, especially to poetry, its symbolism is blurred. The comprehension of meaning in music relies, therefore, on its connection with physical reality. The nature of this meaning derives from the human condition of symbolic mediation with the world. A consequence of Nietzsche's reflection is that different individuals with different backgrounds, in different times and moods, will interpret the same piece of 'absolute' music differently. Music has a deep inner meaning only if it contains a language of symbols through literature; only through language does music attain symbolic meaning. These thoughts are contrary to Nietzsche's earlier view, based on Schopenhauer, whereby music is seen as the thing-in-itself. He affirms this strongly by stating that music 'does not speak of the "will" or the "thing-in-itself"' (IV, §215). While in *The Birth of Tragedy* Nietzsche adopted Schopenhauer's view of the dichotomy between music and non-musical arts, in *Human, All Too Human* he changed his stance. His ideas seem reminiscent of Jean-Jacques Rousseau's aesthetics on the nature and origin of language, for Rousseau, too, explored in his writings the same aspect of human production of meaning in musical forms and substance.

Nietzsche formulated an antithetical concept to the language of symbols in his fragment *On Music and Words*. There he speaks of music as the language of tones, a Schopenhauerean manifestation of the will 'in the tone of the speaker', where 'tone' has become the universal commonality beyond all difference.[7] This claim elaborates the origin of words from the essence of music. Only because of this shared foundation in tone is music the 'supplement' of language, not as an addition but as its alternate consummation. This same emphasis on tone is evident in Nietzsche's early lectures on the art of speaking as the culture of listening: 'Darstellung der antiken Rhetorik'.[8] Here he describes rhetoric as an art 'which appeals chiefly to the ear, in order to bribe it'. The author's parenthesis '(In our time the reader is almost no longer a listener)' will become the more strident expression heard at the end of his preface to *Beyond Good and Evil* ('one must learn to read').[9] This thought is also developed in *Human, All Too Human* (PREFACE, §8).

In addition to language, a second medium — movement — gives symbolic meaning or content to music (see 'Gesture and language', IV, §216). For Nietzsche, music without explanatory dance and miming (the language of gesture) is, at first, as empty noise. However, long habituation to the juxtaposition of music and gesture teaches the ear of the listener and observer to attain an immediate understanding of the figures presented in tones. Finally, the ear reaches such a level of rapid understanding that it no longer requires visible movement and understands the composer without it (IV, §216). But Nietzsche then seems to contradict himself by making a further distinction between music and absolute music. The latter he defines in the preceding reflection 'Music' (IV, §215) as 'form in itself' and 'symbolism of form speaking to the understanding without poetry'. 'Absolute music', a term used derogatorily by Wagner, before his discovery of Schopenhauer, for purely instrumental music, is defined by Nietzsche as music in which everything has to be understood symbolically without further aid (see IV, §216). The music by itself gives an immediate sense of reality, and thus the addition of symbols, words, or actions is irrelevant. Although Nietzsche makes a distinction between music and absolute music, he, unlike Wagner, does not judge their relative quality in these reflections. Rather, he attempts to remain a neutral observer. The fact that in *Human, All Too Human* the absolute music of ancient Greece is Nietzsche's highest ideal shows his definite departure from Wagner's view. In *The Birth of Tragedy* he was convinced that nothing, and especially not language, could ever adequately render the cosmic symbolism of music. *Human, All Too Human* suggests language and gesture as an enhancement of music's symbolism.

A View of Society through Music and Literature

In the aphorism 'Religious after-effects' (III, §131) Nietzsche considers the relation between music and religion and its meaning for society. Here, music is not simply described as a part of religious life; it has the capacity and power to convey sensations of religion and dogma, of spirituality and the universal. Even for the individual who has no religious affiliation or connection, music will always convey a sense of religious feeling. The function of music in this context is the satisfaction of a spiritual need that it awakens in us and fulfils at the same time. Music, in other words, enables us to enjoy religious sentiment without subscribing to any conceptual content.[10] The relation between music and religion is not only expressed in sentiment and spirituality, but in their interdependence. It was religion that initiated progress and change in music, as Nietzsche remarks in 'Religious origin of modern music' (IV, §219):

> Music of feelings comes into being within the restored Catholicism that followed the Council of Trent, through Palestrina, who assisted the newly awakened spirit to find utterance; with Bach, it extended to Protestantism, too, insofar as Protestantism has been deepened by the Pietists and detached from its original dogmaticism.

Not only have significant changes in religion led to changes in music, but music also becomes the means to convey religious sentiment (as in III, §131). Music reflects upon changes in religion and society, but above all it provides a home for the continued existence of religious feeling.[11]

Before Nietzsche wrote *Human, All Too Human*, literature and especially music served as substitutes for religion. Their function was to satisfy epistemological and sensory needs, a potential that he regarded as equal to a quasi-religious and metaphysical revelation.[12] In *The Birth of Tragedy* he demands a desecularization of society through the deification of art, an idea that he illustrates by taking the example of Greek theatre. Dance, poetry, rite, and music seemed inseparably associated in the early history of music in ancient Greece. Music was described as an art exerting great power, and certain musical styles came to be associated with particular peoples and deities. In *Human, All Too Human* this view is modified, as the arts and religion do not show this kind of deification of art. Music, rather, is seen as the final product of a tradition that is based in Christianity. As such, it is powerful only if it is connected to literature, ultimately in combination with science; in this combination alone does it have the potential to disempower religion by conveying religious sentiments. Nietzsche contends that art raises its head where religions decline (IV, §150). By assuming the feelings and moods of religion that had been dismantled by the Enlightenment, he claims that art gives new form to the life of feeling, and is capable of raising the endeavours of life to an exalted plane.

A different role of music and literature in relation to society becomes obvious in the preface to *Human, All Too Human* (§8):

> This *German* book, which has known how to find its readers in a wide circle of lands and peoples — it has been on its way for about ten years — and must be capable of some kind of music and flute-player's art by which even coy foreign ears are seduced to listen — it is precisely in Germany that this book been read most carelessly and *heard* the worst.

Nietzsche refers not only to reading *Human, All Too Human*, but to listening to it, even to hearing it. He claims that his works have the same ability that music has, particularly flute playing. What words seem incapable of achieving, music is able to attain: it can take hold of the psychological attention of the recipient. Music alone has the power to seduce or control the attention, and to affect and influence the human mind subconsciously. For Nietzsche, one aspect that ideally should connect *Human, All Too Human* to its readers is a basic understanding of music and flute playing. However, in his mention of music he uses a metaphor that would seem to be a direct criticism of German culture. Given Germany's long and significant tradition in music and literature, to say that the Germans are those who have 'heard' the book the worst can be meant only as an insult; consequently, they are not even capable of understanding 'the flute-player's art'. The motif of flute playing seems to allude also to Schopenhauer, whom Nietzsche several years later in *Beyond Good and Evil* (IV, §186) scornfully describes as a 'flute-playing pessimist, a repudiator of God and of the world'.[13] Despite the success of *Human, All Too Human* elsewhere, it is really the German nation that should have understood the book best of all, since the work draws upon (and opposes itself to) Schopenhauer. Since Schopenhauer was so ingrained in German thought, this should be the best perspective from which to appreciate Nietzsche's work.

The flute as metaphor also hints at Wagner, whose music Nietzsche comments upon as music of decadence and no longer the 'flute of Dionysus';[14] in contrast to Wagner's music, he praises flute playing as the expression of the Dionysian man.[15] 'Apollonian' and 'Dionysian' are terms based on Schopenhauerian concepts, used by Nietzsche in *The Birth of Tragedy* to designate the two central principles of Greek culture. The Dionysian, which corresponds roughly to Schopenhauer's concept of

Will, is directly opposed to the Apollonian. Music is the most Dionysian of the arts, since it appeals directly to man's instinctive, chaotic emotions and not to his rationally controlled mind. Beyond the potential sideswipes at Schopenhauer and Wagner, the idea of the flute, with its association with Dionysus, suggests that the reader must somehow be capable of using his instinct, which will ultimately lead him to read *Human, All Too Human*. This would appear to contradict the overall idea of the book, whose theoretical and scientific manner of proceeding represents the antithesis of Nietzsche's own Dionysian nature.[16] Nietzsche's social criticism is further developed in regard to the reception of literature, which might include the reception of his own writings. In his reflection 'Bad writers necessary' (IV, §201) he proclaims that bad authors are indispensable, since they are well received by underdeveloped generations and satisfy the taste of the immature reader. Thus, for Nietzsche, it appears that Germans, having lost their ability to judge literature, consequently prefer bad writers to good ones. His extremely critical opinion of Germany, expressed in the preface, is indirectly articulated once again here.

The Dichotomies of Music and Literature

In his reflection 'Poets as alleviators of life' (IV, §148) Nietzsche presents his conception of the contradictory effects that poetry can have on man in society. Poetry eases life, but at the same time, because of this, hinders us from the task of pursuing that which is of genuine practical importance. Since poets are 'backward-looking creatures', they draw their readers' attention to the past and distract them from the current responsibilities of life in the present. Consequently, poetry leads to inactivity and distraction. The relief from reality and the aesthetic pleasure of poetry both have negative consequences: a society that concentrates too much on the arts does not generally progress.

In the 'Draconian law against writers' (IV, §193) Nietzsche goes so far as to conclude that writing, and especially the 'invasion' of books, has a negative impact on society because of the increasing quantity — 'writers ought to be treated as malefactors'. He vehemently judges literature as counterproductive. This is not only an obvious criticism, but also a clear instance of Nietzsche's self-contradiction. On the one hand, language is significant for the evolution of culture — it gives meaning to music and represents important symbolism; on the other hand, literature and poetry as products of language do not serve society well. This unfavourable consequence of art in society is a leitmotif in *Human, All Too Human*, and can be found, with variations, in many other aphorisms, such as 'The artist's sense of truth' (IV §146), and 'Art as necromancer', where Nietzsche concludes that art is 'a phantom life that here arises' and makes 'mankind childlike' (IV §147). When reflecting more specifically on metre, which appears in both music and literature, Nietzsche expresses with even greater clarity that 'metre lays a veil over reality [...] Art makes the sight of life bearable by laying over it the veil of unclear thinking' (IV, §151).

Another aspect of the contradictory nature of the arts appears in 'Good narrators, bad explainers' (IV, §196). Here the contradiction is seen within the artist or the act of artistic expression itself. In particular, a discrepancy is evident between the psychologically consistent narrative and the author's incompetence in psychological thinking. We can find many examples of this Nietzschean position in fiction: many authors describe professions, procedures, habits, and so on, with meticulous accuracy and detail, without having studied the theory of these subjects for themselves. Nietzsche transfers this observation to the example of a pianist who 'has reflected very little on technical matters and the particular virtue, vice, utility and educability of each finger (dactyl ethics), and blunders badly whenever he speaks of such things' (IV, §151). The contradictory nature of the artist, the poet, and the musician is expressed in the artistic intention versus the artistic understanding. In other words Nietzsche recognizes a discrepancy between practice and theory.

An oppositional tension can also be observed between artist and audience. With regard to literature Nietzsche points out that readers prefer the writing of obscure authors rather than clear-minded ones. This derives from a misjudgement of easily understood writers as not being intellectually challenging enough (IV, §181). It becomes clear that Nietzsche sees an opposition between art and culture, which he expresses even more specifically in a later reflection, 'Too near and too far' (IV, §202):

> The reader and the author often fail to understand one another because the author knows his theme too well and almost finds it boring, so that he dispenses with the examples and illustrations of which he knows hundreds; the reader, however, is unfamiliar with the subject and can easily find it ill-established if examples and illustrations are withheld from him.

The tension between writer and reader seems difficult to overcome. The author, who is not challenged by too much information, finds himself in opposition to the reader, who is overly challenged and ultimately frustrated, since he or she lacks the information that is necessary for understanding. In between stands literature itself, in which both perspectives meet. Literature, the in-between space of two conflicting entities, generates tension and contributes to divergence within society (instead of easing life, as Nietzsche proclaimed in §148). Even if the author compromises, the tension can hardly be overcome. In 'Sacrifice of rhythm' (IV, §198) the author tries to make literature more accessible to the reader and 'alters the rhythm'. Consequently, his art sacrifices its quality and essence to suit the perceiver. Can this still be called art, since art by nature expresses the freedom of its creator?

When reflecting more generally on art, Nietzsche proposes a solution to overcome the gap between artist and receiver, which again demands a compromise from the artist:

> Progress from one stylistic level to the next must proceed so slowly that not only the artists but the auditors and spectators too can participate in this progress and know exactly what is going on. Otherwise there suddenly appears that great gulf between the artist creating his works on a remote height and the public, which, no longer able to attain to that height, at length disconsolately climbs back down again deeper than before. For when the artist no longer raises his public up, it swiftly sinks downwards, and it plunges the deeper and more perilously the higher a genius has borne it, like the eagle from whose claws the tortoise it has carried up into the clouds falls to its death. (IV, §168)

The only way to overcome the essential differences between poet and reader, musician and listener, painter and observer seems to be the repetition of a style, a motif, a genre, or a form. Nietzsche proposes that only after becoming familiar with art by seeing numerous versions of it will the public be able to grasp, understand, and enjoy it (IV: §167). Yet, for the artist, the need to repeat means having to avoid new expression of that which is freely conceived.

In his discourse on the artist–recipient relationship, Nietzsche questions the distinction between objectivity and subjectivity. He sees the claim to objectivity as an attempt to gain a powerful position through a privileged and superior vantage point. Philosophers, scientists, and art critics claim objectivity in virtue of their believed ability to attain a God's-eye view through the exercise of their reason. Nietzsche considers that such a view is not possible, and that claims to objectivity are always unsound. This view is further expressed in 'Art of the ugly soul' (IV, §152):

> One imposes far too narrow limitations on art when one demands that only well-ordered, morally balanced souls may express themselves in it. As in the plastic arts, so in music and poetry too there is an art of the ugly soul besides the art of the beautiful soul; and the mightiest effects of art, that which tames souls, moves stones and humanizes the beast, have perhaps been mostly achieved by precisely that art.

Here Nietzsche's reflections on art oppose a rationalist view and explain it as a simple and direct expression of the mind. Central to his perspective is the apparent dichotomy of the beautiful versus the ugly. On first view it is not clear if beauty and ugliness refer to morality or aesthetics. Nietzsche does not decide between these perspectives, but simply names the ugly and the beautiful. Instead of seeing art from the standpoint of morality, so that its function is to achieve balance and/or order in society, Nietzsche even goes so far as to justify why the ugly *is* art and why it deserves equal attention with the beautiful. The ugly sets the greatest passions free and overcomes borders ('moves stones'), it cultivates and civilizes ('humanizes the beast'), it disciplines and humbles ('tames souls'). When Nietzsche reflects on the ugly and the beautiful, he is referring to aesthetic aspects, but these are things that, independently of ugly or beautiful qualities, have an impact on society's morality.

Nietzsche sees society as an active participant in art. He is convinced that all art is incomplete, so that the observer of art participates in its creation by active perception and by engaging with the work through the imagination. The observer has the potential to integrate himself into the created object (IV, §§178, 185, 199). The contradictory nature of participation in art is exemplified in the recitation or narration of literature and poetry. In the aphorism 'The reciter' (VI, §344) Nietzsche says that whoever reads dramatic poetry aloud makes discoveries about his own character. This exemplifies the power of literature: through representing a passion, a scene, or a mood in recitation, the individual has the opportunity to find analogies or their absence in his own character. This introspection or self-exploration through literature is, therefore, dependent on each person's character. In contradistinction to this positive effect of art, we find a very different expression in the preceding aphorism 'The narrator' (VI, §343): the narrator may be motivated to recite either because the subject interests him, or because he wants to arouse interest in himself.

In both cases, if he chooses to recite for the sake of self-interest, his narration will be exaggerated and consequently dreadful.

Nietzsche generally presents an opposition between two heterogeneous realms or powers: art (music, literature, and the plastic arts) versus science. But he also provides a solution as to how the individual can cope with this tension within culture. He speaks of creating 'such a large edifice of culture out of himself that both powers can live there' (V: §276), which means that the creative individual needs to develop an open-mindedness, a broad and flexible cultural intellect, within which both entities can coexist. Nietzsche demands a free-thinking character, one that does not restrict itself but seeks, rather, to overcome and transgress borders that society has created, thereby achieving a synthesis of art and science. The creation of such a coexistence or synthesis is crucial for rehabilitating music and literature and achieving the balance that both lack: 'We owe to Christianity, to the philosophers, poets and musicians, a superabundance of deeply agitated feelings; to keep these from engulfing us, we must conjure up the spirit of science, which makes us somewhat colder and more sceptical' (V, §244). Only when moderated by the scientific can music and literature manage to overcome their own ambivalences and lead members of societies and cultures to become free and critical thinkers able to negotiate the gaps and disjunctures that keep human beings from having complete power over their lives.

Beyond Music and Literature

Nietzsche's insights into the complex and differing relationships of music and literature implicitly reflect upon the multifaceted interconnection of the two sister arts in the nineteenth century in general. Literature and narrative influenced musical compositions when literary Romanticism entered the musical vocabulary in a variety of genres. Reciprocally, music inspired and shaped works of literature; writers saw music as a paradigm of art, and they wished to bring the qualities of music to literature. The nineteenth century was perhaps the most literary of all centuries, and beyond the mutual influences and analogies, a shift from music to literature may be observed. Paradoxically, nineteenth-century instrumental music linked itself to narrative forms at the same time that it was itself valorized as a model for all the arts.

Human, All Too Human also reveals no consistent position with respect to music and literature. It presents a combination of the philosophical and the artistic, the naturalistic and the creative, the logical or conceptual and the poetic and metaphoric, oppositions that can be found in many aphorisms. Nietzsche's thinking about music and literature entered a new phase in this work. His views seem to regard the free play of the two arts as providing an outlet for spiritual pleasure. An undercurrent of thought devoted to music and literature (including language) is expressed in isolated aphorisms that seem disconnected and randomly dispersed, paradoxical and aporetic. They provide puzzlement through raising philosophical objections without offering any solutions. The presentation of music and literature displays contradictory tendencies, for the two arts are viewed as in between valuable aesthetics and negative distraction. But what seems incoherent is, in fact, not so. Nietzsche openly rejects system building and rationalism in favour of self-inspection. That he does not take a consistent position and often contradicts himself is a result of his concern with free thought. For Nietzsche, there can be no single truth, nothing fixed and concrete. He contradicts himself because he wants the reader to see the many sides of the argument, to force the reader to think for himself, and to reveal the underlying contradictions in the reader's assumptions.[17]

What connects all the contradictory aphorisms is an underlying criticism of the four interconnected concepts of metaphysics, religion, morality, and art. All four are related to music and literature. Nietzsche objects to music and literature (especially poetry) as the metaphysical, since, as such, they seduce people into dealing with tribulations only on a short-lived, inefficient level (unlike science, which provides cures). Music in particular is redundant and pernicious. Its only function is easing the passage from a religious to a secular outlook; it serves as a substitute for religion and as a home for the existence of religious feelings. There is an antithetical tension between art and revelation that is a consequence of the musician's and poet's striving for effect instead of truth, and for inspiration and sensation instead of method and technique.

So, to use Nietzsche's own question: What is left of art? He calls attention to the overall importance of music and literature, and concludes:

> One could give up art, but would not thereby relinquish the capacity one has learned from it [...] As the plastic arts and music are the measure of the wealth of feelings we have actually gained and obtained through religion, so if art disappeared the intensity and multifariousness of the joy in life it has implanted would still continue to demand satisfaction. The scientific man is the further evolution of the artistic. (IV, §222)

The disappearance of art leads to science, the evolutionary successor to the arts, to satisfy the intensity and joy that art formerly provided. Nietzsche seems to dismiss art, whose importance has been inherited by science, and it is now without function. Can this really be true? Such a rejection of art contradicts Nietzsche's overall thinking and line of argument.[18] To state the obvious, it is irreducibly at odds with the simple fact that in a certain number of aphorisms Nietzsche explains the functions of music and literature. So the above cannot be interpreted as a mere dismissal. Nietzsche's treatment of music and literature exemplifies a process of philosophical thinking in transition. *Human, All Too Human*, a work strongly associated with Nietzsche's break from Wagner and Schopenhauer, presents itself as ideas in the process of undergoing evolution and change. Although Nietzsche tried to distance himself from his two idols, it seems as if he could not quite accomplish a complete separation. This is evidenced by the fact that in May 1878 Nietzsche sent Wagner a copy of his book with a motto from Descartes (not Schopenhauer) and a dedication to Voltaire (not Wagner). The book and a copy of Wagner's new opera *Parsifal* all but crossed in the post. Wagner's work struck Nietzsche as an insincere, theatrical obeisance to Christianity and a contemptible glorification of empty tradition. In return Wagner attacked Nietzsche in the *Bayreuther Blätter* of August 1878. *Human, All Too Human* did not seal the break with Wagner — that had already been accomplished — but the book does attempt to articulate the split in written form. Both the possibility of doing so, and its ultimate failure, rest on its contradictory treatment of the eternally recurrent themes of music and literature.

Notes to Chapter 3

This article originated in a 1994 lecture presented in the Department of German Literature at the Gerhard-Mercator-Universität in Duisburg, Germany. Dr Mark Ast and Pryor Dodge made helpful comments on an earlier draft. Special thanks are due to Dr Robert Samuels for his work on the English of the essay.

1. Friedrich Nietzsche, *Human, All Too Human: A Book for Free Spirits*, trans. by R. J. Hollingdale (Cambridge: Cambridge University Press, 1986). Throughout this essay I refer only to the first part of the work, *Human, All Too Human*, published in 1878.

2. As Julian Young observed in *Nietzsche's Philosophy of Art* (Cambridge: Cambridge University Press, 1992), p. 38.

3. Nietzsche, *Human, All Too Human*, pp. 5–12.

4. Giuliano Campioni, 'Wohin man reisen muß', *Nietzsche-Studien*, 16 (1987), 209–26.

5. In this context 'collectivism' can be understood as a doctrine in political (or ethical) philosophy that holds that the individual's actions should benefit some kind of collective organization like a tribe, the members of a certain profession, the state, a community, etc., rather than the individual himself.

6. Henceforth, references in text to particular aphorisms in *Human, All Too Human* will appear in abbreviated form, with section number (except for the Preface) and paragraph number(s) only.

7. Friedrich Nietzsche, 'On Music and Words', trans. by Walter Kaufmann, in *Between Romanticism and Modernism: Four Studies in the Music of the Later 19th Century*, ed. by Carl Dahlhaus (Berkeley: University of California Press, 1980), pp. 106–19 (p. 106). See Arthur Schopenhauer, *Die Welt als Wille und Vorstellung*, 2 vols (Munich: Piper, 1911), II, §39, 511–12.

8. See Friedrich Nietzsche, 'Description of Ancient Rhetoric (1872–73)', trans. by R. J. Hollingdale, in *Friedrich Nietzsche on Rhetoric and Language*, ed. by Sander Gilman, Carole Blair, and David J. Parent (Oxford: Oxford University Press, 1989), pp. 2–193 (pp. 21, 24).

9. Friedrich Nietzsche, *Beyond Good and Evil: Prelude to a Philosophy of the Future*, trans. by Judith Norman (Cambridge: Cambridge University Press, 2001), pp. 3–5.

10. Young, p. 65.

11. Young, p. 66.

12. Peter Heller, *'Von den ersten und letzten Dingen'. Studien und Kommentar zu einer Aphorismenreihe von Friedrich Nietzsche,* Monographien und Texte zur Nietzsche-Forschung, 1 (Berlin: de Gruyter, 1972), pp. 67–69.

13. Nietzsche, *Beyond Good and Evil*, p. 71.

14. Friedrich Nietzsche, *Ecce Homo: How One Becomes What One Is*, trans. by R. J. Hollingdale (New York: Penguin, 1993), p. 89.

15. Friedrich Nietzsche, *The Birth of Tragedy; and, The Case of Wagner*, trans. by Walter Kaufmann (New York: Vintage books, 1967), p. 61.

16. See Young, p. 59.

17. See Wolfgang Müller-Lauter, *Nietzsche: His Philosophy of Contradictions and the Contradictions of his Philosophy*, trans. by David J. Parent (Urbana: University of Illinois, 1999).

18. See Young, pp. 72–73.

CHAPTER 4

The Force of Music in Derrida's Writing

Peter Dayan

'Jacques Derrida [...] has written almost nothing specifically about music.' Whether one can agree with Richard Kurth's affirmation[1] depends on how one interprets the words 'specifically about'. Derrida never wrote at length on a specific work of music, but scattered throughout his own work are references to music that play a crucial role in a certain articulation of his thought. Those references, though numerous, always remain curiously undeveloped, for which there is a very good reason. Music, in Derrida's writing, is at the centre of a series of paradoxes on which his art depends, paradoxes that must be repeatedly lived out, but never argued through.

At this point I shall risk a proposition that will at first seem crude and naive in the extreme, namely: Derrida maintains the old association between the poetic and the musical, the tradition according to which the poetic is defined by an obscure but inescapable relation to music. Take the following example, which is particularly revealing in that it remains so completely undeveloped, so untheorized:

> Je rêve [...] je rêve encore sans doute de savoir vous parler non seulement en brigand mais poétiquement, en poète. Du poème dont je rêve, je ne serai sans doute pas capable. Et d'ailleurs, dans quelle langue aurais-je pu l'écrire ou le chanter?[2]

> [I dream [...] I still dream, I expect, of being able to speak to you not only as a brigand, but also poetically, as a poet. I expect I shall not be capable of the poem of which I dream. And in any case, in what language could I have written or sung it?]

Why 'ou le chanter' ('or sung it')? Nothing other than tradition seems to prepare or justify this evocation of song. But then, there is nothing obvious in the text to say what exactly Derrida means by poetry. One is left with the impression, therefore, that the role of the verb 'chanter' is somehow to explain the noun 'poème', and vice versa. Let us not forget, however, that the notion of song is not introduced until Derrida has made it clear that he has no language in which to write his poem; that the poetry that he would have sung is beyond any language he owns. Music, in Derrida's texts, stands first and foremost for that which remains beyond anything that we can call our own.

In *Glas* Derrida says that there are a small number of phrases that stand out for him and which he remembers and compulsively repeats. The most famous of these is 'il y a là cendre' ('there are ashes here'). Another such phrase is 'ce qui reste à force de musique', which might be translated as 'what remains by dint of music', or 'thanks to music'; or, 'what the work of music leaves'. If we read the sentence, as Derrida sometimes does, without the accent on the word 'a', which turns the preposition into a verb, it would mean 'what remains has the force of music'. Both meanings are played on in Derrida's article 'Ce qui reste à force de musique'.[3] Remains after what? The answer often appears to be: after language, after a speaking voice has been silenced, or, more subtly, replacing or displacing the voice.

In *La Carte postale* Derrida's first person narrator (generally taken as autobiographical) posts to his distant beloved a cassette, and writes:

> tu sonnes dimanche prochain (à minuit chez toi) au moment où tu commenceras à m'écouter (enfin, c'est surtout de la musique, le chant d'une autre voix, mais tu accepteras que ce soit moi [...])
>
> [call next Sunday (at midnight for you) at the moment when you start to listen to me (well, it's mostly music, the song of another voice, but you will accept it as me [...])][4]

Or he leaves music for her to listen to in his absence:

> Tu peux ne pas m'attendre. N'oublie pas la petite musique et le disque laissé sur le plateau.
>
> [You can not wait for me. Don't forget the little tune and the record left on the turntable.][5]

Or he thinks of putting on a record for her to listen to over the phone:

> Tu dors? Et si je t'appelais? Et si près de l'écouteur je plaçais, sans rien dire, ce disque. Lequel? Devine, devine.
>
> [Are you sleeping? And if I called? And if I placed this record near the receiver, without saying anything? Which record? Divine, divine.][6]

As if music's role were to speak for him, to make of him, as it were, a ventriloquist's dummy. This ventriloquial force of music is often apparent in Derrida's work.[7] Music speaks his love, in its own voice, better than he can speak it himself. But to this end it must first remove his own capacity for speech. The musical is what remains only once the letter has gone. Once again we hear in the background the refrain 'ce qui reste a force de musique': 'ce qui resterait de nous a force de musique, pas un mot, pas une lettre' ('what would remain of us thanks to music, not a word, not a letter').[8]

And what happens to the writer at this point where not a word remains? He ceases to be himself; he ceases to be the instance that controls the writing. As the voice comes from elsewhere, he knows not what he does. That, perhaps, is the condition of the writing in which love may be given to be understood:

> Mais vous ne pouvez vous intéresser à ce que je fais ici que dans la mesure où vous auriez raison de croire que — *quelque part* — je ne sais pas ce que je fais.
>
> [You can take interest in what I am doing here only insofar as you would be right [*auriez raison*] to believe that — *somewhere* — I do not know what I am doing.][9]

But if love requires us to go beyond that which we can articulate as self-possessed language, as knowledge, so does literature.

Le nom et la chose nommée 'littérature' auront été et restent pour moi, jusqu'à ce jour, autant que des passions, des énigmes sans fond.[10]

[The name and the thing named 'literature' will have been and remain for me, to this day, as much as they are my passions, bottomless enigmas.]

Or, as Jean Genet puts it, quoted by Derrida in *Glas*:

C'est seulement ces sortes de vérités, celles qui ne sont pas démontrables et même qui sont '*fausses*', celles que l'on ne peut conduire sans absurdité jusqu'à leur extrémité sans aller jusqu'à la négation d'elles et de soi, c'est celles-là qui doivent être exaltées par l'œuvre d'art. Elle n'auront jamais la chance ou la malchance d'être appliquées. Qu'elles vivent par le chant qu'elles sont devenues et qu'elles suscitent.

[Only those kinds of truths, those that are not demonstrable and are even '*false*,' those that we cannot, without absurdity, conduct to their extremes without going to their negation and our own, those are the truths that ought to be exalted by the work of art. They will never have the chance or the mischance of being applied someday. May they live through the song they have become and sustain.][11]

For Genet, the logic governing the relative positions of music and letters would seem to be that the true writer will follow through certain kinds of truth to the point where they negate themselves and him. At that point they are reborn as song. This corresponds to Derrida's sense that 'what remains has the force of music'. But Derrida takes further than Genet the analysis of what precisely is the characteristic of writing that must die for song to arise. It is the exchange value of the word; the possibility of calculating its value.

It was in the context of what turned out to be a spectacular public miscalculation that Derrida produced his clearest exposition of the relations between music and words. In 1997, at Ornette Coleman's invitation, Derrida appeared unannounced on stage in the middle of one of Coleman's concerts at La Villette, Paris, intending to recite an 'improvised' text, with Coleman's music, as part of a sort of jazz dialogue between music and words. He was rapidly booed off stage, an unpleasant experience to which he had never before been subjected. Derrida, with characteristic frankness, gave an interview on the subject to *Jazz Magazine*,[12] and the text of his proposed 'improvisation', together with an interview of Coleman by Derrida, was published in *Les Inrockuptibles* under the title 'La Langue de l'autre' ('The Language of the Other').[13] Its first page is occupied by a striking illustration showing Derrida playing a saxophone while Coleman reads from a book. The natural inference, from title to image, is that music is Coleman's language, writing is Derrida's, and they have been, in a sense, exchanging languages. But in the interview the question of the other's language is never put in these terms. It emerges at the point where Derrida and Coleman talk about the fact that neither of them knows the language of his ancestors; they were raised in the language of an imperial colonial power. Coleman asks: 'Est-ce qu'une langue originaire peut influencer vos pensées?' ('Can the language of your origins have an influence on your thoughts?'). And Derrida replies:

C'est une énigme[14] pour moi. Je ne peux pas le savoir. Je sais que quelque chose parle à travers moi, une langue que je ne comprends pas, que quelquefois je traduis dans ma propre 'langue'.[15]

FIG. 4.1. Ornette Coleman and Jacques Derrida in concert at
La Villette, Paris, 1 July 1997. Photo: Christian Ducasse

[That is an enigma for me. I can't know. I do know that something speaks through me, a language that I don't understand, that I sometimes translate into my own 'language'.]

Once again, ventriloquy: a voice from elsewhere, which he does not understand, speaks through him. The language of this other voice is incommensurable with his own language. That is doubtless the signification of the inverted commas around the second occurrence of the word, to show it is heterogeneous to the first. But how can one translate from a language that one cannot understand? If one takes what Derrida says at face value, as suggesting that he translates from the atavistic language of his ancestors into French, it seems obscure, even spiritualist. However, if one allows oneself to remember that the language of the other appeared, at the start of the article, to be music, all becomes, if not clear, then at least recognizably part of a pattern into which the notion of translation can insert itself without adding much to the pattern's complexity.

Translation, an impossible translation out of an incomprehensible language, is a common enough metaphor for such negotiations between love, music, poetry, and language, and by no means a novel one. One finds it in Baudelaire, Sand, or Proust; and in 'Tympan' Derrida quotes a phrase in which Michel Leiris clearly takes up this tradition: 'la ligne mélodique se présentant comme la traduction, en un idiome purement sonore, de ce qui ne pourrait être dit par le moyen des mots' ('the melodic line presenting itself as the translation, in a purely sonorous idiom, of that which could not be said by means of words').[16] Music as the translation of an inaccessible original is certainly a concept that suits the peculiar dynamics of music and writing, not least because it renders the notion of translation itself infinitely problematic. How can one judge the music as a translation, if it cannot be called to account by comparison with its original? 'A bad translation will always be summoned to stand before the original [...] Anyone impairing the original identity of this text may have to appear before the law'.[17] This legal structure is powerless to deal with music as translation, because one cannot calculate the equivalence between source and target languages. But perhaps this powerlessness is the condition of art. Perhaps the peculiar membrane around music that allows it to be perceived as translation, but forbids any economic analysis of that translation, is that which allows music, or even art in general, to exist.

Poetry, like music, or even thanks to music, is a gift beyond price. This may sound like a cliché, but one might resume under this slogan a remarkably high proportion of Derrida's reflection on both these subjects, including the 'improvisation' for the Coleman concert, which defines music as that for which, precisely, there is no price. It takes as its theme an anecdote that Coleman had recounted to Derrida during their interview. When Coleman had complained to his mother about the unsatisfactory relationship between his art and his income, she had replied: 'Do you want to be paid for your soul?'

> '*Do you want to be paid for your soul?*' [...] Voilà ce que lui a dit sa mère: on n'est pas payé, on n'a pas à être payé pour son âme, et l'âme, c'est ça, c'est ce qui arrive, c'est ça la musique qu'il faut entendre et qu'il faut faire — et qu'il faut écrire: ce pourquoi on n'a pas à être payé parce que c'est incalculable et sans prix.[18]

> ['*Do you want to be paid for your soul?*' [...] That is what his mother said to him;

you don't get paid, you shouldn't get paid for your soul, and the soul is just that, it's what is happening here, it's the music that you have to hear and that you have to make — and that you have to write; what you shouldn't get paid for because it is incalculable, it has no price.][19]

Thus, with music, on the side of the incalculable, we have the soul. What label could we give to the instance on the other side of the divide? The instance that believes it possesses a language, a language in which exchange values can be calculated? For obviously — to revert to being crude and naive — music, like writing, can certainly exist (or be perceived) in a form that is not from the soul; and for that form one can receive a calculable payment. Indeed, that is precisely what Coleman was complaining about: not that he was receiving no money, but that in order to receive money he was having to produce music to order — calculated music, rather than music from the soul.

In *Donner le temps* Derrida provides an answer to my question concerning the label to be applied to the opposite of soul, an answer that may seem surprising, but one that is not only helpful, but highly functional, and could, I think, serve to clarify many debates concerning the status of texts, writing, literature, and music. That answer is: the subject.

> En tant que sujet identifiable, bordé, posé, l'écrivant et son écriture ne donnent jamais rien dont ils ne calculent, consciemment ou inconsciemment, la réappropriation, l'échange ou le retour circulaire — et par définition la réappropriation avec plus-value, une certaine capitalisation. Nous nous risquerons à dire que c'est la définition même du *sujet en tant que tel*. On ne peut le discerner que comme le sujet de cette opération du capital.

> [As an identifiable, bordered, posed subject, the one who writes and his or her writing never give anything without calculating, consciously or unconsciously, its reappropriation, its exchange, or its circular return — and by definition this means reappropriation with surplus-value, a certain capitalization. We will even venture to say that this is the very definition of the *subject as such*. One cannot discern the subject except as the the subject of this operation of capital.][20]

The subject as such, in writing, is that which calculates. The soul is that which does not, and which, when it writes, even if it uses words, writes music.

Later in the 'improvisation', Derrida quotes three texts that he had earlier written about music, all three revolving around the themes of music as a singular voice from elsewhere, and of death-in-music. The third is from 'Tympan', the second from 'Ce qui reste à force de musique', and the first from 'Circonfession'.

> quand je ne rêve pas de faire l'amour, d'être un résistant de la dernière guerre en train de faire sauter des trains, je veux une seule chose, me perdre dans l'orchestre que je formerais avec mes fils, guérir, bénir et séduire le monde en jouant divinement avec mes fils, produire avec eux l'extase musicale du monde, **leur création**, j'accepterai de mourir si c'est là descendre lentement, oui, jusqu'au fond de cette musique bien-aimée.[21]

> [when I'm not dreaming of making love or of being a resistance fighter in the last war, blowing up trains, I want only one thing, to lose myself in an orchestra that I would form with my sons, to heal, bless and seduce the world by playing divinely with my sons, to produce with them the musical ecstasy of the world,

their creation, I will accept death if death means to sink slowly, yes, down to the bottom of that beloved music.]

A banal fantasy, perhaps, but its very banality reveals the extent to which Derrida's relation to music, in its unexamined oddity, is widespread in our culture. Let us note first that this music does not exist in autarky. It is created with his sons — it is indeed their creation — and it has an effect on the world, 'le monde'.[22] Let us also note that Derrida's fantasy involves the loss of himself: 'to lose myself in an orchestra'. What does it mean thus to lose oneself, and which is the self that is lost? We now have our answer. In the orchestral fantasy the subject is lost, but not the soul. Death is acceptable in music, but not outside it, because in music the subject, as it dies, leaves a remainder, a remainder in which the incalculable gift of love is to be found. But that incalculable gift can only occur in the time of rhythm.

> *Là où il y a le don, il y a le temps* [...] Ça demande du temps, la chose, mais ça demande un temps délimité, ni un instant ni un temps infini, mais un temps déterminé par un terme, autrement dit un rythme, une cadence [...] un rythme qui n'advient pas à un temps homogène mais qui le structure originairement.
>
> [*There where there is gift, there is time* [...] It demands time, the thing, but it demands a delimited time, neither an instant nor an infinite time, but a time determined by a term, in other words a rhythm, a cadence [...] a rhythm that does not befall a homogeneous time but that structures it originarily.][23]

Derrida habitually invokes rhythm thus: as that without which our time, *including* the time of the gift, of music, of poetry, and in my terms of soul, is unthinkable. It also remains peculiarly unanalysed; indeed, it is the most incalculable Derridean concept of all. This is particularly striking when, in *Glas*, Derrida weaves together the incalculability of rhythm with that of poetic translation. We have seen that around music perceived as translation there seems to be a peculiar membrane that prevents any calculation of equivalence between the translation and its original. What becomes apparent in *Glas* is that the same membrane surrounds poetry as translation; and that membrane's existence is maintained by the concept, at once musical and poetic, of rhythm.

Derrida is discussing Mallarmé's translation of Poe's poem *The Bells*, and asking what, exactly, Mallarmé has translated. Plainly, it is not simply the referential sense of the words. If it had been, the translation would have been calculable. Indeed, in this sense, says Derrida, what Mallarmé produces, although it is a kind of imitation, is not what we normally call a translation. Is it the sound that is reproduced? Not exactly. The only word that Derrida seems able to find is 'rhythm'.

> la *mimesis* se recharge et opère d'un texte à l'autre, de chaque texte à son thème ou à sa référence sans que les mots ressemblent originellement aux choses et sans qu'ils se ressemblent immédiatement entre eux. Cependant la ressemblance se reconstitue, se surimpose ou surimprime à travers et grâce à des structures différentielles ou relationnelles. Le contenu s'y exténue, parfois jusqu'à être tout près de disparaître. De disparaître comme *qualité*, comme *quantité*, mais plus rarement comme *rythme* [...] Les rimes de Poe ne sont pas conservées, bien sûr, mais à toutes les échelles, le plus possible, les battements d'un rythme, quels qu'en soient le support ou la surface matérielle.

[*mimesis* recharges itself and operates from one text to the other, from each text to its theme or to its reference, without the words originally resembling things and without them immediately resembling each other. And yet the resemblance reconstitutes itself, superimposes or superimprints itself through and thanks to differential or relational structures. There the content is exhausted, sometimes to the point of being about to disappear. To disappear as *quality*, as *quantity*, but more rarely as *rhythm* [...] Poe's rhymes are not preserved, of course, but on all levels, as many as possible, the beats of a rhythm, whatever their support or material surface.][24]

Strangely, rhythm appears opposed here to *quality* and *quantity*. But how can one have a rhythm without quantity? Is not rhythm composed, precisely, of quantities? And can those quantities themselves exist without qualities? In other words, can a rhythm exist independently of its 'support or material surface'? Is there an abstract essence of rhythm that can be translated, transported from one language to another, from one poem to another? At first glance Derrida seems to suggest that there is, simply by the way in which he presents his evidence of the link between Poe's version and Mallarmé's. He juxtaposes quotations of the original and of the translation, and affirms that the conserved rhythm is there. He seems to expect readers to nod their heads, and say, 'Yes, I see it'. And he affirms:

Le sémantique est frappé par le rythme de son autre, s'y expose, ouvert, offert dans son hiatus même.

Cet autre, qu'on serait tenté d'isoler comme une concaténation de signifiants, d'identités d'éléments arbitraires, se réemploie sans cesse selon une mimétique qui ne se rapporte pas à un son réel, à un contenu plein mais bien, comme la transposition le fait apparaître, à des structures rythmiques relationnelles sans aucun contenu invariant, aucun élément ultime.

[The semantic element is struck by the rhythm of its other, exposes, opens, offers itself there, in its very hiatus.

This other, which one would be tempted to isolate as a concatenation of signifiers, of identities of arbitrary elements, is unceasingly reemployed according to a mimetics that is not related to a real sound, to a full content, but indeed, as the transposition makes all that appear, to relational rhythmic structures with no invariable content, no ultimate element.][25]

Derrida is here opposing a 'full content' (which is not what a poetic translation translates) to 'relational rhythmic structures'. But why should we believe in the latter, in the total absence of evidence as to their specific character? We are in dangerous territory here. I would go so far as to say that Derrida is skating on thin ice, indeed on ice that he himself has rendered thin.

The clearest lesson that Derrida has taught us is that there is no meaning without articulation, and no articulation without inscription, without a material trace; hence, meaning is never separate from structure. But, in language, the converse applies just as clearly: structure is never separate from meaning. When we perceive in a poem a 'relational rhythmic structure', we do so in relation to the sense of the words. To state the obvious: if one reads a poem in a language one does not know, one does not perceive rhythmic structures in the same way as someone who knows that language. If this were not the case, then, to the extent that one accepts that it is rhythm that makes the poem, translations of poetry would be a waste of time. The language of a poem would simply not matter, since its rhythm would be perceptible to all. But the language of a poem does matter. Poetic rhythm depends on the specific language of the poem, simply because meaning depends on the specific language, and poetic rhythm depends on meaning. Therefore, the question of the translation of rhythm is no less fraught and complex than the question of the translation of meaning. Now, the translation of meaning is traditionally conceived as the replacement of one signifier by another having the same signified. Thus the English word 'bells', for example, can be replaced by the French word 'cloches'. But this implies an unproblematic view of the relationship between signifier and signified that ignores, precisely, the specificity of each language. In fact, the signified does not simply exist outside language, being itself the product of linguistic structures. No one has done more than Derrida (for example, through his reflection on the notion of single or a universal language, from Babel to Warburton) to demonstrate this, to deconstruct the metaphysical notion of the signified beyond words. But does not the same apply to rhythm? Is it not the case that rhythm, like the signified, cannot simply be separated from the signifying system that produces it? In which case, Derrida's apparent opposition between 'full content' — which is not to be transposed from one language to another — and 'relational rhythmic structures' — which can be and are so transposed — would be simply fallacious, a typical deconstructible logocentric mystification. Like the myth of unarticulated music, the myth of transposable rhythm would be Derrida's means of conserving an essence of art in defiance of the logic of his own method.

But if one looks more closely at the precise expressions Derrida uses, it becomes apparent that things are not so simple. Is he asserting, exactly, that Mallarmé's rhythms translate, take up, imitate, or transpose Poe's? No. He appears, perhaps, to imply it, but he never actually says it. Let us return to our first quotation: 'Les rimes de Poe ne sont pas conservées, bien sûr, mais à toutes les échelles, le plus possible, les battements d'un rythme, quels qu'en soient le support ou la surface matérielle' ('Poe's rhymes are not preserved, of course, but on all levels, as many as possible, the beats of a rhythm, whatever their support or material surface'). Note the indefinite article before the word 'rythme'. Is it specifically Poe's rhythm that is conserved? Or merely a rhythm? Rhythm as a substance as incalculable as soul, as Ornette Coleman's soul's music? Are these rhythmic structures in any sense *present* in Poe's poem? Nothing is less clear. Perhaps we are being referred to the rhythm of the relations between Mallarmé's poem and Poe's, rather than to any rhythm inherent in Poe's poem. There is rhythm. The rhythm is structured by a certain relation of meaning to its other. But on the question of exactly what or where that structure might be, what material element it is inscribed in, and where its trace may be followed, Derrida says nothing. Indeed, it would seem that here is the very limit of the possibility of saying — as symbolized by the blank lines in Derrida's text.

Once one has become alert to this role of rhythm in Derrida, one sees the word everywhere, and always with the same peculiarities. 'Les Morts de Roland Barthes' ('The Deaths of Roland Barthes') shows particularly clearly the close relationship between rhythm and music, and the impossibility of calculating either. The essay begins thus: 'Comment accorder ce pluriel? A qui? Cette question s'entend aussi selon la musique' ('How does one reconcile this plural? With whom might it agree [accorder]? And these questions must also be understood in terms of music').[26] Beyond the association between music and the death of the subject that we saw at work in the orchestral fantasy, what has the question of the plurality of Barthes's deaths to do with music? The connection becomes clearer when Derrida sets to analysing the relationship in Barthes's book *La Chambre claire* (*Camera Lucida*) between the two key concepts of 'studium' and 'punctum'. Between these concepts, says Derrida, there is not simply opposition, but composition, and 'la composition, c'est aussi la musique' ('the composition is also the music').[27] Such a composition is a structure organized according to the logic not of philosophy, but of what Derrida calls 'scansion'. Barthes, in his book, is not setting out an argument leading to a calculated conclusion; rather, he 'fait droit au rythme requis de la composition, d'une composition musicale' ('accedes to the requisite rhythm of the composition, a musical composition').[28] Or, again: 'entre les deux concepts, le rapport n'est ni tautologique, ni oppositionnel, ni dialectique, ni en quoi que ce soit symétrique, il est supplémentaire et musical (contrapuntique)' ('the relationship between the two concepts is neither tautological nor oppositional, neither dialectical nor in any sense symmetrical; it is supplementary and musical (contrapuntal)'.[29] Clearly, behind these affirmations lies the notion, now familiar to us, that there are two types of writing: the writing of the subject, which calculates; and the writing of the soul, which gives, in music. What remains as unclear here as in *Glas* is the specific structure of the rhythm itself — or what it translates. Here as elsewhere, in other words, Derrida describes the laws that govern the emergence of rhythm, the establishment of a space for rhythm: a certain relation to time, to the other, to meaning. The music is somewhere between studium and punctum; somewhere in the 'rapport' between them; somewhere in the composition between them; and Derrida adds to the musical sense of the word 'composition' the sense of ongoing negotiation and compromise. What remains beyond establishment is the laws that govern the internal dynamic of the rhythm itself.

Let us return for a moment to Derrida's difficulty at La Villette in 1997. He said in the interview he subsequently gave to *Jazz Magazine* that it was the first occasion on which he had ever been booed off stage. What went wrong? Derrida himself was tempted to blame it at least partly on the fact that Coleman did not introduce him. But Coleman sees it differently.

> Le public n'a pas compris à qui Derrida s'adressait. A lui? A moi? Il exprimait en fait ce en quoi il croyait, ce qu'il pensait. Et je pensais que tout le monde comprendrait. En fait, Derrida est soudain devenu un personnage trop 'avancé', un corps décalé mis sur scène, alors qu'aussi neuf soit-il, par ce qu'il faisait, Derrida était toujours lui-même, sur scène, contrairement à beaucoup de gens.[30]

[The audience didn't understand whom Derrida was addressing. Himself? Me? He was really just saying what he believed in, what he was thinking. And I thought everyone would understand. But, in fact, Derrida suddenly became a person who had put himself forward too much, a body stuck on stage, out of place, whereas, in what he was doing, however novel it was, Derrida on stage, unlike a lot of people, was still himself.]

Derrida, there on stage, speaking on stage, was clearly a *person*, himself; in other words, a subject. But music, as we have seen, is always the voice of the soul, of the other. It does not address itself, really, to anyone; which is why it can speak to everyone and for everyone, why it is ventriloquial. Derrida's 'improvisation', entitled 'joue — le prénom' ('play — the first name'), is, in fact, for the most part clearly addressed to Coleman, and indeed asks Coleman for a response: Derrida asks him to give his mother's first name. This register of verbal exchange is that in which one remains oneself. One can name oneself and others, one becomes a physical presence on stage, both live and alive on stage, 'still himself' — too much himself for music. Music is the element in which we must accept to lose ourselves, as Derrida does in his orchestral fantasy. Music is born as subjects are replaced by souls, as words cease to have a value of exchange, as the value of exchange is replaced by that of an incalculable rhythm. Had Derrida forgotten this?

Yes and no. Certainly, any such amnesia on his part must have a complex structure. For 'joue — le prénom' plays from beginning to end on all the key concepts of this difficult relation between word and music: the incalculable, translation into music, death in music, speaking with the voice of the other, the gift without price. All are clearly there, for example, in the following passage, which proposes the translation of a name into music, and its transmission as a gift:

> Mourir d'envie. Voilà, maintenant je meurs d'envie, moi aussi, de demander quelque chose à Ornette [...] je lui demande de me faire cadeau, **an unpredictable gift**, du prénom de sa mère **(could you tell me, as a gift, your mother's first name?)** pour que je puisse l'appeler de toutes mes voies (téléphone intérieur, *Tone dialing*, *Faxing*, *Cyber cyber*) et lui faire une déclaration d'amour. Même si tu ne le prononces pas, ce prénom, joue-le, envoie-le pour moi en musique, en saxotéléphonie, en saxotéléphonépiphanie.[31]

> [Dying to. There you are, now, I'm dying, too, dying to ask Ornette for something [...] I'm asking him to give me as a present, as **an unpredictable gift**, his mother's first name **(could you tell me, as a gift, your mother's first name?)** so that I can call her by every means I have (interior telephone, *Tone dialing*, *Faxing*, *Cyber cyber*) and declare to her my love. Even if you don't pronounce this first name, play it, send it to me in music, by saxotelephone, by saxotelephonepiphany.]

But how does the saxotelephone work? How can a name be sent in music? In a sense it cannot, as Derrida had affirmed many years earlier in *Signsponge*. Writers, painters, and sculptors, he says, can inscribe their signatures on their works; but 'a musician [...] is incapable, as such, of inscribing his signature [...] upon the work itself: the musician cannot sign within the text'.[32] If Ornette's mother's name had arrived, it would not have been with the force of music. Fortunately, we can be sure this did not happen. After all, the 'improvisation' has only ever been given in writing, in a form within which there is forever no answer to the question, no name given or saxotelephoned.

Thus the name, the word, the subject, though called for in words, never arise in music; they have to die for music to be born. This birth can never be calculated; no letter can give us to understand it. The death of the subject must be accomplished as an act of faith, not as a payment in exchange. At La Villette, one might say (in theatrical parlance) that Derrida died on stage. And perhaps he remembered, or was reminded, of the necessity of dying. Let us not forget that 'joue — le prénom' presents itself as the text of an improvisation, written up, doubtless, after the live event at which it was not given. As the above passage shows, it condenses, often in almost parodic form, the contradictions on which Derrida elsewhere expends hundreds of scrupulous pages, that demonstrate why philosophical or subjective thought cannot cope with music: the incommensurability between the request and the gift, the inhumanity of the language of love, the indirectness of communication, the singularity, emptiness, and propriety of the name. Had Coleman's audience listened to Derrida's performance, they would at the very least have heard a discourse that clearly refuses the logic of the subject. What would have remained? Here calculation fails. It must fail, by definition, otherwise there would be no soul, and no music.

That is why, it seems to me, Derrida could never write about the value of a musical work as such. To do so would be to deny the incalculability that founds music. Here we have, after all, an essential distinction between music and writing. In writing one can at least perceive and analyse the structure of subjectivity, of self-possessed language. Then, having posited that poetry, or music-in-language, or song, is something else — a remainder, after the subject has been consumed — one can analyse the process of consumption of the subject, and at least point to some marks of the emergence of rhythm, even if the internal laws of that rhythm remain inaccessible. This is what Derrida does when writing on Celan, or Mallarmé, or Baudelaire, Ponge, or Barthes. But music is always already the voice of the other; it is always already rhythm; it is always already, by definition, not the voice of the subject. Therefore, one cannot analyse the process by which it ceases to be the voice of the subject. 'Ce qui reste a force de musique': the quality of music is that of the remainder, not of the present.

This means that there are severe limits on the application of deconstruction to music. Deconstruction of musicological discourse is always possible, of course, as is play with the words that music sets in song. But music itself resists. There is a splendid illustration of this in *La Carte postale*. The narrator sends, it seems, to his beloved a cassette with a fragment of Monteverdi. He says: 'je le lis' ('I am reading it').[33] But, in fact, what he is reading is not the musical score, it is the words, in Italian, German, and English. About Monteverdi, he has nothing to say. His only point about music is an absolutely general one: that the language of music is not his language. It is, as always, foreign; he cannot possess it; he cannot, as a subject, speak it or write it. Similarly, deconstruction, as a writing practice, cannot speak or write music; it can only work to efface the subject, the calculable, the exchange, to create the space in which the soul, the incalculable, the gift, the music might remain, though it might never speak. For music one must lose one's life, one's life as a subject. Even that death cannot guarantee music; it can only give music its chance to speak or not to speak, neither of which seems strictly possible. Nonetheless, if we have a soul it seems worth giving music that chance. It is plainly not with regret that Derrida had written, a few pages earlier: 'J'ai ainsi perdu ma vie à écrire pour donner une chance à ce chant, à moins que ce ne soit pour le laisser se taire, de lui-même' ('Thus I have lost my life in writing in order to give this song a chance, unless it were in order to let it silence itself, by itself').[34]

Notes to Chapter 4

1. Richard Kurth, 'Music and Poetry, a Wilderness of Doubles: Heine — Nietzsche — Schubert — Derrida', *19th-Century Music*, 21 (1997), 3–37 (p. 3).

2. Jacques Derrida, 'La Langue de l'étranger, discours de réception du prix Adorno à Francfort', *Le Monde diplomatique* (January 2002), 24–27 (p. 25). (My thanks to Vaughan Rogers for drawing my attention to this article.) The translation is my own. In general, my policy in this essay has been (*a*) to quote Derrida's original French except where I am working from a text published in English for which no precisely equivalent French original exists; (*b*) to provide my own translations where no published translation is available; and (*c*) to quote published translations where they exist, but to gloss them where they do not convey the sense of the French on which my argument is working.

3. Jacques Derrida, *Psyché. Inventions de l'autre* (Paris: Galilée, 1987), pp. 95–104. I have not found a published translation of this article.

4. Jacques Derrida, *La Carte postale, de Socrate à Freud et au-delà* (Paris: Flammarion, 1980), p. 182; *The Post Card, from Socrates to Freud and beyond*, trans. by Alan Bass (Chicago: University of Chicago Press, 1987), p. 118.

5. Derrida, *La Carte postale*, p. 140; *The Post Card*, p. 128.

6. Derrida, *La Carte postale*, p. 100; *The Post Card*, p. 90.

7. To give another example: 'But the eschatological tone of this yes-laughter also seems to me to be worked or traversed — I prefer to say *haunted* — joyously ventriloquised by a completely different music, by the vowels of a completely different song' (Jacques Derrida, 'Ulysses Gramophone', in *Acts of Literature*, ed. by Derek Attridge (London: Routledge, 1992), p. 294).

8. Derrida, *La Carte postale*, pp. 37–38; *The Post Card*, p. 32. Here, the translator seems not to have noticed that there is no accent on the word 'a'; I would have translated it: 'what would remain of us has the force of music, not a word, not a letter'.

9. Jacques Derrida, *Glas* (Paris: Galilée, 1974), p. 76; Eng. trans. by John P. Leavey and Richard Rand (Lincoln: University of Nebraska Press: 1986), p. 65.

10. Jacques Derrida, 'Demeure. Fiction et témoignage', *Passions de la littérature*, ed. by Michel Lisse (Paris: Galilée, 1996), pp. 13–74 (p. 16). The translation is mine.

11. Derrida, *Glas*, p. 54; trans. by Leavey and Rand, p. 45.

12. 'Le Musicien, le philosophe et les fanatiques' (unsigned), *Jazz Magazine*, 473 (1997), pp. 26–28.

13. Jacques Derrida, 'La Langue de l'autre', *Les Inrockuptibles*, 115 (20 August–2 September 1997), 36–43. (Translations from this text are mine.) Note the similarity with the title, quoted in note 2 above, of 'discours de réception du prix Adorno': 'La Langue de l'étranger'. What remains, what has the force of music, is always another's language.

14. It will be remembered that Derrida used the same word to describe literature (see the quotation, above, from 'Demeure. Fiction et témoignage').

15. Derrida, 'La Langue de l'autre', p. 40.

16. Jacques Derrida, 'Tympan', in *Marges de la philosophie* (Paris: Minuit, 1972), pp. i–xxv (p. xx); Eng. trans. in *A Derrida Reader: Between the Blinds*, ed. by Peggy Kamuf (New York: Harvester Wheatsheaf, 1991), pp. 148–68 (pp. 164–65).

17. Jacques Derrida, 'Before the Law', in *Acts of Literature*, ed. by Attridge, pp. 181–220 (p. 211).

18. Derrida, 'La Langue de l'autre', p. 42.

19. Or perhaps: 'that's why you shouldn't get paid, because it is incalculable and has no price'.

20. Derrida, *Donner le temps 1. La fausse monnaie* (Paris: Galilée, 1991), pp. 131–32; *Given Time: I. Counterfeit Money*, trans. by Peggy Kamuf (Chicago, University of Chicago Press, 1992), p. 101.

21. Derrida, 'La Langue de l'autre', p. 42. Derrida is quoting somewhat freely from his text 'Circonfession', which runs through *Jacques Derrida* by Geoffrey Bennington and Jacques Derrida (Paris: Seuil, 1991), p. 194.

22. I have translated this word, which occurs twice, as 'the world', but it could also mean, especially the first time, 'people'.

23. Derrida, *Donner le temps I*, p. 60; *Given Time*, p. 42.

24. Derrida, *Glas*, p. 174; Eng. trans. by Leavey and Rand, p. 154.

25. Derrida, *Glas*, p. 178; Eng. trans. by Leavey and Rand, pp. 157–58. Between the two paragraphs I have quoted there is a blank space corresponding, in the original, to about four lines.

26. Jacques Derrida, 'Les Morts de Roland Barthes', in *Psyché*, pp. 273–304 (p. 273); 'The Deaths of Roland Barthes', trans. by Pascale-Anne Brault and Michael Naas, in *Philosophy and Non-Philosophy since Merleau-Ponty*, ed. by Hugh J. Silberman (London: Routledge, 1988), pp. 259–96 (p. 259). The key words in these sentences are highly ambiguous. One might just as well translate it thus: 'How could this plural be tuned? With what might it agree? With whom? This question should also be heard in terms of music.'

27. Derrida, 'Les Morts de Roland Barthes', p. 280; 'The Deaths of Roland Barthes', p. 268.

28. Derrida, 'Les Morts de Roland Barthes', p. 295; 'The Deaths of Roland Barthes', p. 285.

29. Derrida, 'Les Morts de Roland Barthes', p. 296; 'The Deaths of Roland Barthes', p. 286.

30. 'Le Musicien, le philosophe et les fanatiques', p. 26.

31. Derrida, 'La Langue de l'autre', p. 42. The words in bold and in italics are in English in the original. Translating into English a text that already contains some translation of itself into English has an inescapably ridiculous but nicely Derridean aspect.

32. Derrida, *Acts of Literature*, ed. by Attridge, p. 362. It is true that Derrida is here talking of signatures, rather than names in general, but the same conditions may be said to apply. Both, conventionally, have a form that may be inscribed on paper, stone, or canvas, but not in music.

33. Derrida, *La Carte postale*, p. 170; *The Post Card*, p. 157.

34. Derrida, *La Carte postale*, 156; *The Post Card*, p. 143. Another possible translation would be: 'So I've thrown my life away in writing, writing to give this song a chance, unless I did it to let the song silence itself, of its own accord'.

PART II

Generic Alliances

CHAPTER 5

Music and Realism: Samuel Richardson, Italian Opera, and English Oratorio

Lawrence Woof

What does music have to do with the 'realism' that emerged during the eighteenth century, the defining medium of which was the novel? Not very much, it may appear, if we contrast music's role in the eighteenth-century novel with its role in, for example, cinema. The private nature of reading did not allow for a multimedia approach: music could feature within novels only as subject matter. And indeed, in the novels of Henry Fielding, music is mentioned no more than a social historian might expect: an occasional reference, one theme amongst many. The impetus for Fielding's initial fiction, Samuel Richardson's first novel *Pamela* (1741), similarly lacks any particular interest in music. It is Richardson's two subsequent novels, the hugely influential texts that led to 'the novel of sensibility', that are extensively concerned with music. The reasons for Richardson's fixation with music throughout *Clarissa* (1747–48) and *Sir Charles Grandison* (1753–54), I would suggest, relate to structural aspects of the novel. To establish his new art the author needed to borrow authority from another genre. Richardson's manoeuvre takes place against a background of eighteenth-century political and cultural ideas, which, as we shall see, were thrown into sharp relief by the contrasting musical genres of English oratorio and Italian opera. To create realism Richardson's fiction had to embody what his society would recognize as truth or knowledge, and during the eighteenth century this was understood in relation to the contrasting concepts of (civic) virtue and luxury. In this essay I first examine the tensions between virtue and luxury, and then ask why music was understood to be particularly important in this context. I subsequently turn to Richardson's use of music in *Clarissa* and *Sir Charles Grandison*, and consider its role in establishing realism.

In order to make sense of the world, Richardson's fiction — and, indeed, the culture he inhabited — needed to combine the (emerging) interest in sensibility, associated in general terms with the concept of luxury, with the neo-classical discourse of civic virtue. Jean-Jacques Rousseau (1712–78) wrote the following in his *First Discourse*, translated into English in 1750: 'WHAT is it then that we are contending for in this Dispute about Luxury? Why it is to know, which is of the greatest Importance to an Empire, to be brilliant and momentary, or virtuous and durable.'[1] Virtue, at least at the beginning of the century, referred to republican values inherited from ancient Greece that envisage landowning, independent citizens co-operating within a stable civic framework.[2] Luxury was used to refer to any kind of excess above that which is strictly necessary, and was particularly applied to emergent consumerism.[3] These terms had a wide scope and were applied to both the body and the state. The cautionary example of the consequences of a decline of virtue and a rise in luxury was the Roman Empire. As Edward Gibbon wrote in his *Decline and Fall* (1781):

> the decline of Rome was the natural and inevitable effect of immoderate greatness. Prosperity ripened the principle of decay; the causes of destruction multiplied with the extent of conquest; and, as soon as time or accident had removed the artificial supports, the stupendous fabric yielded to the pressure of its own weight.[4]

Empire created an appetite for luxury within its citizens that made that society unsustainable.[5]

A virtuous society and a luxurious one held differing approaches to property. As the historian J. G. A. Pocock summarizes it, 'The function of property, in this view, is to furnish the individual with independence; independence is the prerequisite of political engagement; and political engagement is the prerequisite of public virtue'.[6] 'Independence' in this context is meant both economically and conceptually. Political engagement is the exclusive prerogative of the financially autonomous, leisured landowner. This was because his thoughts alone are neither encumbered by material considerations, nor cluttered with the compromising specificity of professional knowledge.[7] The disinterested man of leisure, apparently unprejudiced by dependent economic relationships, was understood to be capable of making observations that had a quality of detachment denied to others.[8]

Civic virtue's paradigm for establishing knowledge (and hence political authority), however coherent it may have appeared under earlier conditions, became troubled as the eighteenth century progressed. With the emergence of the specialization of labour, this concept of a disinterested overview became increasingly untenable. As more professions were created, each with a specialized field of knowledge, so the likelihood of any individual's being able to master all of this new information seemed more and more impossible. As Adam Smith famously observed, with the beginnings of industrialization the manufacture of even the humble pin came to involve the interaction of up to eighteen new and distinct professions.[9] This seemed to be creating a society beyond the comprehension of any one of its constituent members.[10]

The rise of luxury not only questioned the subject's conceptual objectivity, it also questioned the objectivity of that subject's empirical perception through the emerging phenomenon of sensibility. George Cheyne (1671–1743), in his influential study of nervous disorders *The English Malady* (1733), relates the distortion of the nervous system, and hence of perception, to luxury:

> SINCE our Wealth has increas'd, and our Navigation has been extended, we have ransack'd all the Parts of the *Globe* to bring together its whole Stock of Materials for *Riot*, *Luxury*, and to provoke *Excess* [...] the intellectual Operations [...] can never be perform'd in the best Manner without proper Instruments. The Works of *Imagination* and *Memory*, of *Study*, *Thinking*, and *Reflecting*, from whatever Source the Principle on which they depend springs, must necessarily require bodily Organs.[11]

As Tobias Smollett (1721–71) has Matthew Bramble ask in his novel *Humphry Clinker* (1771):

> What kind of taste and organs must those people have, who really prefer the adulterate enjoyments of the town to the genuine pleasures of a country retreat? [...] in the course of this gratification, their very organs of sense are perverted, and they become habitually lost to every relish of what is genuine in its own nature.[12]

This awareness of the malleability of the nervous system deprived empirical observation of certainty: if one's nerves were distorted, how could one trust what they related to the mind?

Luxury presented a problem for musical genres in the age of Rationalism because it was understood that music had a particular ability to sway the emotions. In 1736 Handel set Dryden's 'Alexander's Feast; or the Power of Musique. An Ode in Honour of St Cecilia's Day', a work that examines this issue. Dryden's poem concerns the musician Timotheus who manipulates the feasting Alexander, who becomes successively celebratory, sad, amorous, and, finally, vengeful. The poem celebrates, yet also displays the dangers of, music's capacity to manipulate the passions. It concludes by celebrating Cecilia, the patron saint of music, who is identified with a more virtuous and apparently less manipulative model of music production.

An early poetic account of Handel's *Alexander's Feast* entitled *The Tears of the Muses* (1737) demonstrates the way in which this contrast was understood:

> NEAR *Opera's* fribling *Fugues*, what Muse can stay?
> Where wordless Warblings winnow *Thought* away!
> Music, when *Purpose* points her not the Road,
> Charms, to betray, and softens, to *corrode*.

This is contrasted with the oratorio:

> HENCE, to the Realms of *Fame*, ye Muses fly.
> There, to the Drum's big Beat, the Heart leaps high.
> [...]
> The manly Pipe, there, scorns th'expanded *Shakes*,
> That wind wav'd Nothings, till Attention *akes*.
> There *now*, concurring Keys and Chords increase
> The Heart's soft social Tyes, and cherish *Peace*.

Whereas Italian 'corrode[s]' the nervous system and hence the capacity for 'Thought', English oratorio communicates 'concurring Keys and Chords', which, on the contrary, encourage 'social Tyes'.

Why would the Italian opera's 'wordless Warblings winnow *Thought* away'? The physician John Gregory wrote in 1763 that:

> The influence of Music over the Mind is perhaps greater than that of any of the fine arts. It is capable of raising and soothing every passion and emotion of the Soul. Yet the real effects produced by it are inconsiderable. This is entirely owing to its being in the hands of practical Musicians, and not under the direction of Taste and Philosophy.[13]

The musician requires 'Taste and Philosophy', attributes he is debarred from possessing, according to the discourse of civic virtue, as a direct consequence of his professional status (taste meant above all a capacity to abstract truths from the complexities of the world).[14]

This point about the inability of musicians to think extensively about social issues that extend beyond their own professional horizon is made throughout the century. A writer observes in 1718 that 'still there is no Inconsistence between a *Fool*, and a *Musician*'.[15] In 1735 *The Prompter* states that '[i]t is observed of those that give themselves to Musick, that they *give* themselves QUITE UP to it, and are fit for no one thing besides'.[16] In an essay published in *The World* (1754), the Earl of Chesterfield, that arbiter of social propriety, states sarcastically that musicians 'have from their infancy devoted their time and labour to the various combinations of seven notes: a study that must unquestionably have formed their minds, enlarged their notions, and have rendered them most agreeable and instructive companions'.[17]

Gregory goes on to consider the difficulties facing the creative professional musician in terms of the arguments associated with civic virtue. Since, he argues, 'no Science ever flourished while it was confined to a set of Men who lived by it as a profession', the burgeoning commercial music of London would never be able to innovate or reach its full potential:

> The interested views of a trade are far different from the enlarged and liberal prospects of Genius and Science. When the knowledge of an Art is confined in this manner, every private Practitioner must attend to the general Principles of his craft, or starve. If he goes out of the common path [...] he can neither find Judges nor Patrons.[18]

This point is made in more detail by the Scottish divine Thomas Robertson, writing in 1784, who identifies the division of operatic labour as the major problem:

> The Poet, the Musician, the Dancer, the Painter, the Directors of the Machinery, of the decoration, and of the Dress, press all forward upon the Public, vie with each other to gain the public favour, and each in their turn predominating to the prejudice of the rest, have, for the greater part, kept the most perfect of all Fine Entertainments, from attaining to that subordination of the Parts and Unity of the whole; upon which its excellence so much depends.[19]

Dr John Brown's influential *Estimate of the Manners and Principles of the Times* locates this same division between empty rhetoric and virtue in the world of modern music, stating that music, potentially the highest of the arts,

> [has] dwindled into a Woman's or an Eunuch's effeminate Trill [...] we go not to admire the *Composition*, but the *Tricks* of the *Performer*, who is then surest of our ignorant Applause, when he runs through the Compass of the *Throat*, or traverses the *Finger-board* with the *swiftest Dexterity*.[20]

Brown continues in a later publication that argued along Rousseauesque lines about music's role in cultural decline. The rise in luxury, he argues, would be disseminated and magnified *through* music: if musicians are educated by a 'corrupt State', then 'they would be apt to debase their Art to vile and immoral Purposes, as the means of gaining that Applause which would be the natural Object of their Ambition'. For Brown, the market-driven logic of commercial opera led to 'artificial Execution'

— style replacing content. Consequently, 'the *Castrati* were introduced into all Sorts of Characters [...] The flourished Close or Cadence arose naturally from the same Sources: From a total Neglect of the Subject and Expression, and an attention to the mere Circumstance of Execution only.' As a result of the various elements within opera vying for pre-eminence, 'the *tragic Influence* is *overlaid* and *lost*'.[21]

The trill, it could be argued, is in some ways a concentrated symbol of luxury. A note that has a role to play in the larger perspective of the harmony and melody, as well as the still-broader context of the overall moral narrative of virtue, is subverted through (in Gregory's phrase) the 'interested views of a trade'. This latter takes the form of a neighbour-note (usually the tone or semitone above) that alternates with the principal note. Because the principal note has in this way conflated its functional (and hence its moral) content with self-display and self-interest, its message has become intertwined with what is in effect an advertisement for its medium. Brown, in his later, posthumously published work on Italian opera, describes such decorative passages, stating that 'in general, the means are here confounded with the end'.[22] The supplementary neighbour-note has the relative effect of rendering the principal note its own lower neighbour-note, just as the proponents of civic virtue would argue that culture, in a luxurious society, is mistaken for an end rather than a means. The decline from virtue towards luxury was widely understood in terms of effeminization, and castration was understood to be the end result of this process that variously detracted from the physically whole body of the virtuous citizen.[23] The castrati were the most physically/professionally specialized group of workers, whose bodies had literally been 'specialized' in order that they may carry out their labours. The division of labour has modified their bodies to such an extent as literally to effeminize them. This highly-charged combination of symbols made the castrati's vocal decorations both metaphor and metonym of luxury, and accounts for Brown's linking the castrati with the trill as the twinned 'clear and evident Principles' into which he understands the opera to resolve. According to Brown, what Gregory called 'Taste and Philosophy' — that which would have promoted a '*tragic influence*' in opera and so formed a didactic narrative of civic virtue — is fundamentally undermined through the division of labour. This division divorces rhetoric from its moral context, allowing rhetoric — artificial execution — to take the place of civic virtue.

So why might Richardson want to engage with this charged subject matter? Richardson's achievement in *Pamela* and the secret to its success lay in the author's ability to unite feminine sensibility with masculine civic virtue within his fiction. The letters that make up his novels are apparently written by highly sensitive and truthful women, yet Richardson is also able to claim to be the 'editor' of these letters, to have silently sifted the writing in order to generate from it a masculine, virtuous overview of society. So sensibility created a crucial sense of somatic veracity for his epistolary novels through the pathologizing, bodily interrogation of the novels' heroines. This is a crucial element of the plot. As these novels are told in the first person, the eponymous heroines' physical sensibilities must be subjected to a barrage of tests to establish the psychophysical basis upon which the truthfulness of the novels depends. The problem with Richardson's *Pamela* was that the heroine was suspected of duplicity (hence satires such as *Shamela*). If Pamela may have dissembled her rejection of Mr B., might she not have made up other things too? In his two final novels Richardson looked for strategies to evade this charge. In both *Clarissa* and *Sir Charles Grandison* the cultural associations of music were used to achieve these ends.

Clarissa or, the History of a Young Lady: Comprehending the Most Important Concerns of Private Life … Published by the Editor of Pamela announces from the outset both that its medium consists of the feminine 'Concerns of Private Life', and that this domestic sensibility has been silently overseen by a masculine editor. This sense of the woman as pure medium of emotion is brought to the surface of the narrative, for instance, when Lovelace describes his mentioning to Clarissa an evocative subject in the following terms: 'I touched a delicate string, on purpose to set her in such a passion before the women' (p. 775).[24] All women may similarly be played, according to Lovelace. As such, the music they make originates in the intentionality of the player and has little meaning distinct from this. At one point Sally, one of the prostitutes, imitates Clarissa's behaviour:

> never was my lovely girl so well aped; and I was almost taken in; for I could have fancied I had her before me once more.
>
> Oh this sex! this artful sex! There's no minding them. At first, indeed, their grief and their concern may be real: but give way to the hurricane, and it will soon die away in soft murmurs, trilling upon your ears like the notes of a well-tuned viol. (p. 1217)

The speech or music of women that originates from them without being prompted by a man may appear to have meaning, but, like the Italianate operatic trill, it dissolves into the condition of pure music. Lovelace's interrogation of Clarissa's body is one in which he strives to prove that she is a medium under his control. Once her body becomes sexual and/or maternal, Lovelace is able to see himself as the originator of a message expressed though the medium of her body (Lovelace imagines 'the smiling Boy, amply, even in *her own* opinion, rewarding the suffering Mother' (p. 922)). Once this is established, he would retrospectively legitimate all of his actions against her by proving what he suspects, that she has all the time dissimulated her resistance to his advances.

However, if this were the case it would sabotage the empirical veracity of Richardson's novel and provoke another *Shamela*. Richardson's novel needs access to the more delicate nervous-system of women, but does not want the accompanying charge of duplicity with which the female sex was associated. The only solution to this difficulty, therefore, was that Clarissa's sex had been misclassified. If Clarissa does not dissemble (in either her prose or her rejection of Lovelace), it follows that she is not like other women. Lovelace belatedly comes to this conclusion. After Sally has aped Clarissa he writes: 'Miss Harlowe, indeed, is the only woman in the world, I believe, that can say, in the words of her favourite Job (for I can quote a text as well as she), *But it is not so with me*' (p. 1217). Clarissa is not a woman, because, as the reader is frequently informed, she is an 'angel', and as such she is a being, and a gender, of a different order. Lovelace's tragic attempt to insist that Clarissa conform to the expected behaviour of her sex is, in this sense, based upon mistaken classification. She is not a pure medium to be appropriated, but is rather a medium that somehow also creates her own message. As Lovelace later writes,

> Curse upon my contriving genius! [...] To sport with the fame, with the honour, with the life, of such an angel of a woman! — O my damn'd incredulity! that, believing her to *be* a woman, I must hope to *find* her a woman! — On my incredulity that there could be such virtue (virtue for *virtue*'s sake) in the sex, founded I my hope of succeeding with her. (p. 1344)

The paradox of Richardson's entire novel as well as of his heroine is not so much resolved as simply named by the term 'angel'. Richardson claims for both his eponymous heroine and his text a feminine form that nevertheless also contains a real, yet impalpable, masculine moral authority.

Clarissa's musical aptitude is not simply an index of her conventional femininity, but of her capacity — like that of the editor of her letters — to generate virtue from what Richardson in his *Preface* describes as 'collatoral incidents' (p. 130). 'I HAVE been forced to try to compose my angry passions at my harpsichord', writes Clarissa. She continues:

> I made an essay, a week ago, to set the three last stanzas of [Elizabeth Carter's 'Ode to Wisdom'], as not unsuitable to my unhappy situation [...] and I am sure in the solemn address they contain to the all-wise and all-powerful Deity, my heart went with my fingers.
>
> I enclose the ode and my effort with it. The subject is solemn: my circumstances are affecting; and I flatter myself that I have not been quite unhappy in the performance. (p. 231)

The last three stanzas of Carter's Ode (and the majority of the other thirteen stanzas) concern virtue. The final verse concludes:

> Beneath her clear discerning eye
> The visionary shadows fly
> Of folly's painted show.
> She sees through ev'ry fair disguise,
> That all, but VIRTUE'S solid joys,
> Is vanity and woe.

The music, which Richardson commissioned and had engraved, is written in the manner associated with the English oratorio, both in its musical style and in its moralizing text.

At the dramatic climax of the book Clarissa's identification with the English oratorio is again emphasized. Lovelace, disguised, has entered her apartment in the company of Clarissa's landlady: 'Then stumping towards the closet, over the door of which hung a picture — What picture is that? — Oh! I see: A St Cecilia!' (p. 771). That the print functions as an insignia for Clarissa is emphasized further by the celestial imagery with which her eventual emergence from the closet is described:

> my charmer opened the door, and blazed upon me, as it were in a flood of light, like what one might imagine would strike a man who, born blind, had by some propitious power been blessed with his sight, all at once, in a meridian sun. (p. 772)

Lovelace is the master of rhetoric and affect, like the fabled musician Timotheus, whereas Clarissa displays a saint-like moral consistency and semiotic clarity. Her voice is described in musical terms, and Lovelace's reaction, unusually, in terms of psychophysical sensibility. It is significant that Clarissa, invested here temporarily with all of the non-physical attributes of a saint that she will finally assume in death, seems to achieve momentarily a state of psychophysical stasis in comparison with Lovelace, who, in a sudden role reversal, finds his own body under the spotlight:

> and never did her voice sound so harmonious to me. Oh how my heart bounded again! It even talked to me, in a manner; for I thought I heard, as well as felt, its unruly flutters; and every vein about me seemed a pulse. (p. 771)

It is particularly at the points in the text where the pathology of Clarissa seems complete, when she is hagiographied into this paradoxical, virtuous feminine medium, that the gaze of the novel swings around to examine and pathologize the body of Lovelace.

We are frequently reminded of the essential vacuity of Lovelace, who admits that he would be 'at a loss for a subject' were his stratagems to succeed (p. 143). There is a gendered paradox at the heart of Lovelace's absence relating to his repeated associations with the Italian opera and its emblem, the castrato. As Miss Howe writes to Clarissa: 'Mr Hickman tells me that he heard in town, that he used to be often at plays, and at the opera, with women; and every time with a different one!' (p. 284). And again towards the end of the novel Lovelace writes 'I go frequently to the opera' (p. 1476). The identification between Lovelace and Italian opera becomes proportionally more pronounced as Clarissa's unique, saintly viewpoint, which is at once both masculine and feminine, is established. Clarissa, for instance, with her 'harmony of voice' refutes Lovelace's highly rhetorical and non-referential conception of 'wit' by citing Cowley:

> *Wit*, like a luxuriant vine,
> Unless to *Virtue*'s prop it join,
> Firm and erect, tow'rd heaven bound,
> Tho' it with beauteous leaves and pleasant fruit be crown'd;
> It lies deform'd, and rotting on the ground. (p. 712)

Earlier, Lovelace writes 'the instant I beheld her, I was soberized into awe and reverence: and the majesty of her even *visible* purity first damped, and then extinguished, my *double* flame' (p. 658). The charge levelled against Lovelace, that he consists of rhetoric without substance, echoes criticisms directed against the Italian opera, as does the subtext of impotence. Richardson even has Lovelace directly compare himself, 'a young sinner', to a castrato, as he describes Lord M.'s response to one of his anecdotes:

> To see such an old Trojan as this [...] crying out with pain, and grunting with weakness; yet in the same moment crack his leathern face into an horrible laugh, and call a young sinner charming varlet, encoring him, as formally he used to do the Italian eunuchs; what a preposterous, what an unnatural adherence to old habits!

To complete the operatic imagery, Lovelace goes on to emphasize the theatricality of his rhetoric: 'My two cousins are generally present when I entertain, as the old peer calls it. Those stories must drag horribly that have not more hearers and applauders, than relaters' (p. 1024). As with the opera, it is the execution rather than the substance that the audience admires. Lovelace continues, explaining how he appeased their moral disapproval:

> An Italian air, in my usual careless way, a half-struggled-for kiss from me, and a shrug of the shoulder by way of admiration from each pretty cousin, and *Sad, sad fellow*, from the old peer, attended with a side-shaking laugh, made us all friends. (p. 1024)

This sense is reinforced in a letter Lovelace writes two days later. He describes in distinctly operatic terms a confrontation with his own relatives. Lady Sarah asks him:

> Are all women alike to you?
>   Yes; I could have answered; 'bating the difference which pride makes.
>   Then they *chorused* upon me — Such a character as Miss Harlowe's! cried one — A lady of so much generosity and good sense! [...] Damned, damned doings! vociferated the peer, shaking his loose-fleshed wobbling chaps, which hung in his shoulders like an old cow's dew-lap.
>   For my part I hardly knew whether to sing or say what I had to reply to these all-at-once attacks upon me! — (p. 1027)

The word 'chorused' potentially associates his relatives with the oratorio, whilst Lovelace's musical analogy itself works to reduce morality to rhetoric, removing meaning in order to stress the surface of language in the manner of Italian opera.

There is a dichotomy in *Clarissa* that relates to the figures of Timotheus and St Cecilia. Timotheus (Lovelace) represents the rhetorical use of sensibility and the Italian opera, whilst St Cecilia (Clarissa) stands for semantic consistency and the English oratorio. The difficulty with Richardson's position is that his own medium stands in danger of being misclassified. It may itself be understood as a Timotheus-like exercise in the manipulation of the senses. This is because, just as Lovelace and Clarissa both use language, Timotheus and St Cecilia, finally, both use a medium of sensibility, and are to that extent equivalent. Dryden's verse 'He rais'd a Mortal to the Skies; | She drew an Angel down' emphasizes the equivalence as well as the difference of these two stances.

For Richardson's final novel this strategy of using Italian opera and English oratorio is taken even further. In what can only be a gesture towards the somatic legitimation of *Sir Charles Grandison*, the pathologizing of Harriet is performed by Sir Charles's two sisters. Just as Clarissa must not dissimulate her rejection of Lovelace, so Harriet must not dissimulate her love for Sir Charles. In a typically Lovelacean manner, the two sisters enter Harriet's dressing-room before she is dressed and quiz her about her feelings for Sir Charles. Soon Harriet reports 'I felt my face glow', and in response to this physical sign Charlotte cries 'Confirmation, Lady L.! Confirmation!'. Charlotte continues her physical interrogation:

> — Give me your handkerchief! — What doings are here!
>   She snatch'd it out of my trembling hand, and put it round my neck — Why this sudden palpitation? (I, 418)[25]

Sir Charles's sisters' wish to establish that Harriet loves their brother goes some way towards establishing the somatic veracity of her text.

All this, of course, is a mere shadow of the interrogation meted out to Clarissa, taking up a couple of pages rather than five hundred. One reason for this difference, I would argue, is that in the later novel, because of the particularly authorial role accorded to Sir Charles, the disembodied editor is in danger of becoming physically specific, as the editorial figure (Richardson) is to some extent represented in the person of Sir Charles. Sir Charles, therefore, cannot become too physically specific, and therefore can neither write the text of the novel nor interrogate the body of the woman who does. It is perhaps as a consequence of this that in this novel, and, as it were, in place of Lovelace's interrogations, there are several, more explicitly castrated men (in contradistinction to Sir Charles), and there is also a much more sustained identification between the text and the English oratorio.

Sir Hargrave Pollexfen, who attempts to abduct Harriet and is thwarted by Sir Charles, is threatened with castration twice. The first of these incidents, an allusion, occurs as Sir Charles rescues Harriet. Sir Charles, unusually, relates the incident himself (although this reportage is itself embedded with another's letter in the form of reported speech):

> 'I wrench'd his sword from him, and snapp'd it, and flung the two pieces over my head. [...] One of his legs, in his sprawling, had got between the spokes of his chariot-wheel. I thought that was a fortunate circumstance for preventing further mischief' (I, 140–41)

In the second incident the prevention of further mischief is more explicitly what was intended, this time perpetrated by the vengeful relatives of a wronged lady in whose abduction Sir Hargrave Pollexfen and Mr Mercada have been involved. One of the lady's brothers informs Sir Charles, 'Our design [...] was not to kill the miscreants; but to give them reason to remember their villainy as long as they lived; and to put it out of their power ever to be guilty of the like' (II, 429, 431). We are later informed that

> Merceda [...] has, it seems, a wound in his thigh, which, in the delirium he was thrown into by the fracture, was not duly attended to; and which, but for his *valiant* struggles against the knife which gave the wound, was designed for a still greater mischief. (II, 443)

A parallel plot of castration is given in the story of Clementina's brother, Signor Jeronymo. Against Sir Charles's advice he becomes involved with a lady 'less celebrated for virtue than beauty' (II, 120) and is attacked by 'ruffians' hired by a rival. The implication is similarly that Jeronymo has been wounded in the groin:

> His wounds proved not mortal; but he never will be the man he was: Partly from his having been unskilfully treated by this his first surgeon; and partly from his own impatience, and the difficulty of curing the wound in his hip-joint. Excuse this particularity, madam. The subject requires it. (II, 121)

Jeronymo's mother later hints at her son's impotence: 'Our second son [the Bishop] has great prospects before him, in the church: But you know he cannot marry. Poor Jeronymo! We had not, *before* his misfortune, any great hopes of strengthening the family by his means' (II, 457). Jeronymo was also the name of a famous castrato from an earlier era of Italian opera.

None of these castrations is explicitly associated with Italian opera, although they are all associated with sexual transgression, as are all of the explicit references to Italian opera within the novel. The initial reference to the Italian opera in the novel concerns marital difficulties; Sir T., Sir Charles's father, 'was but little at home in the summer;

and, in the winter, was generally engaged four months in the diversions of this great town; and was the common patron of all the performers, whether at plays, operas, or concerts' (I, 311–12). Sir T., we are told, considers a degree of repentance from this self-indulgent life-style when his mistress dies of smallpox:

> for she was taken ill at the opera, on seeing a lady of her acquaintance there, whose face bore too strongly the marks of the distemper, and who, it seems, had made her first visit to that place, rather than to a better. (I, 323)

Another dangerous woman associated with Italian opera is the Italian noblewoman Olivia. In his first description of her Sir Charles observes: 'the first time I saw her was at the opera' (II, 117). In a later letter Harriet links Olivia with both Italian opera and sexual transgression:

> had Sir Charles Grandison been a man capable of taking advantage of the violence of a Lady's passion for him, the unhappy Olivia would not have scrupled [...] to have been his, without conditions [...] Had Sir Charles been a Rinaldo, Olivia had been an Armida. (II, 376)

Jocelyn Harris, in her edition of the novel, is of the opinion that this refers to Handel's 1711 opera rather than directly to Tasso.

Let us now turn to the English oratorio. The first reference to the oratorio occurs towards the beginning of the novel, when Harriet sings what she describes as 'that fine piece of accompanied recitative', which might more accurately be described as a cantabile aria: '*Softly sweet, in Lydian measures,* | *Soon he sooth'd his soul to pleasures*' (I, 239). Describing Charlotte's [Lady G.'s] wedding, Harriet writes that she played the harpsichord herself whilst Sir Charles sung:

> He has a mellow manly voice, and great command of it. This introduced a little concert. Mr. Beauchamp took the violin; Lord L. the bass-viol; Lord G. the German flute; Lord W. sung base; Lady L. Lady G. and the Earl, joined in the chorus. The song was from Alexander's Feast: The words,
>
> > *Happy, happy, happy pair!*
> > *None but the good deserves the fair,*
>
> Sir Charles, tho' himself equally brave and good, preferring the latter word to the former. (II, 345)

This chorus from *Alexander's Feast* runs throughout the novel. Sir Charles's rival, Mr Greville, for instance, says, ' — Let me have the pride, the glory, Sir Charles Grandison, to quit this dear hand to yours. It is only to yours that I would quit it — *Happy, happy, happy pair! None but the brave deserves the fair* —' (III, 88). Perhaps Richardson expects his reader to imagine Greville singing this extract. The phrase 'Happy, happy' is repeated in conjunction with the nuptials of Sir Charles and Harriet at least a further seven times during the final two volumes of the novel. Furthermore, to stress the link with oratorio, there is a tendency for Richardson's characters to break spontaneously into song.

To complete the identification of Sir Charles and Harriet with *Alexander's Feast*, Sir Charles actually performs (and presumably has composed) an oratorio of his own based upon *Alexander's Feast*:

After dinner [...] Sir Charles led us into the Music-parlour. O madam, you shall hear what honour was done me there! — [...] Here is a noble organ: [...] he was so good himself, on my aunt's referring to him with asking eyes, to shew us it was in tune.

We all seated ourselves round him, on his preparing to oblige us; I between my aunt and Lucy; and he with a voice admirably suited to the instrument (but the words, if I may be allowed to say so, still *more* admirably to the occasion) at once delighted and surprised us all, by the following Lines:

I

Accept, great SOURCE of ev'ry bliss,
The fulness of my heart,
Pour'd out in tuneful ecstasies,
By this celestial art.

II

My soul, with gratitude profound,
Receive a Form so bright!
And yet, I boast a bliss beyond
This angel to the sight.

III

When charms of mind *and person meet,*
How rich our raptures rise!
The Fair that renders earth so sweet,
Prepares me for the skies! (III, 274)

The final couplet of *Alexander's Feast*, 'He rais'd a Mortal to the Skies; | She drew an Angel down', is alluded to here. The dichotomy between Timotheus and St Cecilia is transcended as rhetoric and virtue are blended together. Harriet 'prepares [Sir Charles] for the skies' rather than having 'rais'd [Sir Charles] to the Skies', and so infuses the sense of Dryden's final line with the syntax of his penultimate one.

In *Clarissa* and *Sir Charles Grandison* Richardson manipulated, at the level of plot, cultural oppositions to link his medium with the moral unassailability of English oratorio and so resolve the structural, gendered contradictions between sensibility and virtue that had marred *Pamela*. Richardson's fiction had a pivotal role in establishing a genre that still flourishes today. Once established, the sentimental novel had no special need for music. It remains an intriguing question as to whether the newer genre would have come into being in the way that it did if it were not for this infusion of what we might today call the emerging transcendentalizing qualities of music. Did the new genre need to borrow from the authority of the oratorio in order to take its first few steps?

Notes to Chapter 5

1. Jean-Jacques Rousseau, *A Discourse to which a Prize was Adjudged ... on this Question Proposed by that Academy: Whether the Re-establishment of Arts and Sciences has Contributed to Purify our Morals* [*First Discourse*], trans. by R. Wynne (London, 1750), p. 33.

2. See Shelley Burtt, *Virtue Transformed: Political Argument in England, 1688–1740* (Cambridge: Cambridge University Press, 1992), pp. 4–5.

3. See John Sekora, *Luxury: The Concept in Western Thought, Eden to Smollett* (Baltimore, MD: Johns Hopkins University Press, 1977), pp. 63–131.

4. Edward Gibbon, *The History of the Decline and Fall of the Roman Empire*, ed. by J. B. Bury, 7 vols (London: Methuen, 1896–1900), IV, 161.

5. For an account of this phenomenon, see Gerald Newman, *The Rise of English Nationalism* (London: Weidenfeld & Nicolson, 1987).

6. J. G. A. Pocock, 'The Myth of John Locke and the Obsession with Liberalism', in *John Locke: Papers Read at a Clark Library Seminar, 10 December 1977*, ed. by J. G. A. Pocock and Richard Ashcraft (Los Angeles: William Andrews Clark Memorial Library, 1980), pp. 1–24 (p. 15).

7. The use of 'his' in this passage is not a generic convention, but an acknowledgement of the specifically gendered (male) virtuous citizen.

8. The standard study of this phenomenon is J. G. A. Pocock's *The Machiavellian Moment: Florentine Political Thought and the Atlantic Republican Tradition* (Princeton, NJ: Princeton University Press, 1975).

9. Adam Smith, *An Inquiry into the Nature and Causes of the Wealth of Nations* (1776), ed. by Edwin Cannan, 2 vols (London: Methuen, 1961), I, pp. 8–9.

10. For a detailed discussion of this point, see John Barrell, *English Literature in History, 1730–80: An Equal, Wide Survey* (Hutchinson: London, 1983), pp. 17–50. See also John Barrell, 'The Public Prospect and the Private View: The Politics of Taste in Eighteenth-Century Britain', *The Birth of Pandora and the Division of Knowledge* (London: Macmillan, 1992), pp. 41–61 (esp. p. 42).

11. George Cheyne, *The English Malady* (London, 1733), pp. 49, 53.

12. Tobias Smollett, *The Expedition of Humphry Clinker*, ed. by Lewis M. Knapp, rev. by Paul-Gabriel Boucé (Oxford: Oxford University Press, 1984), p. 118.

13. John Gregory, *A Comparative View of the State and Faculties of Man with Those of the Animal World* (London, 1766), pp. 77–78.

14. See Barrell, 'The Public Prospect', pp. 41–61 (p. 42).

15. [C.R.], *Danger of Masquerades* (London, 1718), p. 13.

16. Anon., *The Prompter*, 106 (Friday, 14 November 1735).

17. Anon. [The Earl of Chesterfield], *The World*, 98 (14 November 1754), pp. 587–92 (p. 590).

18. Gregory, pp. 78–79.

19. Thomas Robertson, *An Inquiry into the Fine Arts* (London, 1784), p. 360.

20. John Brown, *An Estimate of the Manners and Principles of the Times* (London, 1757), pp. 45–47.

21. Ibid., pp. 205–06.

22. He writes that the particularly fast and decorated '[a]ria di bravura, aria di agilita, — is that which is composed *chiefly*, indeed, too often, *merely* to indulge the singer in the display of certain powers in the execution, particularly extraordinary agility or compass of voice. Though this kind of air may be sometimes introduced with some effect, and without any great violation of propriety, yet, in general, the means are here confounded with the end' (*Letters Upon the Poetry and Music of the Italian Opera Addressed to a Friend by the Late John Brown* (London, 1789), p. 39).

23. Support for this implicit historicizing of the Oedipus complex may be found in Gilles Deleuze and Felix Guattari, *Anti-Oedipus*, I: *Capitalism and Schizophrenia*, trans. by Robert Hurley and others (Minneapolis: University of Minnesota Press, 1977). Although a Freudian might object that this makes alienation a fetish for castration, the Oedipus complex can equally be understood as a displacement of alienation.

24. Samuel Richardson, *Clarissa or, the History of a Young Lady: Comprehending the Most Important Concerns of Private Life ... Published by the Editor of Pamela*, ed. by Angus Ross (Harmondsworth: Penguin Books, 1985). All parenthetical references within the text are to this edition.

25. Samuel Richardson, *The History of Sir Charles Grandison ... by the Editor of Pamela and Clarissa* (1753–54), ed. by Jocelyn Harris (Oxford: Oxford University Press, 1985). All parenthetical references within the text are to this edition.

CHAPTER 6

Saving the Ordinary: Beethoven's 'Ghost' Trio and the Wheel of History

Lawrence Kramer

Perhaps we need to expend so much energy and effort on the common and ordinary because for the true human self there is nothing more uncommon, nothing more out of the ordinary, than the commonplace everyday?

NOVALIS (1797)

1. Allegro vivace con brio

It is one of the paradoxes of music history that European instrumental music in the first half of the nineteenth century developed a strong tendency to affiliate itself with literary forms, especially narrative, at the same time that its apparent autonomy was aggressively being celebrated and theorized, eventually to the point of being appointed the model for art in general. The reasons for this situation have never been satisfactorily explained. One possibility is that music was simply recovering the narrative connections it had lost as a result of the progressive 'emancipation' from language that had consolidated around the turn of the century and was enshrined in the reception of Beethoven. Another, perhaps more interesting, possibility is that the narrative turn provided a means of limiting a transcendental power that had come to be ascribed to instrumental music and was felt to be both magnificent and dangerous. If one follows Peter Brooks's model of narrative as a structuring process that seeks to assimilate an untamed energy to manageable paradigms of desire and the hope of satisfaction,[1] then the assimilation of narrative by nineteenth-century music may appear to have been a means of reconciling music's extraordinary powers with the potentialities of ordinary life.

One of the earliest compositions to raise these issues is the so-called 'Ghost' Trio of Beethoven (Piano Trio in D Major, op. 70, no. 1) composed in 1808, with suggestive affinities to several contemporary narratives for which the same issues are paramount. A reading of the Trio in conjunction with these narratives can help write a significant chapter in the history of the ordinary, which is also the history of modernity. Perhaps the best way to get at these issues is to plunge *in medias res*, which is exactly what the music and the narratives tend to do.

2. Largo assai ed espressivo

In 1808 Austria was licking its wounds after a string of three major military defeats by Napoleon in as many years. The country had become little more than a French fiefdom; a year later, and Napoleon's armies would occupy Vienna. Cultural life, though, was thriving amidst the political rubble, especially in the capital. At the University, August Wilhelm von Schlegel delivered a widely noticed series of lectures on dramatic art and literature that became one of the key texts of Romantic criticism. And then there was Beethoven, who in this year finished his Fifth Symphony, composed his Sixth, and also produced the two piano trios of op. 70, works as extraordinary in their own genre as the symphonies are.

The First Trio, the 'Ghost', is particularly extraordinary. Or rather, one movement of it is, and famously so. This slow movement is so very extraordinary, so deliberately out of the ordinary, that it seems to be challenging the very conception of ordinary life. August Strindberg named his 1907 'chamber play' *The Ghost Sonata* partly after this music. The play is set in a new house filled with old secrets, not to mention vampires and mummies. The dramatic action peels away the veneer of the ordinary to reveal it as sheer illusion. Strindberg explained that with this play 'one enters a world of intimations where one expresses oneself in halftones and with a soft pedal, since one is ashamed to be a human being'.[2] Clearly, the sound of Beethoven's slow movement was echoing, ghostlike, in his ears, and it is still possible, another century later, to hear it on the same spectral terms. When we speak of music as extraordinary, we usually have something like excellence or originality or expressive power in mind. But this slow movement, this *Largo assai ed espressivo*, treats these qualities, or for that matter any positive qualities or values, with indifference, even hostility. It seems to take them up only to discard them for something else. To form a sense of why, and what that something might be, it is necessary to hear the movement, and the Trio, as part of the historical and cultural ferment of 1808.

We can begin with a simple description — an ordinary thing. This is from Maynard Solomon's well-known biography of Beethoven: '[This Trio] has two unproblematic and relaxed movements flanking a powerful pre-Romantic Largo, whose atmospheric tremolo effects and sudden dynamic contrasts give rise to the work's nickname'.[3] Any hearing of the Trio will bear out this statement, which is both representative and authoritative. It would be easy to take at face value, which is exactly what I want not to do. What happens when we press it a little?

The terms 'unproblematic' and 'relaxed' connote something normal, sociable, congenial, something that needs no further description. The phrase 'a powerful pre-Romantic Largo' implies something strange and singular, something that does need further description — the references to atmospheric sound effects and mercurial dynamic contrasts. The same distinction applies to Solomon's own statement, which also casts itself as unproblematic and relaxed. The statement implies, as if it goes without saying, that the whole arrangement of ordinary and extraordinary movements makes sense. But does it? Or if it does, what kind of sense does it make? Why choose this particular layout? And why choose to give musical expression to the ideas of the ordinary and the extraordinary? Is that something easy or natural to express? What does this 'ordinary' or 'extraordinary' consist of, anyway? And would this question always have the same answer, or is the ordinary, and therefore the extraordinary, a historical phenomenon, rather than what it seems to be, a universal one?

That I cannot promise to answer all these questions is part of my point. We should not fool ourselves into understanding this music too well. Its power to raise so many questions, and to raise them in just this way, is not simply a property to be taken for granted, a phantom of clichéd profundity. It is a cultural event. When we listen to the 'Ghost' Trio, we can hear the turning of a page in the modern history of the ordinary.

That history begins in the mid-eighteenth century as an increasing fascination with everyday things, at least by people comfortable enough to take a plenitude of everyday things for granted. By fits and starts, still-life painting detaches itself from its original purpose of symbolizing sin and mortality and begins to contemplate objects for their own sake. Literary sentimentalism attaches powerful feelings to trivial objects; for instance, the hero of Goethe's landmark novel of 1774, *The Sufferings of Young Werther*, notoriously meets the woman who inspires his transcendental passion as she slices a loaf of bread. An entire literary genre of 'autobiographies' as told by objects or pets — coins, dogs, coaches, and hairpins — flares into popularity.[4]

These trends develop amidst a consumer revolution already in full swing, a 'buying spree', as Michael Kwass puts it, 'of historic dimensions [...] that fundamentally changed the relationship between people and things'.[5] New modes of manufacture mass-produce objects that seem to transcend themselves, the precursors of Marx's commodity fetishes and the dream-laden goods in Walter Benjamin's Paris arcades. In this context Novalis can celebrate Goethe as 'a practical poet through and through [...] [who] did for German literature what Wedgwood did for English art'.[6] At the turn of the nineteenth century, as Benjamin famously observed, the invention of lithography 'enabled graphic art to illustrate everyday life' on a daily basis, a role that would eventually be taken over by photography.[7] More than mere illustration, this new proximity of art to the everyday was a redefinition and a transvaluation. It established the ordinary as something to be remarked rather than taken for granted, something to be preserved, resignified, commemorated.

The effects of this development on the culture of modernity would be hard to overstate. One of the consequences of the European Enlightenment, something insufficiently recognized, perhaps, because it is so familiar, is the eternal question of the value of the ordinary. It almost seems as if ordinary life were something the Enlightenment had invented.

In what sense could this be true? One famous consequence of the Enlightenment was what Max Weber called 'the disenchantment of the world'. By elevating the status of human reason and attacking the credibility of 'superstition', Enlightenment thinking promoted not only a new way of understanding the world but also a new way of experiencing it. A daily life that was once touched everywhere by magical, numinous, divine, and demonic forces, by ghosts and spirits and omens, was now denuded of all these and left to its own devices. At least it seemed so in retrospect. In 1819 John Keats wrote of his keen regret at having been born 'too, too late for the fond believing lyre, | When holy were the haunted forest boughs, | Holy the air, the water, and the fire'. Friedrich Hölderlin felt the same way: 'But friend', he wrote, 'we come too late. The gods indeed still live, | But over our heads, up there in another world'.[8] The present world, for many people, had become inert, inanimate; banality was born.

But it is not so easy to disenchant the world. The very concept of a world seems to carry a connotation of mystery in totality that cannot be suppressed for long. As both Heidegger and Merleau-Ponty suggested in their different ways, the experience of inhabiting a world, 'the' world, is preconceptual.[9] No subject can contain the world within reason: its totality is lived rather than grasped. So, virtually as soon as the old forms of enchantment were stripped away, new ones arose to take their place. The glamour that began to attach to everyday things in the eighteenth century was a start. The nineteenth century would add the full-blown romance of commodities, the marvels of technology, and the transformation of sexuality into both an ideal and a pathology. A step higher on the cultural ladder were the so-called fine arts. By the turn of the nineteenth century the arts were enjoying unparalleled prestige, partly on the basis of the recent conceptualization of them as the objects of a unique type of pleasurable contemplation. Here is another famous consequence of the Enlightenment: the discovery of the aesthetic — the cultivated re-enchantment of the world.

As Romantic writers were quick to point out, though, the revival of enchantment had a dark side. August Schlegel made this point in his Vienna lecture on Shakespeare's *Macbeth*. He begins as the play does, with the abrupt introduction of the witches. And he interprets these extraordinary creatures against the horizon of 1808:

> No superstition can be widely diffused without having a foundation in human nature: on this the poet builds; he calls up from their hidden abysses that dread of the unknown, that presage of a dark side of nature, and a world of spirits, which philosophy now imagines it has altogether exploded.[10]

For Schlegel, the endurance of Shakespeare is a foolproof argument against the excesses of Enlightenment. And not just for Schlegel: this line of thinking is far from exhausted. Here is the anthropologist Michael Taussig, writing in 2001:

> So we find ourselves back with spells and magic [...] making amends for the world that we have lost. [...] [A]ll these images and stories lie like ghosts in our modern world. There they sit in libraries and more often than you think in living speech. [...] And for this we are grateful [...] because poetry is what after the death of God [...] can invoke the spirits of the dead.[11]

Like Taussig, Schlegel is grateful for the abysses of reason. His Shakespeare is a kind of Faust, the artist-magician who calls up spirits from those abysses, and who therefore reinstates as experience the world of spirit that reason has repudiated as truth. But there is danger in this calling. The abyss may make amends for the world we have lost, but it is no haven — anything but. Those who experience its extraordinary powers may never find their way back to the ordinary. They may become mad, tormented, alienated, or simply apathetic, unable to connect with ordinary life. As long as art was simply concerned with the beautiful — the original, primary object of aesthetics — the ordinary would be both enhanced and protected. Although it seems natural now to think of beauty as something exceptional, beauty as the object of aesthetics was originally a defense of the ordinary. For Kant, whose account has been more influential than any other, that is the whole point of beauty: it is the means of reconciling our immersion in the physical world with the freedom of thought. But when art concerns itself with awe, terror, and the unknown, the effects of the abyss that the eighteenth century designated as sublime, all bets are off. The vertigo that can result is illustrated in just the right place by the anecdote of an early French listener to the most sublime musical work of 1808: 'When I tried to put on my hat', wrote Jean-François Lesueur after listening to Beethoven's Fifth Symphony, 'I could not find my head!'.

The danger of the sublime is a recurrent theme in the fantastic tales of E. T. A. Hoffmann, who in 1810 and 1813, respectively, would also publish seminal reviews of the Fifth Symphony and the op. 70 trios. A few years later he wrote 'The Mines of Falun', a tale that can stand with the 'Ghost' Trio as a study of how the ordinary can be lost. The tale is based on a popular true story, one that almost became the basis of a Romantic opera by Wagner.

In Hoffmann's version a melancholy young man, Elis Fröbom, meets a mysterious stranger who urges him to seek his fortune as a miner in the town of Falun. That night Elis has a dream of the world underground. Several of its key features, sexual desire and music among them, uncannily reprise ambivalent moments from Elis's recent past. Both sounds and images literally belong to an abyss:

> There arose [...] strange flowers and plants of flashing metal whose blossoms and leaves climbed upwards from the profoundest depths [...] [A]t the very bottom countless lovely maidens [were] embracing one another with white shining arms [...] and whenever [they] smiled, a sweet, melodious sound echoed through the vault [...] An indescribable feeling of pain and pleasure seized the youth [...] As [he] then looked down again [...] he felt his being dissolve into the shining rock. He screamed out in unspeakable terror and awoke from the dream, its joy and horror still echoing deep within his soul.[12]

Elis's dream systematically destroys the ordinary to the sound of enchanting music. Opposites fuse together in strange shapes that also fuse opposite feelings: flowers become metallic, the music echoes a silent smile, the maidens who arouse Elis's longing only long for each other, and Elis's living being dissolves into solid rock. What the story goes on to show is that there can be no real awakening from this dream: its sublime joy and horror never do stop echoing. When Elis arrives at Falun he has every possible success and becomes engaged to the mine-owner's beautiful daughter. But on his wedding night he follows the call of his dream and disappears into the mines. He is simply incapable of living in the ordinary world, even at its best. Fifty years later, his petrified body is discovered. When his now aged beloved passes by, she identifies the body and dies while embracing it in grief and rapture. The imagery of the dream thus comes true: Elis's organic desires are 'fulfilled' in the form of metallic rock. From the standpoint of ordinary life, this is irony piled upon tragedy. But from the standpoint of the extraordinary, it is a true fulfillment, as the Wagnerian 'love-death' of the aged woman testifies.

I like to imagine that the music of Elis's dream sounds something like the Largo of Beethoven's 'Ghost' Trio. The two, at least, share the same 'structure of feeling'; they inhabit a common world of images, inflections, ways of meaning, habits of thought.

What would the Trio sound like if we heard it with that world in mind? What would we hear as the effect of passing through a sublime, tortuous, uncanny slow movement between two 'unproblematic and relaxed' companions?

This way of putting the question begins to highlight a factor I left unspoken earlier. The two outer movements of the Trio are not unproblematic and relaxed in the same way. The opening *Allegro vivace e con brio* is just what its redundant tempo marking announces: a doubling of liveliness by vigour, a raising of the ordinary to a higher power — liveliness squared. But the Presto finale, although it runs even faster, has less to do. Apparently by design, it risks being ordinary in the sense of banal, a perfunctory conclusion to a remarkable journey. Taken by itself, the movement is a charming combination of ebullience and delicacy, with touches of whimsy. But like the famous second finale to the String Quartet op. 130, which replaced the *Grosse Fuge*, the 'Ghost' finale risks sounding too lightweight for its place. Did Beethoven just fall down on the job here, or is there something else at stake?

But we need to begin at the beginning. The 'Ghost' Trio begins by establishing a complementarity between energy and lyricism. First there is a vigorous flourish; then the music relaxes into something warm and singing. There are no expressive surprises here. This Trio, in short, begins by doing something altogether ordinary. Yet it does so reflectively, so that the listener is invited not just to hear the content of its ordinary expressive gestures, but to hear their ordinariness itself as part of what is being expressed. Both the energy and the lyricism belong to the 'first subject' of the sonata exposition rather than being divided between the first subject and the second, the tonic and the dominant. The qualities meet in a lyric juxtaposition, not a dramatic opposition. Their alliance continues in the second subject, a placid theme enveloped by vigorous 'walking' quavers, heard twice as the piano and strings trade roles. The potential for conflict, and with it the lure or danger of the sublime, is unceremoniously brushed aside. The whole exposition, the whole movement, concentrates on the pleasures of combining energy and lyricism in the absence of antagonism, excess, or disruption. The partnership of the qualities makes apparent the value of the stable, ordinary world that is its condition of possibility. More than that, this partnership and its pleasures make it possible to interpret the value of the ordinary in historically resonant ways. The kernel of this possibility is a small detail unmentioned so far, a detail that, once heard, changes everything.

The opening flourish of the Trio is a rough outburst in bare octaves, with the strings sandwiched between the right- and left-hand piano parts. The singing melody that follows is the product of a smooth-running dialogue. Three pairs of voices exchange and vary a single phrase over an oscillating accompaniment: cello and violin, mixed strings and right-hand piano, and again cello and violin. On the second exchange, the piano extends the phrase and engages it in counterpoint with the strings. On the third, the violin extends the phrase while the oscillations of the accompaniment grow faster and its bass deeper. Where the opening flourish is concentrated, the melody is expansive. What links these complementary figures and enlarges their meaning is the cello's decision not to stop playing when the opening flourish is done. As if on a sudden whim or inspiration, the cello holds on to a high note that sounds alone, quite beautifully, for a full bar. It continues over a soft, sustained octave in the bass of the piano, and finally raises itself by a semitone to become the headnote of the lyrical melody.

Heard in relation to the cello's singing note, the opening flourish becomes an outburst of sheer potential energy waiting to be shaped into melody, harmony, and rhythm. The sustained note turns the flourish into a generative force or a pre-formation, something from which something else, something higher, will come. When it arrives, just a moment later, this new formation follows a basic scheme of Romantic thought. It comes as a result of the intervention of mind or spirit on the matter at hand. The lyrical blossoming is the product of reflective awareness. The music conveys this understanding by its dialogical treatment of the lyrical melody, in contrast to the monolithic flourish. The dialogue form implies the idea of voice, which in turn implies the idea of person, personality, subjectivity. Thus the first few moments of the 'Ghost' Trio pass from the impersonal force of nature to its elaboration in the sphere of human enterprise: all in a few seconds, with a mere handful of notes.

I should like to call the result, which occupies the whole rest of the movement, the ordinary at its best. This is not just an agreeable combination of energy and lyricism, but a projection of their interrelationship as a vital, productive force. As the cello, violin, and piano all take turns stating the theme and making it their own, they establish energy and lyricism as the creative poles between which the ordinary unfolds as the sphere of what is viable and what is feasible. This is the ordinary as the very opposite of the banal: as, rather, the helpfully at-hand, the valuably familiar, something with significant potential for growth, variation, and proliferation. The movement inhabits this ordinariness with pleasure and meaning. It contains no high drama, no heaven-storming gestures, no Fifth Symphony stuff. What it offers instead is plenteous variety and adventure. Its ordinariness can rival the sublime without needing or wanting to become sublime.

The formal layout of the movement is designed to show off these qualities. The development is expansive, the recapitulation is full of telling changes, and the whole sequence of development and recapitulation is marked for repetition: abundance rules. The development sets the agenda, turning the exposition's preference for mercurial juxtaposition over dramatic antagonism into a generative principle. With the cello again in the lead, it begins by quietly transforming the opening flourish into a lyrical gesture from which others proliferate. It culminates in an exuberant contrapuntal episode combining rugged and ardent phrases in an intricate, rapidly changing, yet transparent texture: an acoustic kaleidoscope. And it ends by transforming the fadeout of this episode into the act of recollection and self-renewal — an energetic outburst in octaves — that will become the recapitulation. Everywhere one turns an ear, the dynamism of energy and lyricism makes the ordinary come alive.

The movement concludes in the same spirit, suggesting the irrepressibility of this dynamism by ending with the beginning. The coda reverses the first few moments of the piece; it moves from extended, enriched dialogues on the lyrical melody to an exuberant final statement of the first bar of the opening flourish. Set off by pregnant pauses, this gesture interrupts what sounds like the build-up to the final cadence, which it defers with its own statement of pure potentiality. The message is loud and clear: more to come.

But more does not come. It seems fair to say that the dynamism of the first movement is exactly what is lacking in the third. The finale shows us what the ordinary is like after the extraordinary excursion of the Largo. This is an ordinary that is chastened, perhaps even timid: the ordinary as a refuge from the sublime. Here there is plenty of vitality, but little variety or adventure. Most of the melodic material is ingeniously cut from the same cloth, and there are few departures from its rigid patterns. The movement is notably repetitive both locally and sectionally, and its formal layout virtually retracts that of the first movement. The development, modest in both scale and ambition, consists of three heavily reiterative passages that trace a retrograde path through the melodies of the exposition. The impulse is to return to the point of origin by the shortest route. Unlike its first-movement counterpart, this development could not bear repeating, being itself little more than a mode of repetition. The same spirit carries over into the recapitulation, which is largely unvaried. Only the coda strikes out in a new direction, as if it had belatedly realized that one was needed.

Between the first movement and this finale, then, a change overtakes the character of the ordinary. What change, exactly? One answer may be culled from a comparison between Novalis's thesis that the ordinary is really out of the ordinary and a later version of the same idea. Perhaps with Novalis at the back of his mind, Martin Heidegger writes that 'We believe we are at home in the immediate circle of beings. That which is, is familiar, reliable, ordinary. [...] [Yet] at bottom, the ordinary is not ordinary; it is extra-ordinary, uncanny'.[13] The reason we cannot be truly at home in the unhomely (that is, uncanny, 'unheimlich') circle of the ordinary is that familiar things withhold themselves from us 'in the double form of refusal and dissembling'. We have to win our way to the truth of the ordinary through and against this withholding. Novalis would not agree. Not sharing Heidegger's ideological burden of a demand for authenticity, Novalis treats the ordinary as a sheer coming out of itself, a gift of itself in return for our energy and effort. The ordinary, he says, is indispensable: higher things become incomprehensible to us only when we lose touch with it.

The first movement of the 'Ghost' Trio would seem to prove Novalis's point against Heidegger's. In its melodic fertility and contrapuntal vitality the movement gives of itself without reserve. Notable here are its instrumental dialogues, which pass melodic material from one voice to another not just for repetition but for variation — for growth and change. And the rich transparency of the development section's climactic 'kaleidoscope', together with the movement's eagerness to repeat it, suggests the very reverse of dissembling. The movement realizes the ordinary as an energetic combination of just this forthcomingness and transparency.

The finale, though, does just the opposite: its ordinariness is Heideggerian. The movement upholds the thesis that headlong high spirits can exert themselves without loss within narrow boundaries. But the more exuberant the music becomes, the more it turns its own exuberance into a signifier of restraint, a form of subtle dissembling. And most of the dialogical passages, of which there are many, consist in literal or near-literal repetition. They refuse the dynamism of their counterparts in the first movement. Even the principal means of melodic articulation, the abrupt curtailment of running passagework, is a form of withholding.

Standard modes of description and judgment cannot do justice to this situation.

The point is not that there is something 'wrong' with the finale — hardly a burning question — but that the finale is symptomatic of something. The movement follows a cultural mandate, a narrative mandate, which, as in Hoffmann's story, manifests itself as a psychological truth. Part of the same mandate is to prefer psychological truth over a conventional artistic formula. Hoffmann does so by ending with an apparently supplemental narrative that actually contains the story's most important event. Beethoven follows suit, only more so: he tells the truth of banality. This is where you go, he says; this is how it sounds when you have lost the ordinary and have to find it again and cling to it for dear life; this is what it sounds like when you have to take what you can get. The first movement inhabits a culture of feeling in which the ordinary can be remarkable. That is why a reading of it as an exaltation of the ordinary is consistent with its musically remarkable features. The finale has become estranged from that culture, and shows it. But what has intervened, then? What is there about the Largo that casts such a pall over the ordinary? The answer, like the question, requires a detour — back through *Macbeth* via Schlegel.

Beethoven's sketchbook for the 'Pastoral' Symphony and the op. 70 trios contains a brief entry for a projected opera on *Macbeth*; the entry falls on the same page as some sketches for the 'Ghost' Largo. This conjunction has fuelled speculation about a link between the Largo and *Macbeth* ever since the nineteenth century. In 2001 the National Symphony Orchestra of the USA even gave the 'world premiere' of a *Macbeth* Overture based on the sketches. It begins with the opening of the Largo. But the facts do not quite fit the surmises. Although Beethoven began mulling over the *Macbeth* project in 1808, there is no musical relationship between the 'Ghost' sketches and the *Macbeth* sketch plopped in their midst. Beethoven was probably just making handy use of available white space. So there is no specific connection between the 'Ghost' Largo and *Macbeth*, let alone Schlegel's reading of *Macbeth*, any more than with Hoffmann's 'The Mines of Falun'. It cannot be stressed too much that the Largo and these literary works do not resemble each other in any explicit way. What links them is their historical relationship to a particular way of conceiving and inhabiting the world as the place of the ordinary.

What is really pertinent to the 'Ghost' Largo is Beethoven's remark in a different sketchbook that the *Macbeth* Overture should start right up with the witches ('fällt gleich in den Chor der Hexen ein'). For Beethoven, as for Schlegel, the most striking thing about *Macbeth* was apparently the *way* it departs from the ordinary: without compromise, without delay. The opera, like the Trio and the play, was to intrude that departure in one of the places where it least should go. Such a misplaced sublime seems to have felt especially intractable in 1808. It seems to have been regarded as dredged up arbitrarily from the dark realms mistaken by philosophy for exploded fictions, and installed where it could confront the wayfaring subject with a frightening autonomy. A movement like the Largo cannot be rationalized. No higher unity can assimilate it. It sticks in the craw of Enlightenment, and is meant to.

Perhaps the most immediately striking features of the Largo are its pervasive oscillating figures, especially tremolos, and its obsessive harping on a single little melodic phrase. In the context of the key, D minor, the melodic concentration produces a mood of intense, dissatisfied brooding. The tremolos suggest an abnormal vibration of the nerves, the shuddering or 'thrilling' that the early nineteenth century regularly associated with sublime or uncanny states.

Between them, these two features act out a drama of ever-increasing mutual bafflement. The movement begins with a dialogue in which the piano answers a questioning figure on the strings with the little melodic phrase. For the rest of the movement this phrase will belong almost exclusively to the strings, which often exchange it in a dialogue of their own; and the piano devotes itself above all to the oscillations and tremolos, which the strings do not share. As the movement proceeds, the strings seem to be trying to sustain a feeling of individuality and articulation against the stammering of the piano. The little phrase is their sole meagre resource for doing so; it forms their sole link to the ordinary. And in the long run the link snaps.

Just before the end, the movement rises to a terrifying climax when the tremolos come back after seemingly being laid to rest. In quick succession the cello begins to pulsate and the violin tries and fails to rearticulate the little phrase one last time. With its failure both violin and cello are sucked into the all-pervasive stammering and tumble down to silence in a prolonged shudder. The passage is like the voracious dark side of the opening flourish in the first movement. That, and more: for the tremolos and collapse have been present in the first movement, too, and at a very vulnerable, very exposed place — the close of the exposition. The loss of the ordinary has not only come from the outside, but also, far more disturbingly, from a kernel of the sublime lodged within the ordinary itself. The problem is not just Napoleon's armies; it is the witches.

If that is what the music claims, though, we need not respond with the trope of celebrating its insight that is the aesthetic equivalent of credulity. It may be that the impression of an intrinsic sublime helps defend against the impact of an extrinsic sublime that is less glamorous and more destructive. Schlegel's dark side trumps Napoleon's. The fiction of a tragic necessity becomes a means of accommodating the fact of a terrible contingency. The insight that the sublime is immanent within the ordinary is thus (thus also) a gesture of idealization. It is perhaps no accident, after all, that the Fifth Symphony and the 'Ghost' Trio inhabit the same year that is an interregnum between military and political disasters. If the Fifth Symphony can be thought of as fantasizing the triumph of, and over, an external militancy, the 'Ghost' Trio, or its Largo, can be thought of as devising a second fantasy that envisions a means of surviving the death of the first.

And we need not stop with a single recognition. Another one, deliberately esoteric and perhaps still more disturbing, is also invited by this movement. Throughout much of the Largo the harmony feels wrong. Much of the first half of the movement is dominated by C major, a key adumbrated in the opening dialogue and quite an extraordinary choice in relation to D minor. The two keys form a puzzling intimacy with each other during the exposition. They are linked by a kind of mirror reversal, as plagal movement from D to G becomes dominant–tonic movement from G to C. They share an exclusive concern with the same melodic material. And they behave in the same way, each establishing itself early as a point of reference but deferring a full-bodied cadence to the last minute — and beyond. Despite their conventional remoteness from each other, these two keys cannot quite keep their identities from blending. C major comes to appear as an out-of-focus image of D minor, which it renders less gloomy but more enigmatic.

When D minor returns in the recapitulation, its key-feeling remains out of focus, as if the C-major veil had been parted but not fully lifted. At the long-deferred D-minor cadences, the piano's oscillations slur a variety of dissonances into the keynote deep in the bass, producing an ominous rumble in place of a clear chord tone. The cadences form a pair, with the second more muddy than the first; confirmation is replaced by mystification. And this, too, is an echo of C major, which has earlier formed its cadences in the same way. Not until the coda does the texture clarify to reveal D minor whole, but the revelation coincides with the shuddering implosion of the strings.

This process of veiling and unveiling is reminiscent of an esoteric trope known to have interested Beethoven. He and his contemporaries found great symbolic value in the veil of Isis, the Egyptian goddess whose temple stood in the ancient city of Sais. For Beethoven, Novalis, Hoffmann, and others, the veiled goddess represented (among other things) the continued possibility of numinous mystery in a too-Enlightened world. On his work desk, under glass, Beethoven kept the mystical verse supposedly inscribed above Isis's temple: 'I am everything that is, that was, that will be. No mortal man has lifted my veil'. Kant had called this very inscription the most sublime thing ever written; he also identified the veiled goddess with 'the moral law in us, in its inviolable majesty'.[14] In Novalis's fragmentary novel *The Apprentices of Sais*, the mystery of Isis holds out the hope of a regenerated world. In Hoffmann's review of Beethoven's op. 70, the style of the 'Ghost' Trio in particular is said to imply that 'the deeper mysteries can never be spoken of in ordinary words [...] but only in expressions of sublime splendour. The dance of the High Priests of Isis can only be a hymn of exultation'.[15] But as Beethoven knew well from *The Magic Flute*, the realm of Isis could also be dark and intimidating.

3. Presto

Within earshot of another contemporary trope, that realm could be heard (literally heard) as an indefinite liminal space between spirit and matter — what Friedrich Schelling identified as 'the spiritual–corporeal essence' of the world. This primordial essence manifests itself as a kind of fluid substance that emanates from solids and clings about them like a glimmer:

> In even the most corporeal of things there lies a point of transfiguration that is almost sensibly perceptible. [...] There is always an overflow, as it were, playing and streaming around them, an essence that, though indeed ungraspable [*ungreifliches*], is not for that [reason] indiscernible [*unbemerkliches*].[16]

Schelling tends to favour visual tropes for this 'lyric substance', as Daniel Tiffany has called it,[17] but it was more often located in the sounds made by phenomena that seem to be at once embodied and disembodied, especially wind and water. These semi-musical, semi-vocal sounds had an affinity for sublime surroundings, and often seemed to carry across great distances of time and space. William Wordsworth heard them via tropes made popular by the Ossianic poems: 'I would stand, | Beneath some rock, listening to sounds that are | The ghostly language of the ancient earth, | Or make their dim abode in distant winds'. Goethe heard them in the fall of water, which he treats as the tangible semblance of the soul: 'Lovlily [the jet] breaks into mist, | A cloudwave, | On the smooth rock, | And lightly gathered | Wells up veilingly, | Whooshing lightly | To the depths below'.[18] Both images capture the ambivalence of lyric substance, which secures the survival of spirit in the enlightened world by staging spirit at the level of matter itself, but which can do so only in the veiled neighbourhood of ghosts and the abyss.

Like Goethe's rushing water, long stretches of the piano part in Beethoven's Largo break into a cloudwave, their continuous tremolos forming the acoustic equivalent of a veil of mist. Hoffmann recalls playing them *una corda* and with dampers raised to produce 'a susurration [...] that recalls the aeolian harp and glass harmonica. [...] float[ing] sounds that surrounded the soul like hazy figures in a dream, enticing it into a world of curious presentiments'.[19] Crucial to this impression is the enigmatic harmony, which steeps the movement in the uncanny and, at the cadences closing both the exposition and the recapitulation, sends the lyric substance of the music plunging into the depths below. The space held open within both D minor and C major between key as a referential envelope and key as cadential substance becomes the space in which the extraordinary appears, the space that it fills up and overflows.

Far from the tone of Hoffmann's 'hymn of exultation', this movement seems to seek out a dark truth that forbids any 'intimate familiarity'. This truth does not edify, and it will not set you free. What the final D-minor cadence unveils is a travesty of the kind of ultimate meaning that Roland Barthes, in a now classic text, 'The Death of the Author', rejects in the name of pure writing:

> By refusing to assign a 'secret' ultimate meaning to the text (and to the world as text) [writing] liberates what may be called an anti-theological activity [...] since to refuse to fix meaning is, in the end, to refuse God and his hypostases — reason, science, law.[20]

Beethoven's D minor, although it does form a kind of fixed secret, neither is nor has an ultimate meaning. Its occult tie to C major renders it inaccessible to reason, science, or law. This is meaning rendered as a mode of sublimity, ungraspable but not indiscernible, meaning as sheer force.

But if the 'Ghost' Largo presents its D minor as a surrogate mystery of Isis, a darkness unveiled at the last moment to reveal a greater darkness, then we are taught by this to hear the D major of the outer movements as itself a kind of veil, a veil of illusion. This D major is too easy; it is complacent in its ordinariness; it cannot be trusted. The conclusion of the Largo says so plainly. Just before the end, a bare block-chord progression appears out of nowhere — it is like nothing else in the movement — and softly offers up a luminous D-major triad. But the offering is promptly and loudly rejected, leaving the way clear for the whispery final cadence in D minor. D major is thus revealed as a kind of false consciousness of pleasure and practicality that can neither be rejected nor accepted, at least not at face value.

But D major is, of course, the key of the finale, which is thus lamed from the start. With its studied good cheer, with its lack of generative contrast and its restriction on development, with its celebration of the ordinary as stability rather than as potentiality, the finale, despite its overt good spirits, is tinged with nostalgia and regret. It is almost an unhappy ending. Such as it is, it is the pleasure of Hegel's unhappy consciousness, the pleasure achieved by forgetting — trying to forget — one's historical position as 'the consciousness of self as a dual-natured and merely contradictory being'.[21] The cost of living in the ordinary world after visitation by the sublime is just this restrictiveness, this fixed will, not to real pleasure, far less to 'enjoyment', bliss, rapture, but to having a good time.

Not that we don't have a good time. We do. But the paradox of the ordinary in the post-Enlightenment era, and perhaps in our own as well, is that the ordinary was supposed to give us more than that. And so it does, says the 'Ghost' Trio; so it does. But then...

Notes to Chapter 6

1. Peter Brooks, *Reading for the Plot: Design and Intention in Narrative* (New York: Knopf, 1984; repr. Cambridge, MA: Harvard University Press, 1992).
2. August Strindberg *The Chamber Plays*, trans. by Evert Spinchorn, Seabury Quinn, Jr, and Kenneth Petersen (New York: Dutton, 1962), p. xix.
3. Maynard Solomon, *Beethoven* (New York: Schirmer, 1977), p. 208.
4. On still lives and object autobiographies, see Jonathan Lamb, 'Modern Metamorphoses and Disgraceful Tales', *Critical Inquiry*, 28 (2001), 133–66 (esp. pp. 139–42, 147–66).
5. Michael Kwass, 'Ordering the World of Goods: Consumer Revolution and the Classification of Objects in Eighteenth-Century France', *Representations*, 82 (2003), 87–116 (p. 87).
6. Novalis (Friedrich Leopold von Hardenberg), 'On Goethe', in *German Aesthetic and Literary Criticism: The Romantic Ironists and Goethe*, ed. by Kathleen Wheeler (Cambridge: Cambridge University Press, 1984), pp. 102–08 (p. 102).
7. From 'The Work of Art in the Age of Mechanical Reproduction', in Walter Benjamin, *Illuminations*, trans. by Harry Zohn, ed. by Hannah Arendt (New York: Schocken, 1969), p. 219.
8. John Keats, 'Ode to Psyche' (1819), ll. 37–39, from John Keats, *Selected Poems and Letters*, ed. by Douglas Bush (Boston: Houghton Mifflin, [1959]), p. 204; Friedrich Hölderlin, 'Brot und Wein', vii, 1–2 (my translation), from Friedrich Hölderlin and Eduard Mörike, *Selected Poems*, ed. and trans. by Christopher Middleton (Chicago: University of Chicago Press, 1972), p. 43.
9. See Martin Heidegger, 'The Origins of the Work of Art', in *Poetry, Language, Thought*, trans. by Albert Hofstadter (New York: Harper, 1975), pp. 44–55; and Maurice Merleau-Ponty, 'What is Phenomenology', in *Phenomenology of Perception*, trans. by Colin Smith (London: Routledge & Kegan Paul, 1962), pp. vii–xxi.
10. August Wilhelm von Schlegel, *Lectures on Dramatic Art and Literature*, trans. by John Black (1811), repr. in *Four Centuries of Shakespeare Criticism*, ed. by Frank Kermode (New York: Avon, 1965), p. 494.
11. Michael Taussig, '"Dying is an Art, Like Everything Else"', *Critical Inquiry*, 28 (2001), 305–16 (p. 316).
12. E. T. A. Hoffmann, *Tales of Hoffmann*, trans. by R. J. Hollindale, with Stella and Vernon Humphries and Sally Hayward (London: Penguin, 1982), pp. 317–19.
13. Heidegger, p. 54.
14. For Beethoven's work desk, see Maynard Solomon, *Beethoven Studies* (Cambridge, MA: Harvard University Press, 1988), p. 225; for Kant's remarks, see Immanuel Kant, *Critique of Judgment* (1790), trans. by Werner S. Pluhar (Indianapolis: Hackett, 1987), p. 185, and 'On a Newly Arisen Superior Tone in Philosophy' (1796), in *Raising the Tone of Philosophy: Late Essays by Immanuel Kant, Transformative Critique by Jacques Derrida*, ed. by Peter Fenves (Baltimore, MD: Johns Hopkins University Press, 1993), p. 71.
15. E. T. A. Hoffmann, 'Beethoven's Piano Trios, Op. 70', *Allgemeine musikalische Zeitung*, 15 (3 March 1813); repr. in *E. T. A. Hoffmann's Musical Writings: Kreisleriana, The Poet and the Composer, Music Criticism*, ed. by David Charlton, trans. by Martyn Clarke (Cambridge: Cambridge University Press, 1989), p. 312.

16. Slavoj Žižek, *The Abyss of Freedom*; with F. W. Schelling, *Ages of the World*, trans. by Judith Norman (Ann Arbor: University of Michigan Press, 1997), pp. 148–61 (p. 151).

17. Daniel Tiffany, 'Lyric Substance: On Riddles, Materialism, and Poetic Obscurity', *Critical Inquiry*, 28 (2001), 72–99.

18. William Wordsworth, *The Prelude* (1805), II, 226–29, in *The Oxford Authors: William Wordsworth*, ed. by Stephen Gill (Oxford: Oxford University Press, 1984), p. 400; Johann Wolfgang von Goethe, 'Gesang der Geister über den Wasser' (1779), ll. 11–17, my translation from J. W. von Goethe, *Selected Poems*, ed. by Christopher Middleton, trans. by Michael Hamburger and others (Princeton, NJ: Princeton University Press, 1994), p. 70.

19. Hoffmann, *E. T. A. Hoffmann's Musical Writings*, pp. 309–10.

20. Roland Barthes, *Image, Music, Text*, ed. and trans. by Stephen Heath (New York: Hill and Wang, 1977), p. 147.

21. Georg Wilhelm Friedrich Hegel, *The Phenomenology of Spirit*, trans. by A. V. Miller (Oxford: Oxford University Press, 1977), §206, p. 126.

CHAPTER 7

Musical Scores and Literary Form in Modernism: Ezra Pound's *Pisan Cantos* and Samuel Beckett's *Watt*

Mark Byron

> If there is one place where it is idiotic to sham that place is before a work of art.
>
> EZRA POUND, 'The Serious Artist'

The musical scores within Ezra Pound's poetic sequence *The Pisan Cantos*[1] and Samuel Beckett's novel *Watt*[2] challenge conventions of literary form in visually arresting terms, and extend the possibilities of formal literary experimentation. Both of these late-modernist works — a poetic sequence within a larger modernist epic (*The Cantos*), and an experimental novel — were composed during the Second World War under different conditions of personal authorial extremity. Both texts endured precarious journeys from manuscript to print. Their fragile material contingency reflects a major thematic preoccupation of each text: the precarious nature of the artistic enterprise itself. The visual incursion of musical scores in these texts stalls the act of reading and signals an immediate and specific challenge to literary form. *The Pisan Cantos* and *Watt* are not resolved, formally complete texts; they are replete with allusive riddles and half-submerged references, and display residues of accidental and intentional erasures. The theme of music, specifically musical notation, illustrates the way contingency and fragility become abiding preoccupations in these complex texts.

Pound and Beckett were hardly the first to quote from or include musical scores in their texts. Modernist cultural practitioners often combined various artistic media within one 'work', where they would contest with and define each other. These modernist practices exhibit an eminent history, whereby relations between the arts in the Western tradition stem from Greek and Roman antiquity. In the fifteenth century Leonardo da Vinci contested the Horatian notion of *ut pictura poesis* ('as of painting, so of poetry') in his notion of the *paragone*, or hierarchy of the arts. Leonardo's tract asserts the axiological pre-eminence of painting, based on the superiority of sight over the other senses, and thus neatly transcends the historical contingencies and prejudices of courtly patronage whilst at once meaning to influence them. During the German Enlightenment Gotthold Lessing published a critique of the Horatian equation in his

Laocoön; or The Limits of Painting and Poetry (1766). Again, the contingencies of history — Enlightenment discourse on rational faculties and the functions of taste — shape an ostensibly theoretical discourse.

During the nineteenth century numerous important artistic practitioners came to see a deep cognitive relation between the arts, at least partly in response to the disorientations of their modern urban milieux. The French poet Arthur Rimbaud proposed a radical state of synaesthesia, or 'systematic derangement of the senses', as a true aim of art; and his compatriot Charles Baudelaire signified in his poem 'Correspondances' that words 'would cease to be mere signs and participate in the things that they present or evoke'[3] — in this case the colour spectrum and the reader's corresponding expressive tones. Wagner composed operatic works that sought to encompass the gamut of artistic expression in a unified work: the *Gesamtkunstwerk*.

Modernist writers, composers, and artists inherited this rich vein of philosophical inquiry and practical experimentation. Wassily Kandinsky, Robert Delaunay, Marc Chagall, and e.e. cummings, amongst many others, proposed sometimes complex systems of analogues between words, colours, musical pitch, and sculptural shape. Movements such as Dada, Suprematism, Vorticism, and Italian Futurism redefined aesthetic work in fundamentally intermedial terms. Whilst critics have tended to focus on the relation between literature and the visual arts in modernism, the relation between music and literature is significant and widespread.[4] Many Irish, British, and American modernist writers were influenced by and collaborated with musicians. Often writers were musically trained themselves, and occasionally attempted musical projects of their own devising or wrote columns as music critics in contemporary journals (Pound is exemplary in this way, as a poet who wrote three incomplete operas and numerous reviews and essays of music criticism). Music also served as a richly suggestive field for meditation upon the status and purpose of literary production.[5]

With this context and history in mind, how is the reader to apprehend the musical scores in the late-modernist texts of Pound and Beckett? The scores in both *The Pisan Cantos* and *Watt* function as peculiar gateways to these texts. They elicit a temporary pause and invite the reader to situate the scores in some relation to conventional textual interpretation. The very notion of conventional interpretation becomes newly complex and worthy of contemplation. Pound and Beckett were well acquainted with theories of correspondence and the traditions from which they derived or diverged. Pound's *Cantos* attempts a kind of cultural encyclopedism, drawing a vast array of sources and media into his poetic text, and Beckett's novel includes reference to painting, music, and the transience of aesthetic experience. Yet it seems clear that neither *The Pisan Cantos* nor *Watt* attempts to manifest the *Gesamtkunstwerk* or to mount a comparative valuation of the arts. The composition conditions of each text show precisely the reverse: each includes instructions for musical performance (the score) as a means by which to interrogate the creative enterprise itself and the forms it might legitimately take.

Framing Text and Score: *The Pisan Cantos*

Pound's text incorporates a musical score with an independent history: the violin line of Clément Janequin's *Le Chant des oiseaux*. This sixteenth-century choral piece makes up the larger part of Pound's Canto LXXV (450–51), the second of eleven *Pisan Cantos*. Whilst it may be a visually arresting object, it is but one element in a visually kaleidoscopic poetic work. Even the most perfunctory scan of *The Cantos* reveals Chinese ideograms, the Greek alphabet, Egyptian hieroglyphics, Arabic script, geometric shapes, a panoply of languages, and an array of verse forms and typographic arrangements of text on the page. The musical score is perhaps the most striking physical feature of the entire poem, but it is, in the end, only one of many incursions into a traditional poetic space.

Yet its inclusion prompts a question that precedes any actual process of 'reading' the score: Is the score there to be read (by the musically literate) as a self-standing piece of music, or does it function simply to register the concept of scripted music? Are we expected to think of the piece of music to which the score pertains, or is knowledge of the title and a few historical details enough for the purposes of emotive or thematic evocation? The presence of this score contributes to the semantics of the canto and of *The Pisan Cantos* more generally, and as such it demands interpretation. This canto can be seen as a point of meditation, where the relation between the arts opens out to a revaluation of the artistic enterprise itself.

Ezra Pound composed the typescript of *The Pisan Cantos* in the medical compound of the United States Army Detention Training Center (DTC) in the hills outside Pisa, Italy, some time between 24 May and 16 November 1945. He was detained there by virtue of his broadcasts on the 'American Hour' of Rome Radio (Ente Italiano Audizioni Radiofoniche) dating from 1940, for which he was indicted for treason by a Grand Jury in 1943. In a complicated series of events Pound was taken by Italian Partisans to Genoa in May 1945, and then by US Army personnel to the Pisan DTC. After three weeks caged in an open cell reinforced with airstrip steel, Pound suffered a physical breakdown and was transferred to the medical tent, where composition of *The Pisan Cantos* is supposed to have begun.[6] Pound had drafted cantos initially in Italian as early as 1940 when he was living in Rapallo, and various fragments and passages written in English also survived these war years to make their way into what became *The Pisan Cantos*.

By the Second World War Pound was already immersed in a prolonged expatriation from his native United States, having first departed for Europe in 1908. He relocated from London in 1921 to the English-speaking community of artists and writers in Paris, and in 1924 he moved again, settling in Rapallo, a town on the Ligurian coast of Italy near Genoa, with his wife Dorothy, and close to his long-term companion Olga Rudge. Pound courted political and cultural estrangement when he expressed public sympathy with the Fascist cause, and he fell foul of official opinion in his homeland. His isolation and estrangement became formally explicit at the point of his detention in 1945, culminating a process that began socially, linguistically, and psychologically years before the events leading up to *The Pisan Cantos*.

This historical and biographical information is difficult to ignore, particularly when the reader is met with the score in Canto LXXV. Is the music emblematic of these themes of estrangement? The eleven *Pisan Cantos* are framed rhetorically within a mode of poetic immediacy, and comprise a testament to the importance of personal and cultural memory. There is much in the poem to support an argument for the modernist artist-as-hero — the *ego scriptor* that Pound affirms earlier in his epic poem (LXII/250; LXIV/360; and LXXIV/458) — who attempts to shore up the fragments of a ruined civilization into his poetic archive, which itself is not assured a future outside the encampment at Pisa (indeed Pound was heavily reliant upon his family and editors to assemble his text for publication). This 'tragic view' of *The Pisan Cantos* has proved popular with critics and is consistent with the tenor of the poetic suite as a whole.[7]

Canto LXXIV, the first of *The Pisan Cantos*, opens with an elegy for Mussolini's Fascist dream. It also contains a catechism in the Social Credit economics that Pound saw as a viable alternative to a capitalism he believed hollowed out the value of material production and reduced its inherent worth to abstract currency exchange. In addition Canto LXXIV catalogues important events and ideas from Greek, Roman, Chinese, Carolingian, Italian, American, English, and West African cultural spheres. Pound also records his perceptions in the DTC, and his personal memories of writers and of people he met in travel over many years. Canto LXXIV is representative of *The Pisan Cantos* in striking a double pose of poetic immediacy and of memory and reflection.

How might this context bridge Canto LXXIV with the seven lines of poetic text and the score of Canto LXXV? The final line of Canto LXXIV encapsulates the classical motif of estrangement and return: 'we who have passed over Lethe', the river of forgetting in the Greek underworld. This motif concludes a passage that explores patterns of idealist perfection in nature and in ordinary perception in such terms as: 'diamond clearness', 'This liquid is certainly a | property of the mind | nec accidens est', and 'the rose in the steel dust' (449). Canto LXXV begins, echoing Virgil, with reference to another river of the classical underworld, 'Phlegethon', the river of fire:

> Out of Phlegethon!
> out of Phlegethon,
>   Gerhart
>   art thou come forth out of Phlegethon?
> with Buxtehude and Klages in your satchel, with the
> Ständebuch of Sachs in yr/ luggage
>   — not of one bird but of many (LXXV/450)

In the spirit of memory retained through the ordeals of history (the river of fire), the poetic voice blends epic reference with personal experience. Virgil has Aeneas cross Phlegethon in order to escape the Palace of Hades, and in so doing discover the Elysian fields.[8]

But it is 'Gerhart' who crosses the river in this canto: Gerhard Münch, the German pianist and composer who performed in several of Pound's 'Tigullian concerts' in Rapallo during the 1930s. Münch accompanied Olga Rudge's violin in performances of *Le Chant des oiseaux*, the opening piece in the first and last of a series of concerts, beginning on 10 October 1933 and ending on 31 March 1934. In the canto Münch is imagined to be carrying a satchel of composers' scores: those of Dietrich Buxtehude, the master of organ composition and a profound influence upon Bach, and those of Hans Sachs, the sixteenth-century *Meistersinger*. Münch's satchel also contains the work of anthropologist Ludwig Klages, 'to whom Münch addressed a number of letters'.[9] The final line of text introduces Janequin's score with a comment made by Olga Rudge on playing the violin line of *Le Chant des oiseaux*: that it brought the sounds 'not of one bird but of many'. Commentary and historical reference then recede into silence. The page is filled with the score, and poetic recitation defers to the imagined musical performance.

Canto LXXV gestures towards the purity of artistic expression and the function of the text as a repository for cultural and personal memory. Yet crucially it also bears the traces of its earlier material forms. The score is a transcription of Gerhard Münch's arrangement for violin and piano of Janequin's *Le Chant des oiseaux*. At the time Janequin composed the piece, the practice was to score individual parts separately, and thus Münch's separation of the violin part for performance actually mimics its earlier scripted form. Janequin's early sixteenth-century composition was originally scored for choir, and was then scored for lute by Francesco da Milano — hence its Italian title in Canto LXXV, *Canzone degli uccelli*. Münch's arrangement was first printed in Ronald Duncan's journal *Townsman* in January 1938, followed by an article signed by Pound in which he explains the provenance of the violin part and the general significance of Janequin's art.[10] Pound speculates that 'its ancestry I think goes back to Arnaut Daniel and to god knows what "hidden antiquity"'.[11] Arnaut, a troubadour poet, embodied the principle of aesthetic unity, or *motz el son*, that Pound saw in Provençal poetry and in all great poetry since.

Pound placed a premium on this piece of music's ability to retain the 'spirit' of its origins, murky as they may be, through all of its varying scripted forms:

> Clement Janequin wrote a chorus, with words for the singers of the different parts of the chorus. These words would have no literary or poetic value if you took the music away but when Francesco da Milano reduced it for the lute the birds were still in the music. And when Münch transcribed it for modern instruments the birds were still there. They ARE still in the violin parts.[12]

Pound links this piece of music in this particular arrangement with other instances of birdsong in *The Pisan Cantos*: 'with two larks in contrappunto | at sunset' (LXXIV/431); 'three solemn half notes | their white downy chests black-rimmed | on the middle wire | periplum' (LXXXII/527); and, emblematically, 'f f | d | g | write the birds in their treble scale' (LXXXII/525). The birds of the DTC herald a narrative of personal history embodied in music. This narrative is concerned ultimately with the possibility of expressing eternal forms through art — what Pound calls in his prose writings the 'forma', 'concetto', or 'pith'.[13]

Pound's gesture towards transcendence, by means of a musical score in a literary work, seems paradoxical. The score is visually arresting and reveals part of its transmission history within the frame of *The Pisan Cantos*. The manuscripts and typescripts of Canto LXXV[14] do not include the actual score. Pound was hardly in a position to scout for copies of *Townsman* or to locate its publication archives at the time of composition. He directed his editors, T. S. Eliot at Faber & Faber in London and James Laughlin at New Directions in New York, to locate Münch's score for inclusion at the prescribed place in the text. Dorothy Pound and James Laughlin corresponded over the difficulty obtaining the score and over Pound's instructions for its incorporation into his text. Olga Rudge located the music and sent it to Eliot.[15]

The inclusion of this musical score — for all its hermeneutic significance and its historical traces — asks a more urgent question about the very possibility of art. Any conventional notion of authority and agency is clearly not applicable in this case, making the appeal to aesthetic transcendence and artistic transmigration all the more poignant and irresistible to critics. The score does not tell of the music's circuitous path into the text, or of the author's physical estrangement from the piece of scripted music he mentally envisaged in his poem during composition. For all of its other functions in *The Pisan Cantos*, the violin line of *Le Chant des oiseaux* finally embodies the precariousness of the poetic enterprise. Pound's text was not merely under threat because of the contingencies of war and its author's own peculiar predicament within it. Canto LXXV embodies the uncertainty of aesthetic enterprise per se. The score is an emblem not of the unity of the arts, but of the impending threat of their actual and symbolic silence.

Framing Text and Score: *Watt*

Conditions of estrangement, endangerment, and silence also shape the composition of Samuel Beckett's novel *Watt* and inform the thematic substance of its narrative. As with *The Pisan Cantos*, the inclusion of music and its notation in *Watt* can be seen as emblematic of the persistence of literary expression in the face of complex and even extreme historical contingencies. Whilst Pound quotes a real musical work with a complex history of transcription, *Watt* includes scores and songs of the narrator's own devising, several of which seem to be included for comic effect. The frivolous tone of these musical interludes exempt the reader from the kind of seriousness that might pertain to the musical elements of Pound's text. Yet, in *Watt*, music and its transcription appears in a literary work that also ponders the concept of literary composition with considerable critical reflection. Beneath the comic posturing, is there a meditation in process that uses the allied arts to examine critically the notion of the literary (and literary composition) in oblique ways?

The compositional history of *Watt* is complex, and the novel holds a singular place in Beckett's output. It was composed during the Second World War, after Beckett's early prose work in English (*More Pricks Than Kicks*; *Murphy*), but prior to his French novels and plays following the war (*Molloy*; *Malone Meurt*; *En Attendant Godot*; *L'Innomable*). The conditions of exile and estrangement that shape its composition were threefold: Beckett had only recently exiled himself permanently from his native Ireland, after years of travel and prevarication; the outbreak of war reinforced this move and then necessitated his departure in 1942 from his newly established residence in Paris until 1945; and these displacements and estrangements reinforced the internal exile of language and consciousness evident in his texts.

Beckett began composition in the so-called *Watt* notebooks[16] on 2 February 1941, the birthday of his literary mentor James Joyce, who had died only days earlier. The perilous circumstances of Beckett's stay in Paris inform the tone of the three earlier notebooks, written sporadically up to May 1942 between Resistance tasks and when the motivation to write existed. Sighle Kennedy attributes a two-month silence in the third manuscript notebook to the final flurry of activity in Beckett's Resistance unit before it was betrayed, after which Beckett wrote continuously for five weeks until forced to go underground on 8 July.[17] Beckett and his companion Suzanne Deschevaux-Dumesnil lived in and around Paris until September 1942, when they were smuggled into unoccupied France. They walked from Lyon to the town of Roussillon in the Vaucluse, arriving on 6 October 1942.[18] The remaining notebooks were composed at Roussillon between October 1942 and April 1945. In April 1945 Beckett travelled to Dublin via London, stopping at the Routledge offices to see about the possible publication of *Watt*.[19]

The publication history of *Watt* is no less a tale of waiting, suspension, and deferred hope. Beckett's early attempts to have it published began with his former publishers, who in May 1945 rejected the manuscript as 'too wild and unintelligible'.[20] The text passed through the hands of four literary agents and several publishing houses from 1945 until its publication in 1953. By 1953 Beckett had published *Molloy* (1951), *Malone meurt* (1951), *En attendant Godot* (1952), and *L'Innommable* (July 1953), all with the Parisian firm Les Éditions de Minuit. A group of young American expatriates living in Paris caught wind of Beckett's unpublished text and were summarily presented with a typescript of *Watt*.[21] They published an extract in their English-language journal *Merlin*, and orchestrated the publication of *Watt* on 31 August 1953 by Olympia Press in a first printing of 1125 copies.

The text's journey from composition to publication strangely echoes its narrative. The ostensible story is the tale of Watt, a downtrodden 'university man' (p. 23): he travels to the place of his future employment, the house of Knott (Part I); he enters his first year of service and lapses into ignorance concerning the people and events in the house (Part II); he develops even greater ignorance during his second year of employment, punctuated by memories of events and tales recounted at great length (Part III); Watt then returns from the house to the railway, and then to 'the end of the line' (p. 244), to arrive at the unnamed institution where Part III is to be told to the scribe Sam (Part IV). This schema is complicated by the narrator's claim at the opening of Part IV: 'As Watt told the beginning of his story, not first, but second, so not fourth, but third, now he told its end' (p. 215). The four parts actually follow a rough chronological order, but the narrator, discovered to be Sam in Part III, is given the tale in this chiasmic order. From the reader's point of view the meeting between Sam and Watt (beginning Part III) is last chronologically, whilst its nested tale (Watt's second year of employment) keeps the narrative linearity mostly intact. The presence of a narrator within the framing action of Part III places the world of Watt's tale within a diaphanous and intransigent past tense (a change from its conventional narrative past in Parts I and II). The narrator's transcription is at odds with the reading experience: Sam's notation of Watt's tale has been rearranged, just as he transposes his subject's deranged language.

The narrative and the block of text are consistently disrupted or moderated by songs, lists, footnotes, musical scores, and the Addenda fragments. Intentional infelicities and inconsistencies in the text are ascribed to the narrating voice, but it is not certain, for example, that the narrating voice is responsible for the inclusion of the musical scores. On the other hand, the aporias in Sam's 'MS' are reported by a kind of reticent editorial voice, who arranges the manuscript into its final shape.

The incomplete, disordered narrative, the prevarications of its central character towards the nature of reality and truth, and the opacity with which events are recorded have led critics to read *Watt* as a parable of the limits of rationality, a demented application of the Cartesian reduction, or as a way of coping with the difficulties of war, occupation, and displacement. These kinds of reading attempt to make sense of the text surface, but overlook the concept upon which the entire narrative enterprise hinges. For *Watt* — as Beckett wrote of Joyce's *Work in Progress* — 'is not *about* something; *it is that something itself*'.[22] *Watt* is fiction interrogating its textual state.

Scores and lyrics break up the block of text at regular intervals. The first song to appear in the narrative is Mr Hackett's parodic madrigal 'To Nelly' (pp. 11–12). Instead of virtuous love, Mr. Hackett's is a bawdy Irish song of infidelity and sexual puns combined with the language of decorum. During a conversation on the train with Dum Spiro (*Dum spiro, spero*: 'whilst I breathe, I hope'), Watt is absorbed with ineffable voices 'singing, crying, stating, murmuring, things unintelligible, in his ear' (p. 29). These voices return soon after Watt alights from the train, and they sing him a threne (pp. 34–35). Later the servant Arsene interrupts his own diatribe directed at Watt and bursts into song: 'We shall be here all night [...]' (pp. 47–48). This lyric performs the process of waiting in an attenuated physical or perceptual state endemic in much of Beckett's later prose and drama. On Beckett's instruction the 1963 Calder edition of *Watt* excised a four-line sung lyric that appears in the Olympia and Grove editions: '*Now the day is over,* | *Night is drawing nigh–igh,* | *Shadows of the evening* | *Steal across the sky* — ' (p. 57). Musical notation is parodied when Watt listens to 'three frogs croaking Krak!, Krek! and Krik!' (p. 136). The three different croaks are set out as though parts in a choir: an entire system of 120 intervals between simultaneous croaks, the lowest common multiple of three, five, and eight (pp. 137–38). These songs and lyrics embody the thematic significance of music.

The visually striking threne (its parts are arranged separately and are given musical time) draws attention to the physical distribution of the text. The lyrics of the threne[23] were the last words Beckett composed, on 16 August 1942, before a two-month hiatus when Beckett's Resistance group was betrayed.[24] The threne is sung by the 'mixed choir' to Watt as he lies in the ditch on his way from the station to Knott's house in Part I. The musical notes are not given any pitch value, and a footnote asks: 'What, it may be enquired, was the music of this threne? What at least, it may be demanded, did the soprano sing?' (p. 32). The penultimate item in the Addenda provides the answer for the patient reader: 'Threne heard by Watt in ditch on way from station. The soprano sang' (p. 254), followed by the soprano line itself. It makes some sense to think of the threne and its musical time, on the one hand, and the Addenda score, on the other, as separate entities reflected by their separate appearances in the published text. Nonetheless, a footnote links these disparate items, an editorial apparatus residing within the frame of the fictional work. Although the reader may choose not to compile these elements and appraise the resultant musical work, the theme of tenuous aesthetic integrity is imparted in a (fictional) musical composition. Such questions as 'who might have scored the music?' and 'by what means did they obtain knowledge of the melody?' recede before the notion of a text visibly and precariously assembled on several planes at once.

Another significant instance of musical scoring in *Watt* concerns the 'descant heard by Watt on way to station (IV)' that appears in the Addenda (p. 253). The four voice parts are set out in rough time, but without scale or pitch. The reader is provided with the lyrics that tell of Watt's radically exilic state: 'With all our heart breathe head awhile darkly apart the air exile of ended smile of ending care darkly awhile the exile air' (p. 253). The Addenda provides a fertile ground for archiving musical episodes and themes of painting that were removed from the main narrative during the text's transmission from manuscript to print. The manuscript episode in which the descant occurs continues with a series of lyrics and musical images and tropes. The narrating voice recites a lyric that finishes up in the Addenda (p. 247) and, significantly, as the 'Tailpiece' to Beckett's *Collected Poems*:

> Who may tell the tale
> Of the old man?
> Weigh absence in a scale?
> Mete want with a span?
> The sum assess
> Of the world's woes?
> Nothingness
> In words enclose?[25]

It is hardly surprising that such a meditation on vestigiality and diminishment should conclude Beckett's *Collected Poems*. Yet it is worth noting that specific terms of measurement in the poem ('scale', 'span') also belong to the lexicon of musical notation. The placement of this poem in the Addenda to *Watt* might actually gesture towards the significance of these apparent fragments: they belie their apparently redundant status by contributing to the very essence of Beckett's project.

An earlier manuscript episode contributes to the narrative of *Watt* and also provides several fragments to the Addenda. Once again, this episode centres on the theme of music. The house of Knott (Watt's erstwhile master) belongs instead to the Quin family in the manuscripts. Their portraits hang on the walls of the dining room, one of which is painted by 'Black Velvet O'Connery, a product of the great Chinnery-Slattery tradition' (Addenda, p. 247). One of the portraits depicts (save for the sheet of music placed on his lap) a naked and remarkably dirty man at the piano, striking a chord. This image is salvaged in the Addenda (pp. 250–51). Both the bust of Buxtehude and the ravanastron that originally appear in the Quin portrait survive in the published narrative:

> The music room was a large bare white room. The piano was in the window. The head, and neck, in plaster, very white, of Buxtehude, was on the mantelpiece. A ravanastron hung, on the wall, from a nail, like a plover. (p. 71)

Alexander Quin and the painting have disappeared from this scene in *Watt*. Instead, the 'Galls father and son' tune the piano in an Irish Bull episode. Whilst the manuscript *ekphrasis* is divided in time and context from Knott's piano in the published text, the manuscript links written composition (a monograph on the ravanastron composed by Alexander Quin), musicianship (the ravanastron, the bust of Buxtehude, the naked pianist), and painting (the portrait of the naked Alexander Quin). Elsewhere Watt meditates on the meaning of the painting in Erskine's room (pp. 128–30). It is clear that Beckett's compositional process transforms and submerges the roles of artistic media and instruments. This archiving mechanism is made all the more appropriate when artistic production is the ostensible theme and activity. It is a moment of art appraising itself.

The transformation of extended manuscript episodes into abbreviated entries in the Addenda carries specific hermeneutic weight, particularly when the episodes that do survive, however peripherally, often take music or painting as their themes. The allied arts are invoked at precisely the points at which Beckett's compositional process is archived within the published text. The focus upon artistic media draws attention to the status of the literary work. The narrative is unfinished from the respective viewpoints within the text of Watt, his scribe Sam, the narrator, and the editorial persona; but whether or not the novel is read as a finished text will determine what kind of production it is understood to be.

Critics have expressed deep ambivalence towards the Addenda and the apparent stalling of the narrative towards the novel's end. But instead of an ill-fitting scheme of aesthetic completion (or of fragmentary innovation) being imposed upon the text, the material may be better understood by exploring the relation between earlier manuscript composition and its fragmentary archiving in the Addenda. This relation is conducted thematically, in terms of artistic production, particularly music. It can be read as an interrogation of literary form and of artistic enterprise more generally. In this way the Addenda entries can be seen to articulate an ambivalence towards the literary object similar to that of Pound's inclusion of *Le Chant des oiseaux* in Canto LXXV. The radical displacement of each author, and the unsure future of their respective texts at the time of composition may have given both the opportunity to question and examine critically the role of art in society and the relation of practitioner to artwork. Music offers a powerful and symbolically evocative set of tropes in which to conduct this examination in these two literary works composed at the limits of expression.

Conclusion

Ezra Pound's Canto LXXV and Samuel Beckett's *Watt* do much more than establish a frame of reference between music and literature, or attempt to create a *Gesamtkunstwerk*. They each engage in a profound meditation on the efficacy and possibility of the artistic enterprise. This process of aesthetic reflection is intimately connected to the physical and psychic plight of each author during the Second World War. It also inflects the plight of literary and artistic expression in the shadow and aftermath of this war. Musical episodes and scores arise at the points of intense compositional complexity. Music is emblematic, for Pound and Beckett, of a notion of free artistic expression, the validity of which is put under great historical stress in time of war. This demands a response from the artist, who finds that the most legitimate form lies in art.

Notes to Chapter 7

1. Ezra Pound, *The Cantos*, 4th collected edn (London: Faber, 1987), pp. 450–51. Further references to *The Cantos* will be from this edition, and will be incorporated into the text with canto and page number: thus Canto LXXV, page 450 is LXXV/450.

2. Samuel Beckett, *Watt* (1953) (New York: Grove, 1959). All subsequent quotations are taken from this edition, unless otherwise stated, and are incorporated into the text.

3. Martin Turrell, *Baudelaire: A Study of his Poetry* (New York: New Directions, 1954), p. 30.

4. Steven Paul Scher makes a similar point in the preface to his *Music and Text: Critical Inquiries* (Cambridge: Cambridge University Press, 1992), pp. xiii–xvi.

5. Landmark studies of music and literature in modernism include: Roger Shattuck, *The Banquet Years: The Origins of the Avant-Garde in France, 1885 to World War I*, rev. edn (New York: Vintage, 1968); Stephen Adams, 'Ezra Pound and Music' (unpublished doctoral thesis, University of Toronto, 1974); Marjorie Perloff, *The Poetics of Indeterminacy: Rimbaud to Cage* (Princeton, NJ: Princeton University Press, 1981); and Wendy Steiner, ed., *The Sign in Music and Literature* (Austin: University of Texas Press, 1981).

6. A thorough account of Pound's wartime activities that precipitated his detention and the events that ensued can be found in Humphrey Carpenter, *A Serious Character: The Life of Ezra Pound* (New York: Delta, 1988), pp. 566–693.

7. Pound employs the poetic voice to articulate immediacy, personal memory, and aesthetic symbolism in *The Pisan Cantos*: see Ronald Bush, '"Quiet, Not Scornful"? The Composition of *The Pisan Cantos*', in *A Poem Containing History: Textual Studies in 'The Cantos'*, ed. by Lawrence S. Rainey (Ann Arbor: University of Michigan Press, 1997), pp. 169–211 (pp. 170–88). Bush provides a more compelling reading of the text than the 'tragic view', which tends to conflate the poetic voice of the text with Pound's biographical circumstances.

8. Carroll F. Terrell, *A Companion to the Cantos of Ezra Pound* (Berkeley: University of California Press, 1984), pp. 388–89.

9. Terrell, p. 389.

10. Ezra Pound, 'Janequin, Francesco da Milano', *Townsman*, 1 (January 1938), 18.

11. Ezra Pound, *Guide to Kulchur* (London: Faber, 1938), p. 152.

12. Ezra Pound, *ABC of Reading* (London: Routledge, 1934; repr. London: Faber & Faber, 1951), p. 54.

13. Pound, *Guide to Kulchur*, pp. 151–52.

14. Now housed in the Beinecke Rare Book and Manuscript Library at Yale University.

15. This document is filed in the archives of the State University of New York at Buffalo. The letter from Dorothy Pound to James Laughlin is dated 28 December 1945; it is quoted in *Ezra and Dorothy Pound: Letters in Captivity, 1945–1946*, ed. by Omar Pound and Robert Spoo (New York: Oxford University Press, 1999), p. 229. The news of Eliot's receipt of the music is given in another letter, from Dorothy to Ezra Pound, dated 29 December 1945 (also quoted in *Ezra and Dorothy Pound*, p. 229).

16. The manuscript material pertaining to *Watt* comprises six notebooks and gatherings of loose leaves, amounting to 945 pages, housed in the Harry Ransom Humanities Research Center at the University of Texas at Austin. Many pages are covered with geometrical sketches or doodles of human and animal forms: a preoccupation with the visual that emerges in the novel, with its protagonist's visual perplexity in everyday situations and, at one point, before a work of art.

17. Sighle Kennedy, '"Astride of the Grave and a Difficult Birth": Samuel Beckett's *Watt* Struggles to Life', *Dalhousie French Studies*, 42 (1998), 115–47 (p. 139).

18. James Knowlson, *Damned To Fame: The Life of Samuel Beckett* (London: Bloomsbury, 1996), p. 321.

19. Deirdre Bair, *Samuel Beckett: A Biography* (London: Vintage, 1990), pp. 354–56.

20. Quoted in Knowlson, p. 342.

21. Richard Seaver, ed., *I Can't Go On, I'll Go On: A Samuel Beckett Reader* (New York: Grove Weidenfeld, 1976), p. xv (quoted in Knowlson, p. 395).

22. Samuel Beckett, 'Dante... Bruno. Vico.. Joyce', in *Our Exagmination Round his Factification for Incamination of Work in Progress* (1929) (London: Faber, 1972), pp. 3–22 (p. 14).

23. The lyrics simply sound out the number 52·285714 (i.e. fifty-two and two-sevenths), the number of weeks in a leap year to six decimal places. This calculation derives from a manuscript episode

in which the narrator and Arsene debate the terms of literary merit. It enumerates the number of weeks available for a literary text to make the best-seller list in a leap year.

24. Knowlson, pp. 43–44; Lawrence Harvey, *Samuel Beckett: Poet and Critic* (Princeton, NJ: Princeton University Press, 1970), p. 349.

25. Samuel Beckett, *Collected Poems, 1930–1978* (London: Calder, 1984), p. 170.

PART III

The Gendered Text

CHAPTER 8

Revoicing Rousseau: Staël's *Corinne* and the Song of the South

Tili Boon Cuillé

Germaine de Staël, an author in her own right and a critic of literary, philosophical, and political trends, first came to fame by lavishing praise on the works of her celebrated yet controversial predecessor Jean-Jacques Rousseau. But from her own day onwards, Staël was reproached for being insufficiently critical of Rousseau's writings on women, first by contemporary authors, including Isabelle de Charrière and Mary Wollstonecraft,[1] and later by literary critics. More recently, however, scholars such as Monika Bosse, Madelyn Gutwirth, Susan Tenenbaum, and Mary Trouille have begun to trace a gradual evolution in Staël's response to Rousseau's writings, from her initial tentative questioning of his views to her increasingly clear demarcation of her own. This second wave of critics has documented Staël's growing frustration with Rousseau's refusal to grant women access to the domain of artistic inspiration.[2] Lori Jo Marso has further nuanced our understanding of Staël's reading of Rousseau, suggesting that Staël challenged Rousseau's dictates concerning women's role in society by modelling her heroines after his.[3] Staël's treatment of the musical arts in her 1807 novel *Corinne, ou l'Italie*[4] forms part of her muted opposition to the limits that Rousseau saw fit to impose on women's artistic pursuits.[5] In this essay I shall explore a similarly subversive aspect of Staël's critique, in which she draws upon Rousseau's writings on music in order to controvert his views on female creativity. Rather than unilaterally adopting or eschewing Rousseau's views, Staël strategically incorporates his discourse into her novel. By granting Corinne access to a creative realm from which Rousseau considered her sex to be excluded, Staël endows her with a capacity for alternative means of expression, one that Hélène Cixous would later re-locate *in* language.

Staël first demonstrated her familiarity with Rousseau's œuvre in her *Lettres sur les ouvrages et le caractère de J.-J. Rousseau* (1788),[6] the work that brought her recognition for her skills as a literary critic but also established her reputation for blindness to her predecessor's flaws. Here Staël provides ample commentary on Rousseau's two *Discours*, *Lettre à d'Alembert*, *Julie*, *Émile*, *Contrat social*, and *Confessions*, but no analysis of Rousseau's writings on music; in the letter dedicated to music and botany she merely states that 'Rousseau a écrit plusieurs ouvrages sur la musique' ('Rousseau wrote several works on music') and then proceeds to discuss his compositions.[7] Her phrase 'ouvrages sur la musique' suggests that she was aware that Rousseau had written about music as well as having written music. Indeed, she would have known of Rousseau's *Lettre sur la musique française*, his *Dictionnaire de musique*, and his *Essai sur l'origine des langues* from having read his *Confessions*. Moreover, a volume of Rousseau's collected writings on music, entitled *Traités sur la musique*, had been published in 1781, and his complete works came out the following year.[8] By 1788, therefore, Staël would have had both knowledge of and access to Rousseau's writings on music, but her *Lettres* bear no evidence of her having read them.

By the time she completed work on *Corinne, ou l'Italie* in 1807, however, Staël had either perused Rousseau's writings on music or familiarized herself with his discourse, which had come to govern discussions of music in French society during the course of the eighteenth century. Simone Balayé's detailed comparison of Staël's travelogues and literary texts reveals that Staël took frequent notes on the music she heard in the streets, theatres, and cathedrals of Italy as she collected materials for her novel. Yet, as Balayé points out, throughout most of her trip Staël conceived of her heroine as a poet. Not until the end of her journey, after witnessing an exceptional performance by the renowned Signora Mazzei, did she decide to cast her heroine as an *improvisatrice* — one whose poetic production is oral rather than written and is accompanied by the lyre.[9] Corinne's improvisations bear the mark of their poetic origins and, as critics have observed, are singularly devoid of music.[10] Nevertheless, Corinne's salon conversations and the descriptions of her musical sensibility suggest that Staël returned to Rousseau's writings on music in order to enhance the characterization of her heroine. In the following discussion I provide evidence that Staël read Rousseau's *Lettre sur la musique française* and *Essai sur l'origine des langues* and that she was sensitive to the role he assigned music in his novel *Julie, ou La Nouvelle Héloïse*. I demonstrate that Staël first employs and then manipulates Rousseau's language. Drawing upon the terminology, analogies, and oppositions that Rousseau used to structure his reflections on the common origin of music and language and their relative ability to facilitate communication, Staël selectively adapted Rousseau's discourse for her own purposes.

Staël's mastery of the stances characteristic of eighteenth-century aesthetic debate is most readily apparent in the salon conversations that take place between Corinne, her Italian compatriots, and her guests who are passing through Rome on their Italian tour. In the course of their discussion Corinne cedes the laurels for poetry to the English and theatre to the French, reserving those for music and opera for the Italians. Her description of the Italian language harks back to Rousseau's *Lettre sur la musique française* (1753), in which he argued that Italian is a more musical language than French. Rousseau declares: 's'il y a en Europe une langue propre à la Musique, c'est certainement l'Italienne; car cette langue est douce, sonore, harmonieuse, et accentuée plus qu'aucune autre, et ces quatre qualités sont précisément les plus convenables au chant' ('if there is in Europe a language suited to Music it is certainly Italian; for that language is sweet, sonorous, harmonious, and accented more than any other, and these four qualities are precisely those most fitting for song').[11] Rousseau's letter rekindled the *querelle des bouffons* — the debate that raged mid-century in the Parisian journals between proponents of French and Italian opera — and is the subject of a rather

sensational episode in his *Confessions*.[12] Staël would certainly have known of the
letter, which provided an obvious reference for those who sought to characterize the
Italian language or song. In the course of her salon conversation Corinne explains her
observation that Italian is a particularly expressive language:

> il n'est pas de langue dans laquelle un grand acteur pût montrer autant de talents
> que dans la nôtre; car la mélodie des sons ajoute un nouveau charme à la vérité de
> l'accent: c'est une musique continuelle qui se mêle à l'expression des sentiments.
>
> [in no other language might a great actor show as much talent as in ours, for the
> melodious sounds add fresh charm to the sincerity of the tone [accent], thus music
> blends continuously with the expression of feeling.][13]

Corinne's mention of melody and accent echo Rousseau's assertion that the Italian
language's variety of tone naturally gives rise to the unified melodic and simplified
harmonic lines that enable Italian music to speak directly to the soul of the listener.

Although Rousseau claims in his letter that Italian is the most musical of the
European languages, he nevertheless intimates that he is capable of imagining a more
musical language still.[14] This is, presumably, the cry of nature that preceded language's
division into song and speech that Rousseau posits in his *Essai sur l'origine des langues*.
Corinne's salon conversation once again leaves us with little doubt as to Staël's
familiarity with the work. In his essay Rousseau proposes two compelling correlations:
one between music and climate, the other between music and painting. The lyrical
languages of the south, Rousseau alleges, resulted from an original vocal expression
of joy called forth by the plenitude of the warm climate. The harsh languages of the
north, on the other hand, arose from an original expression of need provoked by the
barrenness of the cold.[15] In the theory of the relationship between climate and the
arts that Staël elaborated in *De la littérature* (1800), she confined her discussion to a
theory of literature, not language. The theory of the relationship between climate
and language thus remained Rousseau's exclusive province until Staël drew upon it
for the purpose of characterizing Italian in *Corinne*, having her heroine remark: 'Vous
sentez que c'est au milieu des arts et sous un beau ciel que s'est formé ce langage
mélodieux et coloré' ('You sense that this melodious, highly colored language came
into being amid the arts under a beautiful sky').[16] Furthermore, in the correlation he
establishes between music and painting, Rousseau explains that melody is the musical
equivalent of line in painting, and harmony the musical equivalent of colour. Listeners
can intuitively colour an image once they perceive the form, but not conceptualize
the form given the colour. The melody therefore guides the ear as the line does the
eye.[17] Staël evokes this analogy when Corinne states: 'L'italien a un charme musical
qui fait trouver du plaisir dans le son des mots presque indépendamment des idées;
ces mots d'ailleurs ont presque tous quelque chose de pittoresque, ils peignent ce
qu'ils expriment' ('almost independent of meaning, Italian gives pleasure through
the musical charm of its words; besides there is something picturesque in all of these
words: they paint the image of their meaning').[18] Alhough Rousseau's essay, like his
letter, provided a natural point of reference for those seeking to characterize the
musicality of southern tongues, Staël's familiarity with the text sets her novel apart
from previous literary characterizations of music, most of which were written before
Rousseau's essay was either published or widely known.

Corinne's salon conversations are revelatory not only of Staël's familiarity with two of Rousseau's most influential texts on music, but of her sensitivity to the way in which music functions in Rousseau's novel *Julie*, which Staël read with much the same enthusiasm as her contemporaries. According to Jean Starobinski,[19] music in this novel, like the *fête champêtre*, is associated with the principle of transparency, for it acts as a conduit for pure sentiment, a catalyst for the communion of hearts. The musician's performance and the listener's senses tend to interfere with or disrupt the transference of sentiment from music to the soul of the listener. Yet melody — simple, unified melody alone, as opposed to the harmony that Rousseau eschewed — is able to 'dépasser la sensation pour se faire pur sentiment' ('transcend sensation and become pure feeling').[20] Staël weds Rousseau's theory of the climate's effect on the character of the language to this opposition between transparency and obstacle when she has Corinne account for the Italians' gift for improvisation:

> [C]e talent serait presque impossible dans une société disposée à la moquerie; [...] il faut la bonhomie du midi, ou plutôt des pays où l'on aime à s'amuser sans trouver du plaisir à critiquer ce qui amuse, pour que les poëtes se risquent à cette périlleuse entreprise. Un sourire railleur suffirait pour ôter la présence d'esprit nécessaire à une composition subite et non interrompue.

> [[This talent] could scarcely exist in a society inclined to ridicule. For poets to risk the danger of the enterprise, it takes the simple good-naturedness [...] of the south, or rather of countries whose peoples like to enjoy themselves but take no pleasure in criticizing what entertains them. A mocking smile would be enough to destroy the presence of mind necessary for instantaneous and uninterrupted composition.][21]

According to Corinne, a certain transparency, or communion of hearts (to borrow Starobinski's term), that unites performer and listener is required before the *improvisatrice* can freely express the sentiment that moves her. An ironic look, which suggests a critical distance between performer and listener and renders the performer self-aware, interposes an obstacle to the pure transmission of sentiment to the soul of the listener, and is enough to silence the *improvisatrice*'s muse. In the course of Corinne's salon conversations, therefore, Staël demonstrates that she has mastered the terms of Rousseau's characterization of the Italian language in his *Lettre sur la musique française*, of his analogies between music, climate, and painting in his *Essai sur l'origine des langues*, and of his association of music with transparency in *Julie*. These terms, as we shall see, provide Staël with a veritable arsenal that she directs against Rousseau's statements concerning women's artistic ability.

Once aware that Staël is systematically invoking Rousseau's terminology, we start to detect subtle yet significant differences in usage. Although Staël herself attended a performance of Allegri's *Miserere* in the Sistine Chapel, heard the Venetian gondoliers, and reread Tasso in the course of her travels, her descriptions of the *Miserere* and the verses of Tasso as sung by the gondoliers are also reminiscent of a passage from Rousseau's *Lettre sur la musique française*. In order to demonstrate the variety of expression inherent to the Italian language Rousseau contrasts two of Tasso's verses:

> [Q]ue ceux qui pensent que l'Italien n'est que le langage de la douceur et de la tendresse, prennent la peine de comparer entre elles ces deux strophes du Tasse [...]. Et s'ils désespèrent de rendre en François la douce harmonie de l'une, qu'ils

essayent d'exprimer la rauque dureté de l'autre [...]. Au reste, vous observerez que
cette dureté de la derniere strophe n'est point sourde, mais très-sonore.

[[L]et those who think that Italian is the language only of softness and tenderness
take the trouble to compare these two stanzas from Tasso with one another [...].
And if they despair of rendering into French the sweet harmony of the first, let
them try to express the hoarse harshness of the second. [...] Furthermore, you
will observe that the harshness of the latter stanza is not at all indistinct but quite
sonorous.][22]

Rousseau's characterization of the contrast between the verses and his choice of the
words 'rauque' and 'sourd' reappear, with a couple of significant changes, in Staël's
description of the *Miserere*. Staël immediately counters Rousseau's rather sensual
descriptions of Italian music in his *Confessions* by characterizing the *Miserere* as
pure, ancient, and religious, as opposed to 'voluptueuse et passionnée' ('sensual and
passionate'):

Le *miserere*, c'est-à-dire *ayez pitié de nous*, est un psaume composé de versets qui se
chantent alternativement d'une manière très différente. Tour à tour une musique
céleste se fait entendre, et le verset suivant, dit en récitatif, est murmuré d'un ton
sourd et presque rauque; on dirait que c'est la réponse des caractères durs aux
cœurs sensibles.

[The *miserere* or 'take pity on us' is a psalm composed of verses sung antiphonally
in very different styles. Heavenly music is heard alternating with recitative
murmured in muffled, almost harsh tones; it would seem to be the response of
hard nature[s] to sensitive hearts.][23]

The *Miserere*'s verses alternate, like the verses of Tasso, between the 'céleste'
('heavenly') and the 'sourd' ('indistinct/muffled') or 'rauque' ('hoarse'/'harsh'); yet,
whereas Rousseau claims that 'cette dureté de la derniere strophe n'est point sourde,
mais très sonore', Staël maintains that the second verse is 'sourd' and not 'sonore'. In
Staël's account every alternate verse of the *Miserere* is thus characterized as far more
muted than the sound that Rousseau tended to associate with the Italian lyric line.
Staël provides her own characterization of Tasso's verses when she describes the cant
of the Venetian gondoliers:

On entend quelquefois un gondolier qui, placé sur le pont de Rialto, se met à
chanter une stance du Tasse, tandis qu'un autre gondolier lui répond par la stance
suivante à l'autre extrémité du canal. La musique très ancienne de ces stances
ressemble au chant d'église, et de près on s'aperçoit de sa monotonie.

[Sometimes from the Ponte Rialto, a gondolier bursts into song with a stanza from
Tasso, while from the other end of the canal, another gondolier responds with the
following stanza. The very ancient music of these lines resembles liturgical chant,
monotonous when heard close up.][24]

Staël highlights the similarity between the *Miserere* and the gondoliers' song by likening
the verses — once again sung antiphonally — to a 'chant d'église'. Unlike Rousseau's
characterization of the verses, however, the salient feature in Staël's description is their
pervasive monotony. Although Staël herself appears to have savoured this monotony,
it is strikingly un-Rousseauian, for Rousseau emphasized the sonority of the Italian
language, associating a monotone exclusively with the languages of the north.[25]

Subtle though these distinctions may be, they contribute to a cumulative contrast between the music that pervades the streets, canals, and churches of Italy and the music to which Corinne gives voice. The strategy behind Staël's emphasis on the monotony rather than the sonority of Italian song is revealed when she stipulates that most Italians sing on a monotone despite the sonorous quality of the language: 'La plupart des Italiens ont, en lisant les vers, une sorte de chant monotone, appelé *cantilene*, qui détruit toute émotion. C'est en vain que les paroles sont diverses [...] puisque l'accent [...] ne change presque point' ('Most Italians read verse in a monotonous tone called *cantilena* that destroys all feeling. It makes no difference that the words vary; the effect is the same since the tone of voice [accent] [...] scarcely changes'). Most Italians, that is to say, recite their poetry in a manner that counters their language's natural tendencies, flattening the accent and hence the melodiousness that has the potential to move the listener. With a significant 'mais' Staël reveals that Corinne is the only Italian to possess both a natural sensitivity to the musical qualities of her language and the capacity to render them audible to her listeners: 'Mais Corinne récitait avec une variété de tons qui ne détruisait pas le charme soutenu de l'harmonie; c'était comme des airs différents joués tous par un instrument céleste' ('But Corinne used a variety of tones that did not destroy the sustained charm of the harmony. The effect was of different airs, all played on a celestial instrument'). Without further ado Staël launches into an explanation of what, precisely, sets her heroine's improvisations apart from those of her compatriots, namely her ability to restore variety of tone and accent to the poetic line, or to render it recognizably Rousseauian:

> La prosodie anglaise est uniforme et voilée; ses beautés naturelles sont toutes mélancoliques; [...] mais quand ces paroles italiennes, brillantes comme un jour de fête, retentissantes comme les instruments de victoire que l'on a comparés à l'écarlate parmi les couleurs; quand ces paroles, encore toutes empreintes des joies qu'un beau climat répand dans tous les cœurs, sont prononcées par une voix émue, leur éclat adouci, leur force concentrée, fait éprouver un attendrissement aussi vif qu'imprévu. [...] l'expression de la peine, au milieu de tant de jouissances, étonne, et touche plus profondément que la douleur chantée dans les langues du nord, qui semblent inspirées par elle.

> [English prosody is regular and veiled, its natural beauties all melancholy [...]. But when these Italian words — sparkling like a holiday, resounding like the trumpets of victory so like scarlet among the colors, all imprinted still with the joys a fair climate spreads in every heart; when these same Italian words are pronounced with feeling, their softened brilliance, their concentrated power set off an emotion in the listener as vivid as it is unexpected. [...] amid so many pleasures, the expression of suffering astonishes and moves even deeper than the sorrow sung in the languages of the north which suffering seems to inspire.][26]

Suddenly, the Italian language, neither uniform nor veiled like the cants we have heard thus far, regains its brilliance, resonance, and force, and unexpectedly moves the listener. Staël reveals the intrinsic musicality of the language by evoking its rich modulations, comparing it to instruments, and describing it as sung.

The foregoing passage dispels any remaining doubts as to whether Staël was familiar with Rousseau's *Essai sur l'origine des langues*, for Staël extends the analogy between music and painting, associating the ring of the Italian words with instruments of victory and the colour scarlet, and opposes Italian to English, associating each language with the geographical region in which it arose. Thus 'des joies qu'un beau climat répand dans tous les cœurs' provide a vivid contrast to 'la douleur chantée dans les langues du nord, qui semblent inspirées par elle'. She again employs the notion of transparency, emphasizing the ability of the Italian language to move the listener, as though an unseen obstacle had been precipitously overcome. Here, however, Staël binds this Rousseauian discourse to her heroine's powers of declamation. The backdrop of an Italy devoid of lyricism serves to enhance the exceptional nature both of Corinne's declamatory powers and of the moments of sustained musical exaltation that Oswald experiences in her company. In the salon conversation that ensues, in which the elements of Rousseau's discourse on music that I have examined above are more schematically presented, Staël systematically places Rousseau's words in the mouth of her heroine. It is Corinne who emphasizes the musicality of the Italian language and who draws the analogies between music and climate, music and painting, and music and transparency. The same terms used to characterize her improvisations furnish the substance of her speech. Staël thus appropriates the terms of Rousseau's musical writings on behalf of her heroine, imbuing her conversation with the weight of authority that Rousseau's discourse had acquired and attributing to her the level of artistic accomplishment and degree of musical sensitivity that correspond to Rousseau's musical ideal.

Yet Rousseau himself did not deem this level of accomplishment, this degree of sensitivity to be appropriate for women. Instead, he sought to dissuade women from developing their artistic abilities on the grounds that it would cast doubt upon their moral integrity and compromise their desirability as lifelong companions.[27] Signs of the troubled relationship between music and morality permeate Rousseau's writing. Marie Naudin remarks that if we reread certain passages of Rousseau's *Julie* or *Confessions* (or, I would add, the fifth book of *Émile*), 'on est immédiatement frappé de la fréquence des termes voluptueux qui traduisent ses impressions musicales' ('one is immediately struck by the frequency of the sensual terms that convey his musical impressions').[28] Elsewhere I have demonstrated the widespread association of musical sensibility and sensuality in French eighteenth-century literature and society that is visible in the prejudicial remarks of the secondary characters in Staël's novel.[29] Regula Hohl Trillini, in the next essay in this volume, points to the prevalence of this trope in Victorian poetry. In order to distance her heroine from the immoral overtones that threaten her ability to secure her lover's lasting affection while cultivating her talent, Staël once again artfully employs the opposition between transparency and obstacle at work in Rousseau's writings, precluding the reader from sharing the characters' misgivings about the morality of Corinne's musical sensibility.[30]

The opposition between transparency and obstacle, Starobinski explains, can be likened to the opposition between paradise and paradise lost. In this context 'paradise' is understood to be 'la transparence réciproque des consciences, la communication totale et confiante' ('the state of transparent communication between mind and mind, the conviction that total, reliable communication is possible') and its loss to be a 'disparition de la *confiance*' ('loss of *confidence*') or 'un *voile* qui s'interpose' ('the drawing of a *veil*').[31] The most clear-cut example of Staël's use of this opposition occurs the first time that Corinne and Oswald are alone together. Timidity has rendered Oswald more cold and dignified than usual, and Corinne, afraid of revealing her true feelings, is uncharacteristically quiet. Casting about for something to fill the awkward silence, she absent-mindedly plays a few chords on her lyre, a sound that gives Oswald the courage to meet her gaze and the occasion to notice 'l'inspiration divine qui se peignait dans ses yeux' ('the divine inspiration in her eyes').[32] The combination of the look in Corinne's eye and the 'bonté' ('kindness') of her expression give Oswald the courage to speak. The sound of the harp thus fills the silence, dissipating their mutual embarrassment and enabling Oswald to sense the purity of Corinne's soul. Persuaded of Corinne's merit, Oswald still harbours doubts as to whether his dear departed father would have approved the match. Upon hearing the Aeolian harps that Corinne has placed in her garden at Tivoli, however, he is suddenly 'inspiré par le sentiment le plus pur' ('inspired by the purest feeling') and becomes convinced that his father has sanctioned their union from on high.[33] Unable to share his confidence, Corinne silences the proposal that is on Oswald's lips, thereby renewing his doubts. Together they take a tour of Corinne's art gallery, stopping before a painting of a young Scotsman seated on a tombstone that evokes Oswald's memories of his father. Corinne demonstrates her mastery of the musical idiom by playing her harp and singing the Scottish refrains that might have been sung by the bard in the painting, thus bringing it to life. The sounds, rather than the sight, of his homeland provoke the catharsis that enables Oswald to regret his father and to forgive Corinne.[34] Three times, therefore, a musical interlude helps the lovers overcome an unspoken obstacle.

Oswald is troubled not only by the question of whether his father would have approved the match (or whether a woman can be both artistic and virtuous), but by whether Corinne is overly fond of public recognition (or whether a woman should be allowed to excel). As Corinne takes her seat at a concert, Oswald notes that her heart beats faster when the audience applauds, and he suddenly fears that he will be forced to share Corinne's affections with her public. Sequestering himself in the far corner of their box, he falls silent, nursing his jealous rage while Corinne turns her attention to the music. At this point the narrator remarks:

> De tous les beaux-arts, [la musique] est celui qui agit le plus immédiatement sur l'âme [...] Ce qu'on a dit de la grace divine, qui tout à coup transforme les cœurs, peut, humainement parlant, s'appliquer à la puissance de la mélodie.

> [Of all the arts, [music] is the one that acts most directly upon the soul. [...] What has been said of divine grace suddenly transforming hearts, may — on a human level — be applied to the power of melody.][35]

The description is arresting, for it corresponds to the notion that Starobinski identifies as central to Rousseau's musical theory. The ballad, Starobinski explains, 'se passe du truchement [...] de la sensation, pour atteindre *directement* l'âme de l'auditeur. Car la mélodie a le pouvoir de toucher le cœur à coup sûr: proposition capitale dans la théorie musicale de Rousseau' ('can [...] do without the senses: [it] works *directly* on the soul of the listener. For melody has the power to affect the heart: this is a major tenet of Rousseau's musical theory').[36] Music's ability to bypass the senses en route to the soul ultimately enables it to escape the stigma of sensuality, ennobling the listener in turn. Corinne's awareness of Oswald's presence is purified of all that could be compromising in their love, as she conflates the image of her lover with a sentiment that surpasses it: 'Sans doute l'image d'Oswald était présente à son cœur; mais l'enthousiasme le plus noble se mêlait à cette image' ('the image of Oswald surely was present in her heart; but the noblest enthusiasm blended with that image'). The lovers are simultaneously filled with emotion occasioned not by one another but by the music, which draws them towards their respective ideals: 'le vague de la musique se prête à tous les mouvements de l'ame, et chacun croit retrouver dans cette mélodie [...] l'image de ce qu'il souhaite sur la terre' ('the vagueness of music lends itself to all the modulations of the soul, and each person thinks he has rediscovered in the melody [...] the image of what he wishes for on earth').[37] The emotion on which the lovers are buoyed as they listen to the concert, like the purity of sentiment with which they are filled when they hear the sound of a harp, thus proves to be intrinsically virtuous.

As we have seen, Staël draws upon Rousseau's discourse both to endow her heroine with the power of musical expression and to shield her from its moral repercussions. Although the textual transcriptions of Corinne's improvisations are indeed, as critics have noted, devoid of elaborate descriptions or depictions of the musical accompaniment, music nevertheless permeates her performances at every level. Aware of the lyrical potential of the Italian language, she reveals its inherent musicality with her declamatory style. Her poetry, in contrast to that of her compatriots, is thereby infused with music. She enhances the significance of her words with the sparse but penetrating tones of the lyre, on which she relies at times to convey her thoughts when words fail her.[38] The union of her poetic and musical skills is complemented, completed in a sense, by her execution of the Tarantella, or Neapolitan dance: 'Corinne, en dansant, faisait passer dans l'ame des spectateurs ce qu'elle éprouvait, comme si elle avait improvisé, comme si elle avait joué de la lyre [...] tout était langage pour elle' ('as if she were improvising, as if she were playing the lyre [...], Corinne communicated her feelings directly to the souls of the spectators through her dance: everything was language to her').[39] Corinne's sensitive rendering of the arts of music, improvisation, and dance, along with the art of spiritual conversation to which they are compared, suggests that she does not, in fact, embody the historical ideal of the eighteenth century, the age of Greek lyric poetry, so much as she does Rousseau's a-historical ideal, which Starobinski describes as 'l'âge d'or où parole, musique, danse, poésie étaient confondues' ('the golden age in which language, music, dance, and poetry were inextricably intertwined'.[40] At this early stage in society, midway between nomadic wandering and the birth of civilization, music and language were not yet fully distinct, and the rhythm of verbal expression led 'natural man' to break into the gesture of the dance. The golden age that Rousseau envisions was prior to the corruptive influence that society exercised on the soul's ability to communicate and prior to the assignation of gender roles. Corinne's moments of musical inspiration are accompanied by a state of exaltation that allows her to discourse on subjects that transcend the personal to embrace all of humanity. Music liberates her from the sphere of human egotism, rendering her capable of a sort of divine empathy that makes artistic utterance possible.[41] Staël thereby places the elusive realm of transcendence within reach of her heroine,[42] for Corinne's musicality recalls not the dubious sensibilities that made it hazardous for women to excel in the musical arts in eighteenth-century French society, but rather the authenticity and immediacy of expression associated with Rousseau's pre-social, amoral ideal.

Staël denies the implications of Rousseau's writings on women by recasting his ideal of musical expression in female form, freeing Corinne from the suspicion of sensuality and the supposed limitations of her sex and granting her access to a creative realm that Rousseau suggested only men could attain. The subversive nature of her approach lies in her use of the terminology, analogies, and oppositions that characterize Rousseau's writings on music to distinguish her heroine's talents from the Italian norm and her virtues from those commonly attributed to female musicians. She thus harnesses the power of Rousseau's discourse in order to contest his conclusions. Pitting, as it were, Rousseau against Jean-Jacques, Staël deftly dissociates women's artistic pursuits from their accompanying moral stigma, a creative act that enabled women to participate in the nineteenth-century cult of the artist.[43]

Rousseau theorized language in the eighteenth century as having lost the original power of expression that it had possessed when music and language were one.[44] Since the eighteenth century, however, as Delia da Sousa Correa suggests in her introduction to this volume, music in turn has lost its 'privileged access to the ineffable' as language has come to share its referential uncertainty. Such characterizations of music and language pertain, of course, not to their absolute limits and potential but to the ways in which they have been historically perceived. The evolving distinction between these sign systems has certain implications for gender. Cixous's notion of *écriture féminine*, for instance, is infused with the voice, song, rhythm, and musicality of which Rousseau and his readers considered language to be pitifully devoid.[45] Women writers, therefore, looked to music in the eighteenth century to provide the alternative means of expression for which feminists looked to non-traditional forms of writing in the twentieth. Elsewhere I have argued that music should not be treated as a mere metaphor for language and literature in eighteenth-century women's writing. Here I would go a step further and suggest that music provided women with avenues for self-expression in the eighteenth century that were closed to them via language, deficient as it was thought to be at the time.[46] Therein lay music's potential as well as its menace. Aware of this, Staël endowed her heroine with a gift for (lyric) poetic improvisation — a form of expressive alterity to which Staël herself, constrained as she was by her historical circumstances, could accede by virtue of her poetic imagination alone.[47]

Notes to Chapter 8

1. For Charrière's objections to Staël's writings see Jacqueline Letzter, 'Isabelle de Charrière versus Germaine de Staël: Textual Tactics in the Debate about Rousseau', *Studies on Voltaire and the Eighteenth Century*, 362 (1998), 27–40; for Wollstonecraft's objections see Mary Trouille, 'A Bold New Vision of Woman: Staël and Wollstonecraft Respond to Rousseau', *Studies on Voltaire and the Eighteenth Century*, 292 (1991), 293–324.
2. See Madelyn Gutwirth, 'Madame de Staël, Rousseau and the Woman Question', *PMLA*, 86 (1971), 100–09 (p. 108); and Trouille, pp. 297, 304, 309, 316–17.

3. See Lori Jo Marso, *(Un)Manly Citizens: Jean-Jacques Rousseau's and Germaine de Staël's Subversive Women* (Baltimore, MD: Johns Hopkins University Press, 1999).

4. Germaine de Staël, *Corinne, ou l'Italie* (Paris: Gallimard, 1985); Eng. trans. by Avriel H. Goldberger (New Brunswick, NJ: Rutgers University Press, 1987).

5. See Rousseau's *Lettre à d'Alembert* and the fifth book of *Émile*.

6. Germaine de Staël, *Lettres sur les ouvrages et le caractère de J.-J. Rousseau*, in *Madame de Staël: Œuvres de jeunesse*, ed. by Simone Balayé and John Isbell (Paris: Desjonquères, 1997).

7. Staël comments upon Rousseau's comic opera *Le Devin du village*, his melodrama *Pygmalion*, and his ballads; see Staël, *Lettres*, ed. by Balayé and Isbell, p. 79 (my translation).

8. See Jean-Jacques Rousseau, *Œuvres complètes*, ed. by Bernard Gagnebin and Marcel Raymond (Paris: Gallimard, La Pléiade, 1959–), I: *Les Confessions* (1959), p. 560; and Jean Starobinski, Introduction to Jean-Jacques Rousseau, *Essai sur l'origine des langues*, in *Œuvres complètes*, ed. by Gagnebin and Raymond, V: *Écrits sur la musique, la langue, et le théâtre* (1995), pp. cxcvii–cciii.

9. Simone Balayé, *Les Carnets de voyage de Madame de Staël* (Geneva: Droz, 1971), pp. 113–14.

10. Anne Deneys-Tunney, 'Corinne by Madame de Staël: The Utopia of Feminine Voice as Music within the Novel', *Dalhousie French Studies*, 28 (1944), 55–63 (pp. 61–62).

11. Rousseau, *Œuvres complètes*, V, 297; Jean-Jacques Rousseau, *Collected Writings of Rousseau* (Hanover, NH: University Press of New England, 1990–), VII: *Essay on the Origin of Languages and Writings Related to Music*, ed. and trans. by John T. Scott (1998), p. 148.

12. Rousseau, *Œuvres complètes*, I, 383–85.

13. Staël, *Corinne*, p. 191; Eng. trans., p. 123. Although 'tone' is an acceptable translation of Rousseau's notion of musical accent, it is important to note that Staël preserves Rousseau's terminology.

14. Rousseau, *Œuvres complètes*, V, 297.

15. Rousseau, *Œuvres complètes*, V, 407, 409.

16. Staël, *Corinne*, p. 83 ; Eng. trans., p. 43.

17. Rousseau, *Œuvres complètes*, V, 413.

18. Staël, *Corinne*, p. 83 ; Eng. trans., p. 43.

19. Jean Starobinski, *Jean-Jacques Rousseau: La Transparence et l'obstacle suivi de sept essais sur Rousseau* (Paris: Gallimard, 1971); Eng. trans. by Arthur Goldhammer (Chicago: Chicago University Press, 1988).

20. Starobinski, *La Transparence et l'obstacle*, pp. 111–12; Eng. trans., p. 89.

21. Staël, *Corinne*, p. 84 ; Eng. trans., p. 44.

22. Rousseau, *Œuvres complètes*, V, 297–98; *Collected Writings*, VII, 148–49.

23. Staël, *Corinne*, pp. 266–67 ; Eng. trans., p. 179.

24. Staël, *Corinne*, p. 430; Eng. trans., p. 302.

25. Rousseau, *Œuvres complètes*, V, 409.

26. Staël, *Corinne*, p. 67; Eng. trans., pp. 31–32.

27. Jean-Jacques Rousseau, *Émile ou de l'éducation* (Paris: Garnier Frères, 1964), pp. 518–19.

28. Marie Naudin, 'Mme de Staël précurseur de l'esthétique musicale romantique', *Revue des sciences humaines*, 35, no. 139 (1970), 391–400 (p. 394) (my translation).

29. See my article 'Women Performing Music: Staging a Social Protest', *Women in French Studies*, 8 (2000), 40–54.

30. Frank Bowman invites critics to investigate further the principles of transparency and obstacle in Staël's œuvre in his 'Communication and Power in Germaine de Staël: Transparency and Obstacle', in *Germaine de Staël: Crossing the Borders*, ed. by Madelyn Gutwirth, Avriel Goldberger, and Karyna Szmurlo (New Brunswick, NJ: Rutgers University Press, 1991), pp. 55–68.

31. Starobinski, *La Transparence et l'obstacle*, pp. 19–20; Eng. trans., pp. 8–9 (emphasis Starobinski's).

32. Staël, *Corinne*, p. 81; Eng. trans., p. 42.

33. Staël, *Corinne*, pp. 230–31; Eng. trans., p. 152.

34. Staël, *Corinne*, p. 238.

35. Staël, *Corinne*, p. 247; Eng. trans., p. 165.

36. Starobinski, *La Transparence et l'obstacle*, p. 111; Eng. trans., p. 89 (emphasis Starobinski's).

37. Staël, *Corinne*, pp. 249–50; Eng. trans., p. 166.

38. Staël, *Corinne*, p. 85.

39. Staël, *Corinne*, p. 148; Eng. trans., p. 92.

40. Starobinski, 'Rousseau et l'origine des langues', in *La Transparence et l'obstacle*, p. 375; Eng. trans., p. 319.

41. Claire L. Dehon, 'Corinne. Une artiste héroïne de roman', *Nineteenth-Century French Studies*, 9 (1980–81), 1–9 (pp. 2–3).

42. For the importance of this contribution, which set Staël apart from her predecessors, see Simone Balayé, 'Fonction romanesque de la musique et des sons dans *Corinne*', *Romantisme*, 3 (1972), 2–32 (p. 24); and Madelyn Gutwirth, 'Woman as Mediatrix: From Jean-Jacques Rousseau to Germaine de Staël', in *Woman as Mediatrix: Essays on Nineteenth-Century Women Writers*, ed. by Avriel H. Goldberger (Westport, CT: Greenwood, 1987), pp. 13–29 (p. 23).

43. I allude to Rousseau's work of 1772–76 entitled *Rousseau juge de Jean-Jacques*. In this work Rousseau discusses with one of his detractors, who is unaware that Jean-Jacques and Rousseau are one and the same, whether or not Jean-Jacques's 'sublime jargon' was, in fact, 'dicté par une ame de boue' ('dictated by a soul of mire') (Rousseau, *Œuvres complètes*, I, 667; *Collected Writings of Rousseau*, I: *Rousseau, Judge of Jean-Jacques: Dialogues*, ed. by Roger D. Masters and Christopher Kelly, trans. by Judith R. Bush (1990), p. 8.

44. Although Rousseau reserved his harshest criticism for the French language, he also found Italian to be wanting in comparison with the expressive power of the original cry.

45. See Hélène Cixous, 'Le Rire de la Méduse', *L'Arc*, 61 (1975), 39–54. Note that Cixous's notion of *écriture féminine*, like Corinne's declamation, is (rather notoriously) asexual in that it can be written by either sex.

46. Although Staël completed *Corinne* in 1807, she was raised in the salons of the *Ancien Régime*, her novels are set during the Revolution, and her aesthetic heritage remains, by and large, that of the Enlightenment. I therefore reclaim her, for the purposes of this study, for the long eighteenth century.

47. See also on this subject Marie-Claire Vallois, *Fictions féminines: Mme de Staël et les voix de la Sibylle* (Saratoga, CA: Anma Libri, 1987).

CHAPTER 9

The Dear Dead Past: The Piano in Victorian and Edwardian Poetry

Regula Hohl Trillini

A woman was playing,
A man looking on.
And the mould of her face,
And her neck, and her hair,
Which the rays fell upon
Of the two candles there,
Sent him mentally straying
In some fancy place.

THOMAS HARDY, 'At the Piano'[1]

It has become a commonplace that the piano played a vital part in the life cycle of the female members of the Victorian middle classes. Aristocrats did not need it and the working classes could not afford it, but the vast majority of middle-class girls played the piano during the period from late childhood until marriage as part of a canon of accomplishments that men were conditioned to consider attractive in a potential wife. Once the aim of acquiring a husband was realized, the practice usually ceased, to be revived only occasionally for the sake of whiling away an idle hour or of teaching one's children. Women who had not managed to get a husband were the ones who continued to play, and also to teach the piano as governesses. Serious, passionate, or even professional musicianship in married women was virtually unthinkable, despite a few high-profile and often foreign exceptions such as Lady Hallé, Arabella Goddard, and Clara Schumann, and scarcely exists in the fiction of the period. Instead, countless Victorian novels feature the piano as locus for amorous encounters, as a consoling companion for lonely or distraught women, and as an object of social status. All these link up with that great Victorian institution, matrimony, which, of course, as the classic conclusion or favourite topic of novels, is also a literary institution. But throughout the nineteenth century and up to the Great War the piano features in poems too, and while the scenes that these texts present (with only slight variations in mood throughout the period) at first seem very diverse, they can be read as a different genre's way of handling exactly the same fundamental quandaries about music and women.

Victorian stereotypes, whether expressed in non-fictional texts, novels, or poems, represent a particularly English response to a long-standing ambiguity in music's status. Since the Renaissance at least, music had been associated with women or love for women, and the contradictory connotations that woman and music shared in the Western patriarchal imagination generated many points of identity between them. Like woman, music had theoretically been exalted as divine — complete with a female patron saint; yet many forms of musical practice were considered inferior, and even morally dangerous to performers and listeners. This same ambiguity is discussed by Tili Boon Cuillé in the preceding essay. In England the inferiority of performance was reinforced by its strong association with 'others': foreigners, 'professional people' (a derogatory term), clergymen, and, of course, women.

Whenever women players are specified in Victorian literature, music tends to be synonymous with 'piano'. For centuries women had been restricted to plucked and keyboard instruments, which could be played more decorously than most string and wind instruments. The lute, which was among the piano's closest rivals, was long-obsolete by the nineteenth century, and the harp was also past its fashionable Regency prime. After a century of piano love poems, the terms 'instrument' and 'music' in connection with women had become shorthand for 'piano' — the default option. Leigh Hunt's poem 'The Lover of Music to his Piano-forte' is an extreme expression of such gendering: the piano, instead of being played by a woman, has itself been feminized and answers the male player with a voice that meets all the requirements of ideal Victorian womanhood:

> O friend, whom glad or grave we seek,
> Heav'n holding shrine!
> I ope thee, hear thee speak,
> And peace is mine.
> [...]
> To thee, when our full hearts o'erflow
> In griefs or joys,
> Unspeakable emotions owe
> A fitting voice:
> [...]
> No change, no sullenness, no cheat,
> In thee we find;
> Thy saddest voice is ever sweet,
> — thine answer, kind.[2]

In most other poetic scenarios, however, the piano is played by a woman in the presence of a male listener, and this constellation is so frequent that often neither player nor instrument need be named. Metonymic evocation is sufficient, as at the end of Dante Gabriel Rossetti's 'During Music', where 'small fingers' floating over 'keys' define the sex of the player and the instrument she uses; although even before this, the set-up must have been obvious to the reader:

> What though I lean o'er thee to scan
> The written music cramped and stiff;
> — 'Tis dark to me, as hieroglyph
> On those weird bulks Egyptian.[3]

Fig. 9.1. *Etching* (1900), by Robert Walker Macbeth, 1848–1910 (Scottish);
455 × 615 mm; after Sir Frank Dicksee, *A Reverie*, 1895
Private collection: photograph Gary Irvine

The painting was supplied with an anonymous quotation which reads:
In the years fled
Lips that are dead
Sang me that song

The male listener, far from participating in instrumental performance, is not ashamed to admit that he cannot even read music. This inability is not just a poetic device but represents contemporary reality. As a contributor to *Nature* remarked in 1874, 'Music hardly comes within the scope of a boy's education, at least in this country; while it is almost compulsory on girls, whether they have the talent for it or not'.[4] Notwithstanding the perceived dangers of music, its practice was forced on every girl in order to display her father's earning power and to bring about a desirable marriage. The time-honoured social practice of functionalizing female musical performance for courtship rituals reached a peak in the mid-nineteenth century, both exploiting music's erotic potential and containing it socially.

The literary effects of these inherent contradictions can be traced back to the early modern period, if not earlier. On the one hand, music becomes a favourite metaphor for all that is ordered, sacred and beautiful — 'harmonious' — about love, whereas, on the other, actual representations of music-making — usually women singing and playing the piano — more frequently exploit its earthy, sensual,[5] or quotidian, even commercial aspects. This second aspect has become proverbial through the piano's complicity in marriage and adultery plots in many familiar and much-quoted scenes in the works of Austen, George Eliot, and Thackeray, not to mention Tolstoy's 'Kreutzer Sonata'. In lyrical poems, however, music is free from such concrete narrative obligations. Love is usually in the air, but the social context, the making or breaking of marriages, need not be. Nevertheless, when the piano is put to more strictly 'poetical' uses, it presents a problem. In striking contrast to older instruments such as the harp, trumpet, or lute, the piano completely lacks allegorical or metaphorical potential. It is too modern a contraption to evoke biblical, classical, or truly romantic associations; we cannot see the Heavenly Host, Orpheus, King David, or even Don Juan sitting down to it. Nineteenth-century novels have taught us to imagine 'real people' on the music stool: pretty husband hunters, scheming adulteresses, sinister, exotic virtuosi, and desperate adolescents. This difficulty may explain Thomas Wade's mistaken assumption, in his 'Written after Hearing Great Music' (1869), that he was the first to write a piano poem:

> Pianoforte! Ne'er before, perchance,
> Thy alien name with English verse was blent;
> But now 'tis meet thou to that place advance,
> As rival to whatever instrument.[6]

By 1869, of course, the piano had for a long time been *the* instrument without rival in fiction, real life, and poetry, and a surprising number of sincerely intended Victorian poems feature women at the piano. These texts usually retain the fundamental erotic connotations of the instrument, but attempt to eschew the domestic trappings that are so firmly attached to it in favour of more conventionally poetic associations. However, love scenes outside the drawing room are difficult to manage around a piano, and many 'piano poems', in fact, find the task of getting this clumsy piece of furniture into Heaven, or simply into the open air, very tricky.[7] John Nicholson's 'Dying Lover', for instance, has to transmogrify the instrument at the last second:

> Go, touch my sweet piano's strings,
> And chant me into rest,

> Till angels come, and on their wings
> Convey me to the blest.
> And mourn not as I soar away
> To tune my *harp* on high;
> Useless the tears upon my clay,
> For I'm prepared to die.[8]

To avoid such contortions, the majority of Victorian piano love poems resort to a very particular solution: they kill the pianist. With striking consistency the woman pianist is depicted as actually dead, or at least far enough away in time and space to be no more than a memory.[9]

In Victorian prose fiction the death of a female character is, of course, not at all rare, but in novels women generally die as a punishment for having 'fallen' or for being at least at odds with society (and their transgressions frequently include playing the piano too well or for the wrong purposes). But poems do not need to sustain a narrative span leading to ruin as retribution, or to marriage as reward. They are at greater liberty to celebrate the musical power of an absent woman who never appears in the flesh, or to mourn a dead woman as a paragon of virtue and beauty, without the need for 'poetic' justice, that is, a moral or logical explanation of her death. Whether the poem looks forward to heavenly rapture or back to death or separation long ago, the piano — treasure casket, coffin, or sounding-board — is all that remains of the enchanting player, and thus acquires a peculiar dignity of its own. The inevitable undertone of domestic realism becomes poignant rather than prosaic or silly.

However, the dead woman pianist solves more than just the poetological 'piano problem'. More importantly, the reminiscing male speaker is at liberty to indulge in memories of the woman's seductive power because he is safe from it. This becomes even more apparent when, as frequently happens, the piano itself becomes the addressee. The male speaker talks to the piano *about* the dead woman player, who is thus elided at the very moment of being voluptuously remembered. Female sensuality (vital to matchmaking at the piano, but always a dangerous property) is evoked, but at a safe distance, at which erotic fantasies can turn into an almost religious exercise, as in William Sharp's 'During music' (1884):

> I hear old memories astir
> In dusky twilights of the past:
> O voices telling me of her,
> My soul, whom now I know at last:
> [...]
> On one day yet to come I see
> This body pale and cold and dead:
> The spirit once again made free
> Hovers triumphant overhead.[10]

Once the body is safely disposed of with no less than three unequivocal adjectives, 'pale and cold and dead', the spirit is free to be addressed as female.

These devious proceedings were quite new. Elizabethan texts had been very explicitly naughty in their description of the tactile values of keyboard performance,[11] and its erotic effects used to be pictured quite openly when the fortepiano was young. In 1788 a 'Seraphina playing the piano-forte' was implored:

> Oh! let me burn beneath thy Phoenix eye,
> And all the wiles of love and music try,
> Conceive the angel flame, Promæthean fire,
> And in sweet ravishments of love expire.[12]

Such intensity had become simply unthinkable half a century later. Unusually for a male poetic narrator, Nicholson's 'Dying Lover' (quoted above) does die near a piano, but not from powerful sexual excitement.

Many Victorian 'piano poems' elaborate one of three scenarios: first, an erotically attractive female is dying at the piano or has her death foreshadowed; alternatively, the keyboard instrument itself becomes a sign for 'memory', evoking a private or historical past; or, lastly, the woman pianist is already in the past, usually dead, but in any case only remembered.

The first scenario — death at the keyboard — can be morbidly dramatic, as in Thomas Hardy's 'The Chapel-Organist' (1884),[13] the interior monologue of a too-handsome girl who plays the village organ for free. Before being dismissed for 'the good name of the chapel', she plays, voluptuously and rousingly, for one last time, and then drinks poison while her feet keep the organ booming. The genre-specific conventions outlined above suggest that this death as punishment for sensuality belongs more typically to narrative fiction than to poetic representation of women at the keyboard, and in fact this poem does tell a story. Arthur O'Shaughnessy's 'Music and Moonlight' is more purely evocative, though far longer. After a great ball the speaker, in the sumptuous, now empty house overhears the belle of the evening playing alone. This drives him to more than five hundred lines of mythological rhapsodizing, at the end of which 'Chopin's soul' invites the girl

> to be henceforth where never she need lose
> That fair illumined vision's height
> Then, she said not Yea,
> But with intense emotion inward spoke.
> And therewith something burst asunder — broke!
> Down in that shrouded chamber far away
> The grand piano snapt one string; but oh,
> Pale Lady Eucharis fell back, as though
> Her dream grew deeper; and at dawn of day,
> They found her — dead; as one asleep she lay![14]

But death at the piano can also be a very quiet and veiled affair. In Thomas Edward Brown's 'Preparation', keeping a virginal well tuned means keeping one's soul prepared for meeting God at death, 'for when He comes thou know'st not'.[15] The name of the historical instrument provides an additional echo of the parable of the Wise and Foolish Virgins, the moral of which the poem is elaborating. William Watt's 'Stanzas on Hearing a Young Lady Perform on the Piano Forte' (1860) are not so openly admonitory, but the player, whose skill is favourably compared to that of Orpheus and Jubal, is reminded, albeit in the nicest possible way, of her final destiny:

> Long be the time before thy hand
> Forego to raise such concord grand,
> And join the bright angelic band
> In the realms of bless'd eternity.[16]

The Hereafter, promised as a reward for excellent moral (and musical) behaviour, also looms in Frances Ridley Havergal's 'Moonlight Sonata', which maps the musical work onto a spiritual itinerary, concluding that 'This strange, sad world is but our Father's school; | All chance and change His love shall grandly overrule'.[17]

Piano poems evoking memory — the second scenario — frequently include allusions to pre-piano times. The name of an earlier keyboard instrument — harpsichord, clavichord, dulcimer, or spinet — is frequently sufficient to establish the theme of loss and nostalgia. By 1800 the harpsichord was a thing of the recent past, something old-fashioned or ridiculous; after 1840 it was remote enough to become a dignified sentimental symbol for lost youth or love.[18] Such poems are not to be confused with jolly historical genre scenes that feature spinets as quaint or saucy accessories in 'Merry Old England' contexts;[19] old keyboard instruments are regularly shown as what they have become *since* their own epoch — not only historical, but old, unstrung, broken, and thus doubly apt to set scenes of loss and remembrance. Examples of poems in this vein are Andrew Lang's 'The Spinet',[20] Edward Waite's 'House Fantastic' (1904, an imitation of Poe's 'Raven'),[21] Norman Rowland Gale's 'The Old Piano' (1912),[22] and George Barlow's 'White',[23] where the last sight of the beloved is compared with falling rose petals and the 'last long wailing of a harpsichord'. In Francis William Bourdillon's 'The Spinet' (1888)[24] a widower is reminded of his long-dead wife by the strumming of his grandchildren on an old spinet.

A particularly ghostly version of this nostalgic allusion to instruments of the past became popular after 1890: willowy, pale, dreamy women scarcely 'perform' at the keyboard, but are seen, rather, or felt as a kind of visual emanation of music. Ezra Pound's 'Scriptor Ignotus' (1909) describes a lady organist recorded by an eighteenth-century Dante scholar:

> Dear, an this dream come true,
> Then shall all men say of thee
> 'She 'twas that played him power at life's morn,
> And at the twilight Evensong,
> And God's peace dwelt in the mingled chords
> She drew from out the shadows of the past,
> And old world melodies that else
> He had known only in his dreams
> Of Iseult and of Beatrice.'[25]

In 'Nel Biancheggiar' (1908) Pound audaciously uses the medieval dulcimer to celebrate a pianist friend's concerts in London in this misty way:

> I feel the dusky softness whirr
> of colour as upon a dulcimer
> 'Her' dreaming fingers lay between the tunes,
> As when the living music swoons
> But dies not quite, because of love of us
> — knowing our state /
> How that 'tis troublous —
> It will not die to leave us desolate.[26]

James Joyce's early poem cycle *Chamber Music* (1907) exists in a similar twilight. Again, the instrument is only metonymically present in the 'yellow [i.e. *old*] ivory' of its keys;[27] 'one at twilight shyly played | And one in fear was standing nigh'. The love between these two creatures of course 'came to us in time gone by'.[28] In all these texts the contemporary practice of piano performance by young women is made a vehicle for wistful historicizing.

Finally, poems where the female performer herself exists only in her lover's memory form a large group that is especially representative of certain gender stereotypes. Typically, the male speaker touches a single key or chord — he does not, of course, actually play, let alone perform on the piano. The only audience is the piano itself, whilst the speaker remembers how she, now dead or gone, used to play or sing. Theodore Wratislaw's Verlaine translation 'Le Piano que baise' (1893) depicts such a scene:

> The piano over which a light hand strays
> Shines vaguely in the evening grey and rose,
> While as with rustling of a wing that plays,
> An ancient air most weak and charming flows
> Discreetly and as though heart-broken goes
> Throughout the boudoir where her memory stays.[29]

Similarly, the speaker in Philip Marston's 'A Remembered Tune' records how '[m]y hand strayed o'er the piano keys, | And it chanced on a song that you sang, my dear'.[30] In John Payne's 'At the Piano' (1903), the touching of the keys prompts a sensual resurrection:

> As o'er the answering keys my fingers stray,
> [...]
> The memories of many a bygone day,
> The curtain of the Present drawn away
> Is from my thought and with the veil's undoing,
> The dear dead past arises, the renewing
> Seeking of that which moulders in the clay.
> [...]
>   I, as o'er the abyss
> Of thought I lean and watch the wraiths emerging,
> Feel on my lips once more my first love's kiss.[31]

In Mary Elizabeth Coleridge's 'To a Piano' (1908), the instrument 'only to one hand on earth replieth', but that hand is gone, the speaker cannot play, and the instrument remains mute:

> If I might win me that remembered strain
> By reverent lifting of thy gleamy lid,
> I could forget the sorrowful refrain
> Of all the world shall do — is doing — did.
> Pandora's prisoned hope was not more vain.
> The casket's there, the melody is hid.[32]

The allusion to Pandora's box is, of course, another reminder that it is not only sad but safer if the sensual attractions of music remain locked away. The closed instrument stands in for the objectified female body, which, thus safely displaced and locked up, can be allowed to be erotically responsive to the male touch.[33] The straying fingers

of the dreamy reminiscer figure in all these texts, re-enacting the physical touch of
the vanished woman player who also used only her fingers, a highly erotic and at the
same time decorous body part.

This trope becomes rather gruesome in Thomas Hardy's 'Haunting Fingers' (1884),
where a group of old musical instruments is conversing in an attic, and a harpsichord,
'as 'twere from dampered lips' remembers

> The tender pat
> Of her aery finger-tips
> Upon me daily — I rejoiced thereat!

Macabrely, we are told that its keyboard is

> filmed with fingers
> Like tapering flames — wan, cold —
> Or the nebulous light that lingers
> In charnel mould.[34]

Similarly eerie, Hardy's 'The Re-enactment' (1884) has a ghost entering a woman's
room, first mistaking the speaker for his 'lady fair', then ordering her to rearrange the
furniture in the old way so that he could again envision his long-gone lover serving
him — pouring tea and, of course, playing the piano to him:

> 'Aha — now I can see her!
> [...]
> She serves me: now she rises,
> Goes to play.
> But you obstruct her, fill her
> With dismay,
> And all-embarrassed, scared, she vanishes away!'[35]

This is indeed rather an embarrassing instance of the difficulties of what F. R. Leavis
called 'that most dangerous theme, the irrevocable past'.[36] It is this difficulty together
with a frequent disregard of the practical givens of keyboard music-making that makes
Victorian piano poetry a rather deplorable sub-genre.

Leavis, however, showed himself receptive to the potential power of the piano poem
to evoke memory when he analysed an example of the genre approvingly because
its 'particularity' in remembering an 'unbeglamouring' situation something tangible,
'the presence of something other than directly offered emotion, or mere emotional
flow — the presence of something, a specific situation, concretely grasped'.[37]
The poem in question is the 1918 version of D. H. Lawrence's 'Piano',[38] in which
a woman's singing transports the speaker back to a childhood experience of sitting
under the piano 'in the boom of the tingling strings | And pressing the small, poised
feet of a mother who smiles as she sings'. The mother's 'poised' feet and the tinny
vibrations, more felt than heard, of a modest family instrument playing hymns on 'the
old Sunday evenings at home' retain the realist bearings that suit the piano so well
and lend a particular force to the 'flood of remembrance' provoked by 'the insidious
mastery of song'.

One of Thomas Hardy's best-loved piano poems equally avoids the ridiculous
through particularity, and this is especially impressive because he uses all the tricky

conventional elements of 'piano poetry' that Lawrence avoids.[39] 'The Duettist to her Pianoforte: Song of Silence' (1884) assembles the complete cast of the usual lyric effusion — the male speaker, the dead or absent woman player, the apostrophe to the piano, and the touch of the fingers — but exact historical detail and the domestic realism associated with the instrument join with Hardy's haunting iterations to set this poem apart from others in the genre:

> Since every sound moves memories,
> How can I play you
> Just as I might if your raised no scene,
> By your ivory rows, of a form between
> My vision and your time-worn sheen,
> As when each day you
> Answered our fingers with ecstasy?
> So it's hushed, hushed, hushed, you are for me!
> I fain would second her, strike to her stroke,
> As when she was by,
> Aye, even from the ancient clamorous, 'Fall
> Of Paris,' or 'Battle of Prague' withal,
> To the 'Roving Minstrels,' or 'Elfin Call'
> Sung soft as a sigh:
> But upping ghosts press achefully,
> And mute, mute, mute, you are for me!
>
> Should I fling your polyphones,
> plaints and quavers
> Afresh on the air,
> Too quick would the small white shapes be here
> Of the fellow twain of hands so dear;
> And a black-tressed profile, and pale smooth ear;
>   — The how shall I bear
> Such heavily-haunted harmony?
> Nay: hushed, hushed, hushed you are for me!
> And as I am doomed to counterchord
> Her notes no more
> In those old things I used to know,
> In a fashion, when we practised so,
> 'Good-night! — Good-bye!? to your pleated show
> Of silk, now hoar,
> Each nodding hammer, and pedal and key,
> For dead, dead, dead, you are to me![40]

The concluding line contains a unique touch, in that the instrument — not a dilapidated spinet but a mid-nineteenth-century upright — is no coffin or casket but has itself died with the beloved. But instead of being laboriously made to ascend to Heaven, it is described in earthly detail. Popular sheet-music and the technicalities of four-hand playing are movingly evoked: the beloved's face is remembered in the profile view her duet partner would have seen when the two practised together. The nonce-word 'counterchord' encapsulates a frequent structure of simple four-hand writing (the secondo player, at the lower half of the keyboard, accompanies the double-octave melody of the primo with his chords), and may even allude to the effort it takes a not very advanced pair of players to sound these chords at the right time against the tune. The insistence on the piano's old-fashioned and worn-out trimmings (faded silk front, ivory keys, wood shining with use) further turns this moving poem into a farewell not just to an individual love but to a whole epoch, without having to resort to spinets and pseudo-Elizabethan jargon. The very conventionality, the humdrum quality of the domestic piano is used for a maximum of poetic poignancy.

In nineteenth-century fiction, women protagonists who do not marry suffer 'death or despair or disappearance',[41] that is, they exit the plot, depart this life, or become 'disinfected' as confirmed spinsters. While plot conventions make the actual death of nubile middle-class pianists in novels rather rare,[42] it is poetry's favourite genre-specific strategy for dealing with the sexual power of female musicians who are, as it were, sacrificed on 'the household altar'.[43] The poems discussed in this essay communicate, in a peculiarly direct and absolute fashion, the familiar mixture of fascination and fear that female sensuality provokes: they deal out death far more freely than narrative texts, which need to explain death as retribution. In his extraordinary 'Duettist', Thomas Hardy reveals himself as truly the 'last Victorian' by endorsing the implicit message of most nineteenth-century piano poetry: that the only good woman pianist is — distanced and silenced — a dead woman pianist.

Notes to Chapter 9

I am grateful to the Swiss National Science Foundation for funding the research out of which this article has grown; my warmest thanks are due to Balz Engler and Anne Shreffler for their help in persuading the Foundation to support me in this way. I am also much indebted to Delia da Sousa Correa and Robert Samuels and to Markus Marti for the valuable suggestions that followed their readings of various drafts of this paper.

1. In *The Complete Poetical Works of Thomas Hardy*, ed. by Samuel Hynes, 5 vols (Oxford, Clarendon Press, 1982–95), II (1984), p. 279.

2. James Henry Leigh Hunt, 'The Lover of Music to his Piano-forte', in *The Poetical Works of Leigh Hunt*, ed. by Humphrey Milford (Oxford: Oxford University Press, 1923), p. 355.

3. Dante Gabriel Rossetti, 'During Music', in *The Works of Dante Gabriel Rossetti: Edited with Preface and Notes by William M. Rossetti*, rev. and enlarged edn (London: Ellis, 1911), p. 195.

4. Anon., 'The Education of Women', *Nature*, 10 (17 September 1874), 395–96 (p. 395).

5. In her article in this volume Tili Boon Cuillé describes the similar sensual connotations that music has in Rousseau's writings, as well as the literary tactics that Germaine de Staël employs in order to distance the musical protagonist of her novel *Corinne* from such demeaning associations.

6. Thomas Wade, 'Written after Hearing Great Music', in *The Poems and Plays of Thomas Wade*, ed. by John L. McLean (Troy, NY: Whitston, 1997), p. 368.

7. Compare, for example, Rudyard Kipling's 'The Song of the Banjo', in *The Complete Verse* (London: Kyle Cathie, 1990), pp. 82–84 (p. 82):

> You couldn't pack a Broadwood half a mile —
> You mustn't leave a fiddle in the damp —
> You couldn't raft an organ up the Nile,
> And play it in an Equatorial swamp.

8. John Nicholson, 'The Dying Lover', in *The Poetical Works* (Bradford: Thomas Brear, 1876), p. 243 (my emphasis).

9. I am indebted to Daniel Albright for the interesting piece of information that the end of *Tristan* acquired the title 'Liebestod' only in its form of Franz Liszt's piano transcription.

10. William Sharp, 'During Music', in *Earth's Voices, Transcripts from Nature, Sospitra, and Other Poems* (London: Elliot Stock, 1884), pp. 114–15.

11. Shakespeare's Leontes coins a suggestive verb to express this: 'But to be paddling palms and pinching fingers, | As now they are! [...] Is she | Still virginalling | Upon his palm?' (William Shakespeare, *The Winter's Tale*, in *The Riverside Shakespeare*, ed. by G. Blakemore Evans (Boston: Houghton Mifflin, 1974), pp. 1564–1605: I. 2. 125–26). The allusion is even cruder in Shakespeare's *The Two Noble Kinsmen*: 'She met him in an arbor: | What did she there, coz? play o' th' virginals? *Arcite*. Something she did, sir. *Palamon*. Made her groan a month for't | Or two, or three, or ten' (William Shakespeare, *The Two Noble Kinsmen*, in *The Riverside Shakespeare*, ed. by G. Blakemore Evans (Boston: Houghton Mifflin, 1974), pp. 1639–82: III. 3. 34–37). In Shakespeare's Sonnet 128 ('How oft when thou, my music, music play'st') two male personae (the speaker and the keyboard instrument) are sharing not memories but the actual body of a woman player: 'Since saucy jacks [i.e. keys] so happy are in this, | Give them thy fingers, me thy lips to kiss' (William Shakespeare, *The Sonnets & A Lover's Complaint* (Harmondsworth: Penguin, 1986)).

12. Robert Colvill, 'To the Elegant Seraphina, Performing on the Piano Forte, at a Private Concert', in *The Poetical Works* (London: Dodsley, 1789), pp. 97–99 (p. 99).

13. Thomas Hardy, 'The Chapel-Organist', in *The Complete Poetical Works*, II, 406–12.

14. Arthur Edward William O'Shaughnessy, 'Music and Moonlight', in *Music and Moonlight: Poems and Songs* (London: Chatto and Windus, 1874), pp. 7–37 (p. 137).

15. Thomas Edward Brown, 'Preparation', in *Poems*, 2 vols (Liverpool: University Press of Liverpool, 1952), II, 380–81.

16. William Watt, 'Stanzas on Hearing a Young Lady Perform on the Piano Forte', in *Poems, on Sacred and Other Subjects, Humorous and Sentimental* (Glasgow: William Eadie, 1860), p. 254.

17. Frances Ridley Havergal, 'The Moonlight Sonata', in *The Poetical Works*, 2 vols (London: James Nisbet, 1884), II, 14–31.

18. Mrs Transome in *Felix Holt*, in her mid-fifties in 1832, considers 'her young accomplishments [...] almost ludicrous, like the tone of her first harpsichord and the words of the song long browned with age' (George Eliot, *Felix Holt, the Radical* (Harmondsworth: Penguin, 1972), p. 89). Dickens's hopelessly loyal, faded Miss Tox, who remains devoted to the cold Paul Dombey throughout his two marriages, owns and plays 'an obsolete harpsichord, illuminated round the maker's name with a painted garland of sweet peas' (Charles Dickens, *Dealings with the Firm of Dombey and Son, Wholesale, Retail and for Exportation* (Oxford: Clarendon Press, 1974), p. 86).

19. For example, compare Austin Dobson's 'Gentlewoman of the Old School' (in *Collected Poems*, 9th edn (London: Kegan Paul, Trench, Trübner, 1913), pp. 14–18) —

> Perchance could sum, I doubt she spelt;
> [...]
> I know she played and sang, for yet
> We keep the tumble-down spinet
> To which she quavered ballads set
> By Arne or Jackson

— and many others such as William Thomas Moncrieff's 'Good Old English Gentlewoman' (in *An Original Collection of Songs* (London: John Duncombe, 1850), pp. 150–51); and 'Nell Cook' from the *Ingoldsby Legends* (Thomas Ingoldsby (The Revd Richard H. Barham), *The Ingoldsby Legends, or, Mirth and Marvels* (London: Richard Bentley, 1840), II, 91–99).

20. Andrew Lang, 'The Spinet', in *Poetical Works*, 4 vols (London: Longmans, Green, 1923), II, 25.

21. Edward Waite, 'House Fantastic', in *The Collected Poems of Arthur Edward Waite* (London: William Rider, 1904), p. 112.

22. Norman Rowland Gale, 'The Old Piano', in *Song in September* (London: Constable, 1912), pp. 78–80.

23. George Barlow, 'White', in *The Poetical Works*, 11 vols (London: Henry T. Glaisher, 1902–14), volume II, 119.

24. Francis William Bourdillon, 'The Spinet', in *Young Maids and Old China* (London: Marcus Ward, 1888), n.p.

25. Ezra Pound, 'Scriptor Ignotus', in *Collected Early Poems* (London: Faber, 1977), pp. 24–26.

26. Pound, 'Nel Biancheggiar', in *Collected Early Poems*, p. 72.

27. James Joyce, *Chamber Music*, in *Poems and Shorter Writings* (London: Faber, 1991), pp. 11–48 (p. 14).

28. Joyce, p. 42.

29. Theodore Wratislaw, 'Le Piano que baise', in *Caprices* (London: Gay and Bird, 1893), p. 26.

30. Philip Bourke Marston, 'A Remembered Tune', in *The Collected Poems of Philip Bourke Marston* (London and Melbourne: Ward, Lock, Bowden, 1892), p. 348.

31. John Payne, 'At the Piano', in *Vigil and Vision: New Sonnets* (London: Villon Society, 1903), p. 48.

32. Mary Elizabeth Coleridge, 'To a Piano', in *Poems* (London: Elkin Mathews, 1908), p. 58.

33. I am indebted to Delia da Sousa Correa for suggesting this angle.

34. Hardy, 'Haunting Fingers', in *Complete Poetical Works*, III (1985), pp. 357–59.

35. Hardy, 'The Re-Enactment', in *Complete Poetical Works*, II, 74–77.

36. F. R. Leavis, *The Living Principle: 'English' as a Discipline of Thought* (London: Chatto and Windus, 1977), p. 76.

37. Leavis, p. 78.

38. D. H. Lawrence, 'Piano', in *Complete Poems*, ed. by Vivian de Sola Pinto and Warren Roberts, 2 vols (London: Heinemann, 1972), I, 148.

39. Compare John Lucas's comment that 'Hardy is too intelligent to indulge in a timeless, idyllic past': *Modern English Poetry from Hardy to Hughes* (London: Batsford, 1986), p. 32.

40. Hardy, 'A Duettist to her Pianoforte: Song of Silence', in *Complete Poetical Works*, I (1982), pp. 353–54.

41. This is the frequent fate of John Galsworthy heroines as formulated by the critic Elizabeth Drew in *The Modern Novel: Some Aspects of Contemporary fiction* (London: Jonathan Cape, 1926), pp. 167–68.

42. The strength of such genre conventions also appears in the fact that Mary Elizabeth Coleridge wrote not only 'To a Piano', but also a novel where the overheard piano playing of *The Lady On the Drawing-Room Floor* promotes a late but happy marriage.

43. 'In every house there is an altar [i.e. the piano] devoted to saint Cecilia, and all are taught to serve her to the best of their ability' (Roland Pearsall, *Victorian Popular Music* (Newton Abbot: David and Charles, 1973), p. 74).

CHAPTER 10

Music and Kate Chopin's *The Awakening*

Sue Asbee and Tom Cooper

Kate Chopin is best known for her prose fiction, but her first publication, in fact, was a polka. Though not a professional musician, she was by all accounts a competent pianist, and her keen appreciation of music is apparent in her 1899 novel *The Awakening*, as well as in a number of her short stories.[1] Music is important in this novel in many ways: it informs its structure; allusions to specific pieces and composers enrich the text's emotional depth; and musical sounds of different kinds resonate, with varying effects, throughout. Although music serves complex functions in *The Awakening*, the plot itself is simple. Set in the 1890s at Grand Isle in the Gulf of Mexico, and at New Orleans, the story concerns Edna Pontellier, a woman in her late twenties. Married with two children, she falls in love with Robert Lebrun but has an affair with Alcée Arobin, whom she does not love. Edna's ultimate response to a dawning awareness of society's expectations and of nature's coercion of women for the continuation of the race, and, perhaps most of all, to her realization that sexual fulfilment is not necessarily dependent on romantic love, is to swim out into the Gulf to drown. While suicide and adultery were not new subjects in fiction, Kate Chopin's detached narrative perspective offers neither moral guidance nor judgement. When, therefore, the novel was first published it was generally unfavourably reviewed, mainly on moral grounds.

Among the composers Kate Chopin names in *The Awakening*, Fryderyk Chopin (no relation) recurs consistently; and because of the convention of using last names, any discussion of this aspect engenders confusion, a difficulty to which the author herself must have been alive. There is a moment when one of the characters says, 'I have always said no one could play Chopin like Mademoiselle Reisz!' (p. 30). It is significant that the author's own name is inscribed in the text in such a way, for Kate Chopin consciously draws analogies between the art of the novelist and the art of the composer of music; the connection is emphasized, and the reader struggles to distinguish between the two Chopins. This ambiguity is analogous to the fluidity of form and structure in the novel, which sets out to explore desire, sexuality, identity, and women's roles, rather than to prescribe behaviour or — more importantly — to moralize. Fryderyk Chopin was greatly favoured by the decadent writers of the 1890s (Oscar Wilde, for example), and there is a hint of sexual impropriety in the *fin-de-siècle* vogue for his music that Kate Chopin draws on here.

As a pianist herself in the late nineteenth century, Kate Chopin would have known intimately at least some of Fryderyk Chopin's music, which was not only ubiquitous but synonymous with the piano. This in itself is enough to explain why his music is mentioned specifically at key moments in the novel; but there are also a number of parallels between the two Chopins that are worth exploring, including the terms in which their works were initially received.

Critical reception of *The Awakening* was mostly hostile. The novel was considered morbid, unhealthy and unwomanly,[2] echoing typical contemporary criticisms of Fryderyk Chopin's music — 'morbid', 'diseased', 'feverish and unwholesome', with decided overtones of 'unmanliness'.[3] The Nocturne op. 37, says one critic, 'bewitches and unmans'.[4] James Huneker, writing in his *Chopin: The Man and His Music* (New York, 1900), says of the Chopin Nocturnes that they 'seem to be suffering from anaemia', and that 'the feminine note [... is] overemphasised'.[5] In contrast to Fryderyk, Kate Chopin was criticized for not being 'feminine' enough. Her representation of free-willed female sexuality was too shocking for late nineteenth-century Louisiana in particular, where the belief that Southern white women had no sexual desires was still widely upheld. Fryderyk Chopin was criticized mainly for the emasculated emotional world he was considered to inhabit, but also in contemporary perceptions of his form and harmony. The acknowledged sensuality of Fryderyk Chopin's music may have been a reason for Kate Chopin's choice of this music for her novel. A hint of its dangerous excesses is provided when one listener remarks, 'That last prelude! Bon Dieu! It shakes a man' (p. 30).

The Awakening is a novel full of sound, from the 'fluty notes' of a mocking bird, heard on the first page, to the 'clang' of a cavalry officer's spurs, remembered on the last. During the dinner-party scene the sound of mandolins and the 'soft, monotonous splash of a fountain' create an ambience of privilege and luxury, and contribute to the sense of *fin-de-siècle* decadence (p. 98). Mademoiselle Reisz keeps letters under a bust of Beethoven; indeed, music is pervasive. In addition to Fryderyk Chopin, a number of other composers and compositions are invoked, although at the moments of greatest intensity it is often difficult, if not impossible, to identify specific pieces. This, as we shall see, is almost certainly deliberate. A number of popular classics make an appearance, including the duet from Hérold's *Zampa*, a wildly successful opera in the nineteenth century (produced in New Orleans in 1833), and Franz Suppé's overture *Poet and Peasant* dating from 1846. These are enthusiastically played on the piano by the young twin Farival sisters. The instrument also features in other musical soirées. In one it is played by the magnificently named Mrs Highcamp, who gives renditions of Grieg that 'apprehended all of the composer's coldness and none of his poetry' (p. 83); and the pianist Mademoiselle Reisz plays a crucial role in the novel.

Discussion of music in *The Awakening* inevitably leads to the related imagery in the novel to do with the sea. Both are intimately associated with Edna's changing sense of identity. After hearing Mademoiselle Reisz play, she is disturbed and excited by the performance, and later the same night she swims properly for the first time. This is one of her awakenings, and in terms of her emotional development, music and swimming become inextricably linked. This key episode takes place in Section IX of the novel, which describes a Saturday night's entertainment on Grand Isle. To begin with, Madame Ratignolle, one of the other wives, plays the piano for others to dance. Edna, having danced first with her husband, then Robert, then Monsieur Ratignolle, withdraws from the company and sits 'on the low windowsill' out on the gallery where she can see everything that is going on in the hall but where she can also 'look out toward the Gulf' (p. 28). Her positioning is important, for she is literally and metaphorically poised between two worlds, neither indoors nor out, neither simply part of nature nor of society. The description that follows is deeply romantic, foreshadowing the transformations that are to follow Edna's liminal state: 'There was a soft effulgence in the east. The moon was coming up, and its mystic shimmer was casting a million lights across the distant, restless water' (p. 28). The imagery in this passage also contributes to a cumulative effect whereby descriptions of the sea act as refrains throughout the novel. Edna first appears making her way out of the sea up the shore towards her husband, 'advancing at snail's pace from the beach' (p. 4), and at the end she returns to it (p. 128).

Earlier, the narrator comments that Madame Ratignolle 'played very well [...]. She was keeping up her music on account of the children, she said; because she and her husband both considered it a means of brightening the home and making it attractive' (p. 27). (The customary role of music in the family is discussed by Regula Hohl Trillini in the previous essay in the present collection.) Here, in a deadpan tone suggesting that an artistic disposition is not involved, the narrator says, 'Edna was what she herself called very fond of music' (p. 29). But her response to Madame Ratignolle's playing or practising in the mornings is very interesting, and includes a moment of analeptic slippage that the narrator chooses to explain. Like contemporary publishers who, for sales reasons, gave Fryderyk Chopin's Nocturnes such titles as 'Les Zéphyrs' (for op. 15) without the composer's consent (or even knowledge in some cases), Edna has her own names for some pieces, emphasizing the subjective nature of her response to the music:

> One piece which [Madame Ratignolle] played Edna had entitled 'Solitude'. [...] When she heard it there came before her imagination the figure of a man standing beside a desolate rock on the seashore. He was naked. His attitude was one of hopeless resignation as he looked toward a distant bird winging its flight away from him.
>
> Another piece called to mind a dainty young woman clad in an Empire gown, taking mincing dancing steps as she came down a long avenue between tall hedges. Again, another reminded her of children at play, and still another of nothing on earth but a demure lady stroking a cat (p. 29).

Music evokes visual images in Edna's mind, and that first image of 'Solitude' becomes one of the incremental refrains used to structure the novel. Here the imagery prefigures the end of the novel when Edna returns to Grand Isle and prepares for her last swim: 'All along the white beach, up and down, there was no living thing in sight. A bird with a broken wing was beating the air above, reeling, fluttering, circling disabled down, down to the water', while, for the first time in Edna's life, 'she stood naked in the open air, at the mercy of the sun, the breeze that beat upon her, and the waves that invited her'; she stood 'naked under the sky!' (p. 127). The gender reversal of the solitary figures is interesting; but the main point is that imagery works in the manner of variations on a theme. The man stripped of civilizing garments conjured up by 'Solitude' is at odds with the other images Madame Ratignolle's playing suggests: nature here is artificial, planted and tamed; the cat is a domestic animal.

However, when Mademoiselle Reisz, the novel's serious pianist, takes over at the piano, Edna's habitual visual response is replaced by a more immediate physical reaction. Mademoiselle Reisz's appearance is witch-like: an artist-as-outsider figure, she is capable of enchantment through her art. She makes a point of deferring to Edna, who, embarrassed, 'would not dare to choose' what should be played, asking that Mademoiselle Reisz 'please herself in her selections' (p. 29). Tonight,

> the very first chords which Mademoiselle Reisz struck upon the piano sent a keen tremor down Mrs Pontellier's spinal column. It was not the first time she had heard an artist at the piano. Perhaps it was the first time she was ready, perhaps the first time her being was tempered to take an impress of the abiding truth. (p.29)

The rhythmical repetitions draw our attention to the magnitude of what happens to Edna, and the same rhetorical pattern is used in the next paragraph:

> She waited for the material pictures which she thought would gather and blaze before her imagination. She waited in vain. She saw no pictures of solitude, of hope, of longing, or of despair. But the very passions themselves were aroused within her soul, swaying it, lashing it, as the waves daily beat upon her splendid body. (pp. 29–30)

Edna's response to the music here is intensely physical: 'she trembled, she was choking, and the tears blinded her' (p. 30). When Mademoiselle Reisz asks 'how did you like my music?', Edna is unable to answer; and when the pianist 'perceived her agitation and even her tears', she says Edna is 'the only one worth playing for'. In fact, Mademoiselle Reisz has aroused a 'fever of enthusiasm' in several of her listeners (p. 30).

Edna is still poised on the gallery between interior and exterior worlds, neither quite within the social gathering, nor out of doors. Which will ultimately claim her? From the refined sensibility of Fryderyk Chopin interpreted by an artist who paradoxically depends on, but cares little for, society, Edna moves to the seduction of the sea. As the party breaks up, someone, 'perhaps it was Robert, thought of a bath at that mystic hour and under that mystic moon' (p. 30), and under the heady influence of the music Edna finally learns to swim. In its portrayal of Edna's physical response to music, the novel's interactions with the music of Fryderyk Chopin and other Romantic composers overlap with the traces of biological theories of emotional response. Kate Chopin had read both Charles Darwin and Herbert Spencer. Music's arousal of Edna's animal sexuality re-enacts Darwin's view of musical expression as an echo of its primary original function in sexual selection. Kate Chopin has Edna rebel against Darwin's notion of women's passive role in human sexual selection, by attempting to do the selecting herself.[6] She also shows Edna recoiling from the domestically musical Madame Ratignolle's acquiescence in constant sexual reproduction. Edna's despair after witnessing the latter give birth to her latest child is instrumental in her final return to the sea — as if seeking to reverse the tide of evolution.

Music gives expression to Edna's awakening sexuality and also to her subsequent disillusionment. On one occasion Mademoiselle Reisz's playing has 'penetrated her whole being like an effulgence, warming and brightening the dark places of her soul. It prepared her for joy and exultation' (p. 89). Towards the end of the novel Kate Chopin constructs a scene that forms a variation on her earlier description of Edna listening to music. She is again positioned by a window; this time, however, the piano stool is occupied by Robert, long the object of her romantic yearnings and at whose initiative Edna heard Mademoiselle Reisz play and learned to swim on Grand Isle. When Robert returns after a prolonged absence, his hollow explanation of his failure to seek her out is accompanied by 'a crash of discordant sound' as he leans his arms onto the keys; this dramatizes Edna's dismay and Robert's complete failure to understand her desires (p. 108). She had 'always fancied him expressing or betraying in some way his love for her. And here, the reality was that they sat ten feet apart, she at the window, crushing geranium leaves [...] he twirling around on the piano stool' (p. 108).

Kate Chopin builds up her novel through a series of such suggestive episodes, rather than providing comprehensive detail. The brevity of *The Awakening* marks a break from the scale and inclusivity of the nineteenth-century novel. Elaine Showalter remarks on the way in which 'incremental repetition and circularity gradually replace the forward dynamism of the plot' in Kate Chopin's writing.[7] This is entirely appropriate, for Edna's psychological and emotional awakenings are far from straightforward. Others have specifically noticed the way in which *The Awakening* 'moves away from the representational conventions embraced by the nineteenth-century novel or short story and begins to model itself on the discourse of music'.[8]

This affinity with musical discourse can be explored by investigating particular formal analogies between Kate Chopin's novel and Fryderyk Chopin's compositions. In certain pieces, such as the Nocturne in G minor, op. 15 (1832) for example, his music avoids a literal repeat of the first section (which was very common for short pieces in the nineteenth century, particularly piano pieces) and instead moves away into another style of music altogether, with remote echoes of earlier motifs and pitch intervals providing formal coherence. *The Awakening* consists of thirty-nine numbered sections of unequal length rather than conventional chapters. Within these, in a manner similar to that used by Chopin in the G minor Nocturne, images repeat and accumulate, exploring variations of themes rather than furthering the plot. Rhythm is also an important structural device, achieved through these repetitions and through the juxtaposition of the thirty-nine sections. Kate Chopin's prose rhythms vary: some sentences are short and convey a practical if not sardonic tone, often when the narrator offers straightforward descriptions; others are lengthy, fluid, hypnotic, most frequently when Edna's emotional states are being expressed.

Repeated and varied movement also contributes to the rhythms of the novel. We see Edna emerging from the sea at the start of the novel, and at the end she returns to it. After Edna had read Robert's letter and left, Mademoiselle Reisz 'reentered' the room, 'restored' the letter to the envelope, and 'replaced it in the table drawer' from which she had originally taken it (p. 71). Mademoiselle Reisz's improvisation also goes away from and comes back to the Fryderyk Chopin 'Impromptu'. We have already described such repetition in *The Awakening* as operating as an 'incremental refrain', a feature of Fryderyk Chopin's own approach to form, particularly in the smaller-scale pieces such as the Preludes op. 28 (1838–39). His E minor Prelude op. 28, no. 4, for example, continually returns to the opening theme but varies it constantly: the initial right-hand line is repeated a tone lower in bars 5–8; bars 8–12 move away to another idea; in bars 13–18 the opening takes another turn but comes back to the same place as in bars 8–12; and the opening right-hand line appears in the bass in bars 18–23. Characteristically for this piece, the note values and harmonies are altered each time.

While it is unlikely that Kate Chopin thought of Fryderyk Chopin's works in this way — only recently has criticism of his music tended to celebrate his skill with manipulations of form — it is probable that the descriptions of his music in the novel as fluid, both in form and content, refer to his position as a key signifier of femininity and transgression in the nineteenth century. These in turn reinforce the subversive, enigmatic aspects of Kate Chopin's novel, not least in its formal structure.

In Kate Chopin's short story 'Wiser than a God', the heroine plays one of Fryderyk Chopin's best-known works, the *Berceuse* op. 57 (1844), a set of variations over a repeated harmony. Here also, Kate Chopin's writing style imitates the form of the music to which it alludes. This example is one of the few pieces of music named — and played in full — in her fiction, and such closure is significant in the context of the story: Paula's mother is soothed when her daughter plays the *Berceuse* at her request, 'the wonderful strains that came like an ethereal voice out of the past' lull her spirit 'into the quiet of sweet memories' (p. 130). The lullaby reconciles mother to daughter, evokes joyful memories of the past, and allows her to drift peacefully — romantically and sentimentally — to her death. Texted music is rarer in *The Awakening* and presents a slightly different case when it does occur: words Victor sings to Edna provoke her dismay and the subsequent disruption that brings her dinner party to an embarrassed end. As the guests leave, in a curious reversal the silent street scene is described in terms of music: 'The mandolin players had long since stolen away. A profound stillness had fallen upon the broad, beautiful street. The voices of Edna's disbanding guests jarred like a discordant note upon the quiet harmony of the night' (p. 101). Once again, emotions are at the heart of the musical imagery, but here discordances represent people out of sorts with each other after an evening of rather too much sensuous decadence and self-indulgence.

'Wiser than a God' was first published in 1889 in the *Philadelphia Musical Journal*, indicating that Kate Chopin had a particularly musical audience in mind when placing her story, one that would have no trouble in recognizing her reference. Appearing ten years before *The Awakening*, it is hardly surprising that the relationship between subject matter and music is more complex in the later, longer work. Chopin gives details to an informed audience, and paradoxically leaves her more general readers in the dark. In the novel, types of music are indicated, and an individual performance of some excellence is evoked, but details are deliberately elusive. Ultimately, language is unequal to the task of recreating the experience of hearing instrumental music, and the narrative falls back on describing the physical and emotional effects it produces on its listeners.

Being at a loss for words, inarticulate in the face of extreme emotion, is indeed one of Edna's chief characteristics. Unlike some nineteenth-century heroines — Dorothea Brooke or Jane Eyre, for example — Edna is neither an intellectual nor given to self-analysis; rather, she abandons herself to emotion:

There were days when she was very happy without knowing why. She was happy to be alive and breathing, when her whole being seemed to be one with the sunlight, the color, the odors, the luxuriant warmth of some perfect Southern day [...]. She discovered many a sunny sleepy corner, fashioned to dream in. And she found it good to dream and to be alone and unmolested.

Then there were days when she was unhappy, she did not know why, — when it did not seem worth while to be glad or sorry, to be alive or dead; when life appeared to her like a grotesque pandemonium and humanity like worms struggling blindly towards inevitable annihilation. She could not work on such a day, nor weave fancies to stir her pulses and warm her blood. (pp. 64–65)

Two very different versions of nature, idyllic then brutal, are set up for comparison by repetition and rhythm in these two paragraphs that bring Section XIX to a close.

Edna cannot reconcile her newly awakened sensibilities with her daily life as wife and mother. Longing for news of Robert, who has abruptly departed for Mexico, she visits Mademoiselle Reisz. Robert has written to her enquiring about Edna: '"If Mrs Pontellier should call upon you, play for her that Impromptu of Chopin's, my favourite [...]. I should like to know how it affects her"' (p. 70). As Mademoiselle Reisz plays, Edna reads Robert's letter:

Mademoiselle played a soft interlude. It was an improvisation [...].Gradually and imperceptibly the interlude melted into the soft opening minor chords of the Chopin Impromptu.

Edna did not know when the Impromptu began or ended. She sat in the sofa corner reading Robert's letter by the fading light. Mademoiselle had glided from the Chopin into the quivering love-notes of Isolde's song, and back again to the Impromptu with its soulful and poignant longing.

The shadows deepened in the little room. The music grew strange and fantastic — turbulent, insistent, plaintive and soft with entreaty. The shadows grew deeper. The music filled the room. It floated out upon the night, over the housetops, the crescent of the river, losing itself in the silence of the upper air. (p. 71)

Music does the work of expressing the intense range of emotions Edna goes through, before she leaves, blinded by tears. Once again, repetitions and rhythms generate the effects as much as the sense of the words. Successive sentences begin 'The shadows ...', 'The music ...', 'The shadows ...', 'The music ...', recreating in prose the subtle cadences of the piano.

On a practical level there are obvious parallels between contemporary performance practice and what we are told Mademoiselle Reisz does — the initial improvisation before the piece begins, for example. However, the identity of the piece seems deliberately mysterious. None of the actual Chopin Impromptus have 'soft opening minor chords', although the second Impromptu does have soft major ones. However, to pin down the identity of the piece is to miss the point, which is that the music forms a counterpoint to the ambiguous changes taking place in Edna's soul. Not only are these are too complex to be named or catalogued, but a specific label might suggest the experience could be shared — or recreated. This would be contrary to the extreme subjectivity of Edna's response, and her feeling that she goes out beyond where any woman has been before. The novel is an adventure and an exploration for Edna. It is thus significant that she does not know when the piece begins and ends, and that the 'Impromptu' encapsulates another piece altogether, identified as 'Isolde's song'. This is probably a reference to the transfiguring *Liebestod* or 'Love-Death' that brings Wagner's *Tristan und Isolde* to a close: a telling choice, both of composer and work. First performed in 1865 (and in New York in 1886), the opera had become notorious for its revolutionary musical content and its supposed difficulty. Isolde's singing in the *Liebestod* of the eternal joys that await her in her dissolution from this world, 'Unbewusst, höchste Lust' ('Oblivious, utter rapture'), resonates with Edna's essentially indescribable emotional experiences. The consolations of religion are replaced in the opera by a thoroughly Romantic yearning for annihilation that borders on the erotic.

The close links between Edna's sexual awakening and her final suicide suggest a parallel with Wagner's opera, as do the unconsummated adulterous desires that feature in both works. In addition, there are implicit parallels between Wagner's compositional technique and Kate Chopin's structure in *The Awakening*. Wagner typically moves away from the set-piece format of earlier composers (with self-contained arias, duets, etc.) and instead sets his texts in a continuous flow of unending melody. Structure is provided not by literal repetition, as in some older operatic styles, but through variation and development, particularly applied to 'leitmotif', the use of a theme or harmonic sequence that is expressively identified in the music with a character, idea, or artefact. Wagner's subtle use of harmony frequently creates a dramatic sense of instability. Isolde's 'Liebestod' is full of such moments, where key slides into key by imperceptible means, creating a mood of fluidity perfectly suited to illustrate Isolde's impending dissolution. This fluidity owes some debt to the harmonic procedures also found in Fryderyk Chopin's music. In the Prelude in E minor mentioned earlier, the harmonies shift and melt into each other, continually drawing upon the downward stepwise movement that characterizes the melody.

The music comes to a momentary rest in bar 23 after a chord that can be interpreted aurally, though not visually, as having a dominant relationship to the key of F major (see Ex. 10.1). This remote key is based on the flattened second degree of the scale of E minor (bearing what is technically known as a Neapolitan relationship to the tonic). As the music resumes in the penultimate bar, this chord, which at its first hearing seems to point the piece in a whole new harmonic direction, is reconstrued in hindsight as a chromatically altered chord belonging to a conventional final cadence that reasserts the tonic key of E minor. Such disguise of the identity of chords is an example of Chopin's fluid and evasive treatment of final cadences found throughout his music. A similar liquidity characterizes the formal configurations of Kate Chopin's novel. The episode where 'Isolde's song' is interpolated into a piece by Fryderyk Chopin begins by drawing the reader's attention to the way light and air float in through the windows of Mademoiselle Reisz's apartment (p. 68). At the end of the passage the motif is recalled, but it is music that floats out 'losing itself', dissolving and dissipating as Edna herself dissolves back into nature as she swims out to sea at the end of the novel (p. 71).

Kate Chopin's fictions constantly echo one another, signalling that this formal fluidity operated between, as well as within, discrete works. Characters, resonant phrases, and visual imagery from *The Awakening* are found in some of the short stories, suggesting that Chopin did not necessarily think of each piece of fiction as self-

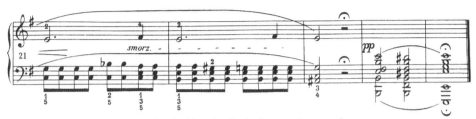

Ex. 10.1 Fryderyk Chopin, Prelude op. 28, no. 4, bars 21–25

contained. Gouvernail, who attends Edna's dinner party in *The Awakening*, also appears as a character in 'Athénaïse' and 'A Respectable Woman'. Other minor characters from *The Awakening* are developed more fully in 'Tonie (At Chénière Caminada)', and the 'red lateen sail' of Tonie's boat at the end of Section XIII of *The Awakening* reappears in the short story too (p. 44).[9] In 'Tonie' music is also crucial to the protagonist's confused desires in a way that mirrors *The Awakening*. This inter-textuality indicates a fluid approach to composition, significant given the kind of romantic music on which Kate Chopin draws. Contemporary musical parallels abound. The 'Rheingold' theme in Wagner's Ring Cycle (first performed in its entirety in 1876), for example, recurs in all four operas, while Gustav Mahler makes similar use of a falling chromatic motif in his symphonies (composed between 1888 and 1911).

However, as other essays in this collection are more expressly designed to show, drawing direct links between literature and music is a highly problematic venture. In addition, to argue that Kate Chopin saw and consciously employed the same fluidity of structure when constructing her fiction that modern analysts celebrate in Fryderyk Chopin's music would be to overlook the point made earlier concerning contemporary critical reactions to Chopin's work. Such a link between the procedures of novelist and composer would be speculative at best. Nevertheless, reading Kate Chopin's novel with her musical counterpart in mind demonstrates the value of such affinities in alerting us to the effects of musical analogy within literature. Musical parallels in Kate Chopin's novel assist in creating the fluidity of structure, mood, and language that is such a feature of the work. They help to impart significance to the temporal shifts in the narrative, and to lend credence to the departures from the traditionally linear plot still favoured by many of Kate Chopin's contemporaries. They also contribute to the imagery and metaphor that provide a rich account of the emotional world of the novel's heroine while leaving the author free from the necessity of describing it in detail. *The Awakening* ends with a striking description of the fleeting sounds and images that present themselves forcibly to Edna as she swims out into the gulf:

> She looked into the distance, and the old terror flamed up for an instant, then sank again. Edna heard her father's voice and her sister Margaret's. She heard the barking of an old dog that was chained to the sycamore tree. The spurs of the cavalry officer clanged as he walked across the porch. There was the hum of bees, and the musky odor of pinks filled the air. (p. 128)

Notes to Chapter 10

1. Kate Chopin, *The Awakening; and Other Stories*, ed. by Pamela Knights (Oxford: Oxford University Press, 2000). All page references in text are to this edition.
2. See Chopin, ed. Knights, p. ix.
3. Jim Samson, ed., *The Cambridge Companion to Chopin* (Cambridge: Cambridge University Press, 1992), p. 227.
4. Samson, p. 227.
5. Jeffery Kallberg, *Chopin at the Boundaries: Sex, History and Musical Genre* (Cambridge, MA, and London: Harvard University Press, 1996), pp. 42–43.
6. Charles Darwin, *The Descent of Man, and Selection in Relation to Sex*, 2 vols (London: John Murray, 1871), II, 333–37. For discussion of Darwin and Spencer's views on music and literary responses to these, see Delia da Sousa Correa, *George Eliot, Music and Victorian Culture* (Basingstoke: Palgrave, 2002).
7. Elaine Showalter, 'Tradition and the Female Talent: *The Awakening* as a Solitary Talent', in *New Essays on The Awakening*, ed. by Wendy Martin (Cambridge: Cambridge University Press, 1988), pp. 33–57 (pp. 46–47).
8. Avril Horner and Sue Zlosnik, *Landscapes of Desire* (London: Harvester Wheatsheaf, 1990), p. 53.
9. Chopin, 'Tonie (At Chénière Caminada)', in *The Awakening; and Other Stories*, pp. 231, 233, and, with a slight variation ('taut, red sail'), p. 234.

CHAPTER 11

Narratives of Masculinity and Femininity: Two Schumann Song Cycles

Robert Samuels

Song cycles present one of the most fascinating modes in which words and music collaborate in the creation of an artwork.[1] Any example of song composition raises issues of signification. A song setting suggests that its lyric (which has usually been conceived by its author as self-sufficient) is in need of the supplement of musical accompaniment in order to signify. In a song cycle these issues are enlarged by the potential narrative that arises from the sequence of songs. The qualification 'potential' is needed, because this narrative may not be straightforwardly legible from the texts themselves. Sometimes, as in Schubert's *Die schöne Müllerin*, the 'story' is entirely explicit, so that the song cycle appears to be close to an unstaged opera; but often the narrative remains latent, requiring interpretation by the performer and listener to bring it to light. This need for interpretive effort signals at the outset the frequently enigmatic nature of the musical and literary (or intermedial) signification of the genre.

When presented as a cycle, rather than simply as a collection (the term *Liederzyklus* was first used on the title-page of Beethoven's *An die ferne Geliebte* of 1816), a work claims to achieve the nineteenth-century aesthetic goals of overarching coherence in an extended form, and unity of connotative purpose between the small and large scale. Song cycles are not the only nineteenth-century genre where self-sufficient individual pieces are grouped together into a larger cohesive form. The term 'multi-piece' has been used to cover cases where this can be argued to be true; sets of piano miniatures (another genre beloved by Schumann) are the other most common example of this form.[2] Where the connections between the songs of a cycle are left unstated by the texts, and even more so where the selection of texts as a group is the work of composer rather than poet (as is the case with Schumann's *Dichterliebe*), these aesthetic goals are left in the sole care of the musical settings. In other words, the song cycle takes its place alongside many other nineteenth-century musical genres, where the coveted goal of organic unity is at once the preserve of the 'purely musical', and simultaneously a product of the interaction between that musical structuring and a literary narrative. The paradox of the song cycle as a form is that it makes explicit the need for language to identify the nature of the unifying process of the work, and denies to the words of the poetry the articulation of that very process.

It is a commonplace of writing on Robert Schumann that his so-called 'year of song', 1840, coincided with the conclusion of his tortuous courtship of Clara Wieck, their marriage following a successful legal action brought by the couple against her father, who refused to consent to the union. Amongst the fruits of that year are two song cycles in which the poetry has romantic love as its theme. Before rushing to the inevitable interpretive conclusion of the vast majority of CD liner and programme notes, a pause might be in order: *Dichterliebe* (op. 48, written between 23 May and 1 June 1840) presents a tale of unrequited passion culminating in the renunciation of the love affair by the (male) protagonist, whilst *Frauenliebe und Leben* (op. 42, written on 11 and 12 July 1840) concludes with the death of the (female) protagonist's husband and her retreat behind the widow's veil. These profiles might suggest caution in reading these works as biography in notes. Denying any connection between Schumann's circumstances and the cycles is pointless; although reading them in this naïve fashion is unilluminating. However, what these cycles do encapsulate is an exploration of the kinds of narrative that can be viably adopted by the personae of male and female lover respectively; thus, an exploration of the nature of masculinity and femininity themselves at this stage of the nineteenth century.

The issue of the narrating persona or 'voice' in these song cycles is central. The embarrassment of many modern performers with *Frauenliebe und Leben* in particular has to do with the perceived identity of performer and poetic voice. Its eight songs describe successive episodes narrated by a woman, all of which centre entirely on the man who is effectively the silent protagonist of the work. The *Leben* of the title begins when she first sees him, climaxes with their wedding (which occupies the central two songs), and ends with his death, 'the first pain you have ever caused me'. This is difficult to stomach for any interpreter with even moderately feminist sympathies. Ruth Solie surveys common (male) attempts to justify affection for the cycle whilst wriggling away from its ideology; most such attempts rely on excuses broadly along the lines of 'that was then, this is now'. Solie's counter is understandably dismissive: 'such defensive arguments are merely sloppy intellectual habits, and historically inaccurate as well'.[3] Any rehabilitation of Schumann's work has to begin with acceptance of its ideology, rather than these symptoms of denial. This is a song cycle describing a woman's experience, composed by a man using words written by another man — an apparent act of ventriloquism that in recent years has led sopranos to attempt to perform it 'as if in quotation marks', in an effort to create properly sceptical (and postmodern) ironic distance between performer and nineteenth-century patriarchal ideology.[4]

It is significant, in the light of this embarrassment, to register that Schumann himself regarded the performer as having some distance from the narratives. The near-universal convention of today, that *Frauenliebe und Leben* should be sung by a woman and *Dichterliebe* by a man, respecting the explicit gendering of the texts, does not derive from their nineteenth-century performance history.[5] This is demonstrated by the dedication of *Dichterliebe*: originally the cycle was to be dedicated to Felix Mendelssohn, presumably as an act of homage to a fellow composer rather than in the expectation that Mendelssohn would sing it (although he possessed a fine amateur tenor voice); but by the time of its publication the dedication had been altered to Wilhelmine Schröder-Devrient. As possibly the foremost female singer of the time, it is inconceivable that she was not intended as a performer of the cycle. *Frauenliebe und*

Leben does not have a similar dedication, but it was, later in the century, frequently performed by Julius Stockhausen with Clara Schumann as accompanist. Both cycles are described on the title-page as 'für eine Singstimme mit Begleitung des Pianoforte' ('for voice with piano accompaniment'); the fact that each could acceptably be performed by a singer of either gender perhaps shows that contemporary listeners had a keener awareness than present-day ones that the works embody representation of experience rather than its articulation.

Not that this is itself intended as excuse-making. Before judgment is passed on *Frauenliebe und Leben* as an aesthetic or moral experience, it is worth comparing the form of its narrative with that of *Dichterliebe*. The comparison of musical detail reveals depths to what Schumann's (admittedly patriarchal) aesthetic can credibly ascribe to a 'woman's story' and a 'man's story'.

Frauenliebe und Leben: A Closed Circle

The songs of *Frauenliebe und Leben* are linked by several different sorts of musical device. One of Schumann's favourite textures, where repeated chords in the piano right hand accompany a prominent, often chromatically rising bass line, is used in songs 2, 4, 5, and 6 (in comparison, this is a texture used only once in the sixteen songs of *Dichterliebe*). In addition, songs 2, 6, and 7 all close with motivically linked gestures, where a chromatic falling line approaches a suspended cadence. Here, the reminiscence underlines the connection between the poems, which are the three in which the woman is overcome with admiration of her beloved: 'the most manly of men', her 'sweet friend', and then in the person of her baby, who is 'your image'. These isolated moments, however, are not the primary articulation of the musical narrative.

The most immediately striking gesture towards 'multi-piece form' in *Frauenliebe und Leben* is the repetition at the end of song 8, as a postlude to the cycle, of the piano accompaniment to song 1. The repeated material is a virtually literal repeat of one strophe with the concluding cadence, giving twenty bars of postlude rather than the thirty-six bars of the first song. The postlude returns to the key of the opening, B flat major, contrasting with the D minor of song 8. If this provides an aural marker of coherence in the cycle, then investigating the sequence of keys in the whole cycle seems a good way to continue (see Table 11. 1):

TABLE 11.1. Key structure of Schumann's *Frauenlieben und Leben*

No.	Song title	Key
1	Seit ich ihn gesehen	B flat major
2	Er, der Herrlichste von Allen	E flat major
3	Ich kann's nicht fassen, nicht glauben	C minor
4	Du Ring an meinem Finger	E flat major
5	Helft mir, ihr Schwestern	B flat major
6	Süsser Freund	G major
7	An meinem Herzen, an meiner Brust	D major
8	Nun hast du mir den ersten Schmerz gethan	D minor (B flat at end)

This is a song cycle of two halves. The first five songs present a palindrome of keys, beginning and ending in B flat major and moving to the closely related keys of the subdominant and supertonic minor. The last three songs also share closely related keys, which in relation to B flat are the submediant major, the mediant major, and the mediant minor: in other words, a third above and below, so that the note D natural connects the tonic triads of all these keys.

Ex. 11.1. Schumann, *Frauenliebe und Leben*, end of song 5 and opening of song 6

It is hardly surprising that this division of the eight songs corresponds to a grouping within the texts: first the courtship ending with the wedding march that closes song 5, then the married life of songs 6–8, ending with the husband's death. But the key structure does more than divide the 'woman's life' into two phases. A much more ideologically charged narrative appears if the voice-leading that connects the two halves and introduces the postlude is considered. The rather distant modulation from B flat major to G major between songs 5 and 6 is smoothed over by linear connections between the two songs. These are analysed by the two voice-leading graphs in Ex. 11.1. Song 5 closes with the wedding march of the happy couple fading out of earshot, with a diminuendo and the music descending to the bass register, following an unproblematic structural close to the song in bar 44. The first graph in Ex. 11.1 shows how the chromatic opening of song 6 follows this cadence by establishing B natural as the primary tone in the new key. The chromatic lines pick up the B flat (enharmonically A sharp) and D natural of the previous song, effectively converting them into neighbour notes, as the second graph shows.

Ex. 11.2. Schumann, *Frauenliebe und Leben*, end of song 8 and beginning of postlude

This technique is recalled by Schumann's handling of the end of song 8. This never reaches a definite close in D minor: the dominant chord accompanying the final word of the poem is converted into the dominant chord of the postlude. Ex. 11.2 again suggests two ways of accounting for the voice-leading here. The descent of the fundamental line in song 8 is relatively easily discernible, and chiefly notable for the lengthy concentration on $\hat{4}$ (G natural) for the spine-chilling descent of the widow's veil. The line is summarized in the first graph in Ex. 11.2, showing how it comes to rest on $\hat{2}$, the E natural of bar 22, before a chromatic chord progression is then used by Schumann, as between songs 5 and 6, to join the imperfect cadence to the B flat triad that opens the postlude. The second graph shows how this pivotal chord (a dominant seventh on F) effectively consigns the top-line descent to the status of an inner part, continuing from E natural through E flat to the D natural in the alto of the B flat tonic triad; meanwhile, the A natural at the top of the chord reinterprets the opening note of song 8 as the leading note of the new key.

Such moments are not just elegant devices creating logical continuity at these points. They create a specific narrative in which songs 6, 7, and 8 appear as an interpolation between the B flat cadence that closed song 5 so confidently, and the recurrence of this triad, at the same registral level, at the opening of the postlude. The cadence at the end of song 5 turns out to be the structural close of the entire cycle, the subsequent exploration of slightly more distant keys serving to prolong this B flat tonic sonority. It is no great leap from this tonal structure to an ideological narrative. The culminating moment of the woman's entire experience is the wedding march that secures her union with the beloved. Her married life is ultimately only a prolongation — in the literal as in the music-analytic sense — of this single event. After her wedding begins an interlude forever destined for its definitive close — again, literal as musical — with her beloved's death. She is left with memory alone, living behind the veil in that place where she still possesses 'you and my lost happiness'. That place is identified musically as the B flat major which becomes the tonic key for the whole cycle, creating a closed circle of experience.

Dichterliebe: Love Springs Forth

TABLE 11.2. Key structure of Schumann's *Dichterliebe*

No.	Song title	Key
1	Im wunderschönen Monat Mai	F sharp minor/A major
2	Aus meinen Tränen spriessen	A major
3	Die Rose, die Lilie, die Taube, die Sonne	D major
4	Wenn ich in deine Augen seh	G major
5	Ich will meine Seele tauchen	B minor
6	Im Rhein, im heiligen Strome	E minor
7	Ich grolle nicht	C major
8	Und wüssten's die Blumen, die kleinen	A minor
9	Das ist ein Flöten und Geigen	D minor
10	Hör' ich das Liedchen klingen	G minor
11	Ein Jüngling und ein Mädchen	E flat major
12	Am leuchtenden Sommermorgen	B flat major
13	Ich hab im Traum geweinet	E flat minor
14	Allnächtlich im Traume seh ich dich	B major
15	Aus alten Märchen winkt es	E major
16	Die alten, bösen Lieder	C sharp minor (D flat major at end)

The tonal integration of *Frauenliebe und Leben*, with B flat major functioning as a tonic key for the whole cycle, contrasts with the approach taken in the sixteen songs of *Dichterliebe*. Once again, a summary of the keys involved is the starting point (see Table 11.2). There is clearly no 'central key' here. Neither is there any tonal disjunction as great as the B flat followed by G major that marks the division of the two parts of *Frauenliebe und Leben*. The cohesion of the tonal journey here derives from the fact that whilst no two consecutive songs are in the same key, they are always in fairly close relationship: never more than one sharp or flat's difference between the two key signatures (the only exception is song 13's E flat minor, following the B flat major of song 12; song 14's B major takes the previous key enharmonically as D sharp minor). Despite Arthur Komar's efforts to argue that A major is a 'central' key for the cycle,[6] there is much more sense of a continuous tonal journey. The connection between each song and the next is also frequently reinforced by motivic detail, as will be seen below.

As in *Frauenliebe und Leben*, the tonal architecture of *Dichterliebe* produces an ideological narrative within the cycle. Whilst Schumann set almost all of Adalbert von Chamisso's poems in *Frauenliebe und Leben* (he omits only one, in which the heroine's mother has to explain to her that her strange malady is pregnancy), in *Dichterliebe* he made a careful selection from Heinrich Heine's sixty-six poems in his *Lyrisches Intermezzo*, aiming, as Rufus Hallmark puts it, 'to condense a drama from Heine's wide-ranging anthology of lyrics of frustrated and embittered love'.[7] The drama that results begins promisingly: the first song celebrates the 'wonderfully beautiful month of May', when 'love springs forth', and this finds fulfilment in the second song, when 'blooming flowers' sprout 'from my tears'. All continues well as far as song 4, although here, in a 'reversal' typical of Heine, the long-awaited declaration 'Ich liebe dich' makes the narrator 'weep bitterly'. From this moment the progress is downhill: by song 7 the protagonist is protesting far too much that 'I bear no grudge, even if my heart breaks'; in song 9 the beloved is seen dancing at her marriage to a rival; and a lengthy process of gradual consolation ensues, until in the final song the lover is able to call for an immense coffin in which to consign 'my love and suffering' to the depths of the sea. This overall narrative is complex and subtle, but the point I wish to emphazise here is that it is different in nature from the 'woman's life' of *Frauenliebe und Leben*. The male lover's story develops continuously, each song providing a new event, a new emotional circumstance. There is no central event after which the cycle is structurally closed, and indeed there is a telling contrast between the wedding scenes in the two cycles: although his beloved's marriage is pivotal to *Dichterliebe*, it does not dictate what course the protagonist has to follow thereafter.

To emphasize the nature of this 'man's story', I shall consider the tonal processes of the opening and closing songs of the cycle. The first song is described by Komar as 'justly famous for the ambiguity of its key'.[8] The very first interval heard in the work is striking: a compound major seventh (D natural and C sharp), which turns out to be a suspension of a 6/3 chord of B minor, the D in the bass resolving downwards to C sharp, the root of a dominant seventh chord in bar 2. This suggests F sharp minor as the key, but this key is nowhere properly established: there is no F sharp minor triad anywhere, and although the opening chord progression returns at the end, the song finishes on an unresolved dominant seventh. By contrast, when the voice enters, it is with a firm and unambiguous cadence in A major, recasting the opening B minor triad as chord IIb. Schumann has turned usual processes inside out, so that chromatic uncertainty defines the frame of the song rather than a central section. Not only does this encapsulate the unresolved yearning of the 'longing and desire' of the poetry, but the true main key of the song is confirmed by the opening of song 2, where the dyad C sharp/A natural is heard against a descending bass line that hints at an F sharp minor triad before resolving definitely into A major as the flowers begin to bloom. So the resolution of the ambiguous key in the first song is provided by something outside it altogether. This establishes the constant forward movement of the narrative from each song to the next, and the importance of motivic connections between the songs, which characterize the entire cycle.

No such ambiguity of key marks the close of the cycle. The final postlude is in D flat major, the enharmonic major of the key of the final song, and it is in fact a transposed and slightly altered repeat of the postlude of an earlier song (no. 12). After a cycle in which virtually every pair of songs displays a connection of some kind between the end of one and the beginning of the next, it is revealing to place this

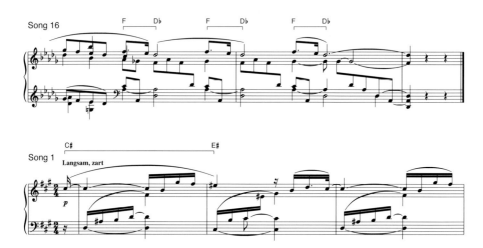

Ex. 11.3. Schumann's *Dichterliebe*, end of song 16 and opening of song 1

D flat major cadence next to the opening of song 1. This is done in Ex. 11.3. The motivic connection is apparent at once: the oscillation of C sharp and E sharp that opens song 1 is reversed as the tonally conclusive descent from F natural to D flat in song 16 (enharmonically the same notes and at the same register). Whilst D flat major is a different key from either of those implied in song 1, the final chord of the whole cycle presents the same note at the top of the texture as the opening chord, and it is (literally) a small step from the D flat in the bass to the D natural of song 1. Indeed, if the opening of the cycle is played again immediately after the end of the last song, the logic is aurally apparent: exactly the same kind of motivic connection as is found between almost all adjacent songs elsewhere in the cycle.

The interpretive point, and the contrast with *Frauenliebe und Leben*, should by now be clear. After the terrifyingly painful loss of his beloved, the protagonist of *Dichterliebe* ends the cycle implying that the whole process could begin again: another wonderfully beautiful month of May might bring better luck. The conceit of the 'cycle' (and *Dichterliebe* was the only one of the song collections of 1840 described as *Liedercyclus* on its title page) means that the wheel has indeed turned full circle, and the beginning can follow logically from the end of the work, as if *ad infinitum*. This is the exact opposite of the 'woman's life and love', where the metaphor of a cycle can mean only final completion at the end, with no prospect of any further event: the life truly ends with the love.

It is mildly ironic, given the usual gendering of interpretations, that the 'man's story' should turn out to be one of openness and possible continuation, whilst the 'woman's story' is about completion and closure. This irony is perhaps sufficient proof that these are both, at a deep level, a man's story. It is part of the richness of Schumann's admittedly patriarchal view that it is the protagonist of *Frauenliebe und Leben* who is able to sing of certainty and fulfilment, whilst the masculinity depicted in *Dichterliebe* is endlessly at the mercy of events: fragile, threatened by extinction in tears and grief. However, ultimately it is the man who can go on, and the woman who is condemned to endless mourning. The contrast in the final states of the two protagonists turns on another aspect of the narratives dear to Schumann — the musical representation of memory.

Mixing Memory with Desire

To return to the postlude to the final song of *Dichterliebe*, it was mentioned above that this is a transposition of the postlude to song 12. That is not the end of the matter, since this postlude is itself reminiscent of earlier events.

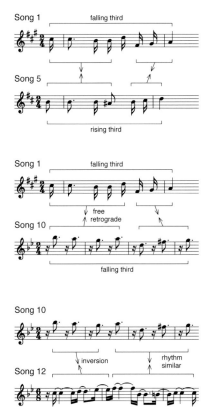

Ex. 11.4. Schumann *Dichterliebe*, connections between songs 1, 5, 10, and 12

A web of motivic connections can be traced that link the melodies of songs 1, 5, 10, 12, and 16. These start with the opening vocal phrase of the first song, and are presented in Ex. 11.4. The connections are subtle, and open to dispute; but they are evident to my ear, and I believe that their rationale becomes clearer through consideration of the texts set to the extracts of the melodies of songs 1, 5, and 10 that are presented in Ex. 11.4.

> Song 1, bars 5–8
> 'Im wunderschönen Monat Mai, als alle Knospen sprangen'
> [In the magically beautiful month of May, when all the buds were bursting]

Song 5, bars 9–12
'Das Lied soll schauern und beben wie der Kuss von ihrem Mund'
[The song shall shiver and tremble like the kiss of her lips]

Song 10, bars 1–8
'Hör' ich das Liedchen klingen, das einst die Liebste sang'
[When I hear the song that my dearest once sang]

Whilst the first line of song 1 is the originatory experience for the cycle, the other two songs relate memories of the beloved after the love affair breaks down. In both cases she is equated with song, in a musical representation of memory. Song 10 is particularly striking as an image of the melody that one cannot quite recall, always slightly off the beat but insistently repeated. The motivic connections, loose as they are, to my mind suggest that 'the song that my dearest once sang' is the melody of that first 'wunderschönen Monat Mai'. This concern with memory is evident too in song 12, set in a garden like song 1, where the flowers speak to and console the unhappy lover.

Dichterliebe, then, turns out to be a narrative concerned with the mastery of experience through its varied recollection in memory. The depiction of human experience is complex and multi-layered throughout the cycle, always mediated through perception. Schumann clearly revelled in the sort of conundrum presented by song 9, in which the hero is standing outside the dance hall where his beloved is dancing with her new husband; the music consists of an accompaniment which must be the dance music itself, but which the hero *cannot hear* (instead, he hears 'the dear angels' who 'sob and groan'). Schumann's representation of memory and the act of remembrance blends with the recurrent imagery of flowers, tears, and song, until the final song can list several features of earlier songs as part of the great funeral procession for the poet's (finally dead) 'love and suffering'.

Memory is also part of the narrative of *Frauenliebe und Leben*, but here the process is not one of mastery of experience through recollection, but rather the equation of the two. The final postlude was described above as a repeat of one strophe's worth of the first song, plus its cadence. But here is no sense that the cycle is beginning all over again, in the manner of the linking of end and beginning in *Dichterliebe*. I said above that the postlude is 'a virtually literal repeat' of the earlier material. The differences may be tiny, but they are far from insignificant. They consist of minuscule alterations to the rhythm of the melody line: two crotchets at the beginning of bar 7 of song 1 become two quavers and a crotchet rest; some other quavers become dotted. The point of these changes is that the piano is adopting some of the expressive gestures of the vocal line in the original song. In other words, the wordless accompanying instrument is attempting to imitate the now mute voice. The cycle is not beginning again; rather, the narrative suggestion seems to be that the experience now exists only in memory, and it is memory that will ceaselessly replay itself behind the descending widow's veil.

Ideology and Experience

It has not been my intention to defend Schumann in the face of attacks like Solie's, or to dissociate him from the patriarchal narrative conventions of his time. The complexity of the narratives of the two song cycles, however, and the place of memory in the experience of grief or suffering, goes some way towards accounting for the enduring popularity of both works. Perhaps the challenge of hearing them performed by the 'wrong' voice, as Schumann clearly could envisage, is a salutary one for modern ears. In the case of *Frauenliebe und Leben*, a male voice foregrounds the status of the work as a fundamentally male view of the ideal wife. In *Dichterliebe*, a female voice emphasizes the distance between the events of the hero's life and the enactment of them within the songs, where the story is mediated through many levels of memory and representation. In both cases there is a distinction between the persona of the narrator, the persona of the protagonist, and the persona of the performer. Recognizing this fact takes us away from the idea of a musical performance as an act of (imagined) self-expression, towards an understanding of music as an image of the complexity of human experience. In making this interpretive move, we leave behind some of the more self-centred aspects of twentieth-century hermeneutics; and the evidence seems to indicate that we regain some of what Schumann and his contemporaries believed about the nature of music's powers.

Notes to Chapter 11

1. This chapter draws in part on material jointly written by the author and David Rowland for an Open University course. I should therefore like to acknowledge my general indebtedness to David Rowland's research. See David Rowland and Robert Samuels, 'Unit 15: Gender Studies II: Schumann Song Cycles and their Singers', in *Motive, Gender and Large-Scale Form, c. 1840–1900*, Studies in Music, 1750–2000: Interpretation and Analysis, 4 (Milton Keynes: Open University, 2001), pp. 1–36.
2. The term 'multi-piece' was coined by Jonathan Dunsby in his chapter 'The Multi-Piece in Brahms: *Fantasien* Op. 116', in *Brahms: Biographical, Documentary and Analytical Studies*, ed. by Robert Pascall (Cambridge: Cambridge University Press, 1983), pp. 163–89.
3. Ruth Solie, 'Whose Life? The Gendered Self in Schumann's *Frauenliebe* Songs', in *Music and Text: Critical Inquiries*, ed. by Stephen Paul Scher (Cambridge: Cambridge University Press, 1992), pp. 219–40 (p. 221).
4. The phrase 'within quotation marks' is one used by Will Crutchfield as a warning to interpreters (cited by Solie, p. 220). Maria Ewing is one singer who has embraced the performer's dilemma as a challenge.
5. The convention that certain songs or song cycles are normally performed by a singer of a particular gender is frequently more revealing of twentieth-century assumptions than those of the composer. An example is Mahler's *Kindertotenlieder* ('Songs on the Death of Children'), much more often today performed by a female singer, although some of the texts are written in the persona of a father, some in that of a mother, whilst some are not gender-specific. Mahler himself conducted performances by both soprano and tenor soloists, expressing some preference for the latter.
6. Arthur Komar (ed.), *Robert Schumann: Dichterliebe* (New York: Norton, 1971), pp. 77–81.
7. Rufus E. Hallmark, *The Genesis of Schumann's Dichterliebe: A Source Study* (Ann Arbor: University of Michigan Press, 1979), p. 115.
8. Komar, p. 66.

PART IV

Narrative Modes

CHAPTER 12

The Concert as a Literary Genre: Berlioz's *Lélio*

Guillaume Bordry

In an article published on 5 October 1835, Berlioz states that the great French poet Alfred de Vigny once called him 'un homme de lettres', a description that Berlioz treats with humour and irony, and rejects as absurd.[1] Yet Vigny was right. Berlioz could definitely be called a man of letters: his literary production is substantial; his concert reviews reveal a very interesting style; and, moreover, Berlioz himself collected these reviews into books, where the same poetics can be seen to underlie both his musical and his literary works.[2] This chapter will explore the nature of these poetics within two important works: the *Symphonie fantastique* of 1830, first called *Épisode de la vie d'un artiste* (op. 18a), and the second part of that symphony, *Le Retour à la vie* (op. 18b), dating from 1832, whose title Berlioz changed to *Lélio* in 1855.[3] Berlioz said of *Le Retour à la vie* that it was his 'first attempt in literature'.[4] Rather than being merely a musical work, it embodies the union of music and literature.

The *Épisode de la vie d'un artiste* and *Le Retour à la vie* are two parts of a single work. More precisely, the *Épisode de la vie d'un artiste* forms the first panel of a diptych, completed by the composition of *Le Retour à la vie*.[5] These two symphonic works have a protagonist in common, the Artist, who dies (or believes he dies) at the end of the first work, and rises again in the second. Nevertheless, many factors have conspired to separate the two parts and to split the unity of the work. Today, the audience remembers only the symphony — under the name *Symphonie fantastique* — and has forgotten *Lélio*; and Berlioz himself wrote in 1855 that it was not necessary to play *Lélio* after the *Symphonie fantastique*.[6] Though very different, these two parts share a most important feature: they are both symphonic works based on a literary text. The *Épisode* has a written libretto — a 'programme' — and *Lélio* is a theatrical work. Both explore the complex links between text and music, between a literary form and a musical one, between a theatrical form and a symphonic one. And beneath these two experiments lurks the influence of opera — Berlioz had not yet completed an opera in 1832.[7]

The composer compares the programme of his *Épisode de la vie d'un artiste* with the 'spoken text of an opera',[8] and says that his symphony belongs to the 'expressive and instrumental genre'.[9] In *Le Retour à la vie* he combines poetic and theatrical texts with a variety of musical forms, and calls the result a 'mélologue'.[10] But if Berlioz subsumes his two works under two different genres, an expressive symphony and a mélologue, how may their union be described? What kind of genre might include the two works?

Throughout his musical œuvre Berlioz seems to be obsessed by the idea of a sort of semi-opera, an imaginary opera, and he explores and creates unexpected forms of musical drama. This obsession can be seen in other works, such as *Roméo et Juliette*, *L'Enfance du Christ*, and *La Damnation de Faust*. As with the 'dramatic legend' of *La Damnation de Faust* and the 'dramatic symphony'[11] of *Roméo et Juliette*, the union of the *Épisode de la vie d'un artiste* and *Le Retour à la vie* results in the creation of a new genre conceived by Berlioz. I would call this form, which already existed but was not consciously and dramatically arranged, the 'concert form'.

Both the *Épisode de la vie d'un artiste* and the *Retour à la vie* are built on a text, the most obvious function of which is to ensure, through the words, the coherence of each part, and to link their various sections. At first the *Épisode de la vie d'un artiste* was presented to the audience with its 'programme' (libretto). We could even say *after* its programme, since this was published in newspapers the day before the concert. Here, written language is being used to explain music. This fact was clearly understood by the journalist of *Le Figaro*, who wrote on 6 December 1830: 'This is the first time somebody has tried to give a precise direction to an instrumental piece of music'. The opposition between a 'precise' direction, a precise language (the language of the text), and a vaguer musical language had already been postulated in the eighteenth century by the Abbé Dubos, the Abbé Batteux, and, of course, Jean-Jacques Rousseau.[12] The words of the programme were intended to prepare the feelings of the listener and to guide, to frame his imagination. Whilst the *Épisode de la vie d'un artiste* is based on a standard symphonic framework — the first movement is divided into two parts, a slow introduction followed by a symphonic Allegro — this musical structure is coupled with a narrative structure. For a French audience of 1830 the story of an artist unfortunately obsessed by the *idée fixe* of a woman was perhaps easier to conceive than a purely musical structure.[13]

Similarly, two years later, a text provided the link between the symphony and its continuation. The textual introduction to *Le Retour à la vie* looks like a long transition, resuming the narration where Berlioz had left it. The character of the Artist, who now speaks in this second part, is no longer described by an anonymous narrator. He starts with a verbal paraphrase of the *Songe d'une nuit de Sabbat*, which was the last movement of the symphony. This rather artificial preliminary speech confirms that the two works are two parts of a whole. The new episode in the musical proceedings reveals a coherent and crafted construction, which in the initial symphony had remained latent.

Berlioz's text seems to be a kind of didactic artifice. In the *Épisode de la vie d'un artiste* the programme supports and sustains the attention of the audience. Berlioz compares it to 'the spoken text of an opera', since opera is a more familiar genre to an audience than is the symphony. In *Le Retour à la vie* Berlioz writes continuous spoken transitions — monologues — to explain clearly and justify the meaning of each musical number. This didactic function of words is called 'Lesueurisme' by Jacques Barzun,[14] who maintains that Berlioz is following the rules of Jean-François Lesueur, the composer's teacher at the Paris Conservatoire and a man known to be highly suspicious of instrumental music; the use of a literary text can be put down to 'Berlioz the student'. Afterwards, 'Berlioz the composer' will gradually be emancipated from the idea of a verbally constructed music. Surprisingly enough, *Le Retour à la vie* does not confirm a progression towards 'absolute music'.[15]

Music in *Le Retour à la vie*, instead of gaining independence from the text, leaves more room for it. The programme of the *Épisode de la vie d'un artiste* was simply conceived as a guide: it was a written document, and also a silent one. In the mélologue Berlioz chooses to employ a spoken text whose words and meaning clearly cannot be ignored by the audience. Purely instrumental music plays a restricted role here: *La Harpe éolienne — Souvenirs* is, in fact, the only instrumental number, and the shortest part of the work. The text between the numbers is longer than the short explanations of the symphony, as if the musical basis of the work were not self-sufficient. It seems impossible, therefore, to perform *Le Retour à la vie* without the monologues, since the speech provides justification for the musical numbers. Moreover, the words of the Artist do not function simply as narrative support: though connecting or distinguishing the musical numbers, the various monologues also take on a semantic content of their own. The Artist praises his favourite authors, especially Shakespeare and Goethe, but Beethoven is also mentioned in the first version.[16] A number of literary references that are already evident in the symphony's libretto, even if they are not always explicit (Chateaubriand and Hugo, for instance), are now clarified;[17] and many characters, such as Hamlet or Ossian, are convened here as doubles and models for the Artist.

Spoken language, as it gains autonomous sense and function, ventures into the territory of music; instead of simply specifying the subject and guiding the attention of the audience, it reveals the feelings and emotions of the protagonist. In a letter to his friend Humbert Ferrand, Berlioz describes his symphony as a 'novel, the hero of which is not hard to recognize'.[18] The autobiographical and even autographic genre, both literary and musical, is clearer and more explicit in the new work. Although the programme of the *Épisode de la vie d'un artiste* has been clearly and gradually dismantled (only the titles of the movements remain, and the complete programme is no longer given in many performances), *Le Retour à la vie* retains to this day all its verbal support. According to Berlioz himself, the programme must still be given to the audience when an orchestra plays both the symphony and *Le Retour à la vie*.[19] The unity of these two works remains, in spite of an autonomous *Symphonie fantastique*, which has become a 'symphony without programme'.

Let us reconsider the genre of *Le Retour à la vie* itself. Rather than regarding *Lélio* as a failure, a superfluous production, one can instead try to reconstitute what associates it logically with the *Épisode de la vie d'un artiste*. Berlioz is haunted by the dream of a complex creation, in which the poet and the musician, the critic and the dramatist, and also the conductor could share their ideas and their aspirations. As I mentioned above, Berlioz called *Le Retour à la vie* his 'first attempt in literature'.[20] The greater role of the words is not a regression, however, but an innovation. After the instrumental genre Berlioz now creates the 'expressive musical poem', and for this literary attempt he uses very different kinds of writing: lyrical poetry, popular song, critical text, and even, in the 'Chant de bonheur', rhythmic prose ('prose cadencée').[21] He also exploits every possible link between text and music, such as succession, overlapping, and interpolation; and he explores many different musical forms with his chosen resources: numbers, for example, for tenor and piano, for soloist, choir, and orchestra, and for instruments alone.[22] This catalogue of spoken and musical forms gives birth to a new genre, the 'mélologue', the inspiration for which Berlioz discovered in Thomas Moore's poetry, and which is not so far from Rousseau's melodrama (Berlioz later called *Le Retour à la vie* a 'monodrame lyrique'). The mélologue is a musical and a literary genre, but also a dramatic form. Despite its theatrical and musical form, it is not an opera, but a hybrid genre that seems only to exist in its association with *the Épisode de la vie d'un artiste*. Berlioz dramatizes a pre-existent musical practice: he turns the concert into a theatrical form. In a letter to his friend Gounet, Berlioz states specifically that he created *Le Retour à la vie* as a complement to the *Épisode de la vie d'un artiste*: 'I have completed a mélologue to accompany the *Épisode de la vie d'un artiste*; it will be played after the symphony and that will complete a concert'.[23]

The concerts that Berlioz reviewed each week all had similarly conceived programmes: an incoherent mixture of solo, orchestral, and choral pieces, among which a symphony was often the most significant item; the other pieces were varied and shorter.[24] After the *Épisode de la vie d'un artiste*, *Le Retour à la vie* resembles all these other pieces commonly found in an 1830 concert, here gathered together in a single work. Reviewing a Wagner concert in Paris,[25] Berlioz regretted that every piece of music was symphonic; there were neither songs nor choir, and no variety or difference between the genres — elements that seemed to him to be absolutely necessary for a concert audience. Berlioz creates a way to mix genres, to vary the forms and the instrumental structures. The logic of his work is unquestionably that of the concert; yet he adds an essential element to this pre-existent machinery. He thinks of the concert as a theatrical genre, and uses the juxtaposition of the various parts as a dramatic engine, which the text and the presence of a protagonist unify and clarify. Spoken language, in fact, will provide a justifiable rationale and coherence to such a concert, whose stucture would otherwise be largely random. Berlioz creates here a 'concert with programme'. The *Épisode de la vie d'un artiste* kept the musical structure of a symphony, but a text made it comprehensible and relevant; similarly, *Le Retour à la vie* preserves the musical form of the concert, but the presence of the Artist's monologue makes it understandable and coherent. It is a kind of ideal concert, which is played in the mind of the Artist and brought to the stage, just as the *Scenes of Faust*, Berlioz's imaginary opera, could be played a few years earlier in the mind of the composer.

The *Épisode de la vie d'un artiste* belongs to the 'expressive instrumental genre' that Berlioz had himself developed and theorized. *Le Retour à la vie* is a mélologue, a hapax, a singular mixture of text and music. As two parts of a single work, they can be considered as a concert form, a coherently organized sequence of various musical pieces that retains the contemporary customs and rules of the concert, while justifying and dramatizing them. In 1855 the published libretto described *Lélio* as a 'weak sketch';[26] perhaps Berlioz deemed it a mere sketch in comparison with the ideal opera that he aspired to write, an ideal towards which he so often, as in *Lélio*, makes an indirect approach.

Notes to Chapter 12

I should like to thank Robert Samuels, Sophie Vasset, and Véronique Magista for their comments on the text of this chapter.

1. Hector Berlioz, 'Le Rénovateur', *La Revue musicale*, 5 October 1835; repr. in *La Critique musicale, 1823–1863*, ed. by H. Robert Cohen and Yves Gérard (Paris: Buchet-Chastel, 1996–), II: *1835–1836* (1998), p. 305.
2. Berlioz's own published books are: *Les Soirées de l'orchestre* (1852), *Les Grotesques de la musique* (1859), *À travers chants* (1862), and the (posthumous) *Mémoires* (1870).
3. After the character of that name in George Sand's *La Marquise*.
4. 14 June 1831: Hector Berlioz, *Correspondance générale*, ed. by Pierre Citron, 8 vols (Paris: Flammarion, 1972–2003), I (1972), p. 429.
5. Compare the complete programme notes for these works in the New Berlioz Edition: Hector Berlioz, *Symphonie fantastique*, ed. by Nicholas Temperley, New Berlioz Edition, 16 (Kassel and London: Bärenreiter, 1972); and *Lélio, ou Le Retour à la vie*, ed. by Peter Bloom, New Berlioz Edition, 7 (Kassel and London: Bärenreiter, 1992).
6. Hector Berlioz, *Symphonie fantastique* (Paris: Schlesinger, 1855).
7. His first opera was *Benvenuto Cellini* of 1838.
8. 'Le texte parlé d'un opéra': Berlioz, *Episode de la vie d'un artiste* (livret de 1830), repr. in *Symphonie fantastique*, ed. by Nicholas Temperley (Kassel: Bärenreiter, 1972), p. 170.
9. This genre appears in Berlioz's article 'Aperçu sur la musique classique et la musique romantique', *Le Correspondant*, 22 October 1830 (two weeks before the first performance of his symphony).
10. Berlioz will replace this term, inspired by Thomas Moore, with the more usual 'monodrame' after 1855. Cf. the footnote written by Pierre Citron in his edition of the *Mémoires* (Paris: Flammarion, 1991), p. 243.
11. The terms 'mélologue', 'légende dramatique', and 'symphonie dramatique' are placed on the cover of the respective scores.
12. Jean-Baptiste Dubos, *Réflexions critiques sur la poésie et sur la peinture* (Paris: Mariette, 1719); Charles Batteux, *Les Beaux-Arts réduits à un même principe* (Paris: Durand, 1746); Jean-Jacques Rousseau, *Essai sur l'origine des langues* (1781) (Bordeaux: Ducros, 1968).
13. On the importance of a the narrative frame see Jean-Pierre Bartoli, 'Symphonie fantastique', in *Dictionnaire Berlioz*, ed. by Pierre Citron and Cécile Reynaud (Paris: Fayard, 2003), pp. 537–41.
14. Jacques Barzun, *Berlioz and the Romantic Century* (New York: Columbia University Press, 1950), pp. 144–56.
15. Barzun, p. 181.
16. Hector Berlioz, *Le Retour à la vie. Mélologue, faisant suite à la Symphonie fantastique* (Paris, Schlesinger, 1832), p. 12.
17. Nicholas Temperley, 'Avant-propos. Sources littéraires et autobiographiques', in *Symphonie fantastique*, ed. by Temperley (New Berlioz Edition), p. xix.
18. Berlioz to Ferrand, 16 April 1830: *Correspondance générale*, I, 318.
19. Berlioz, Symphonie fantastique (1855), p. i.
20. Letter to Thomas Gounet, 14 June 1831: *Correspondance générale*, I, 429.
21. Berlioz, *Le Retour à la vie*, IV: 'Chant de bonheur' (1832), p. 16.
22. Tenor and piano: 'Ballade' (I); soloist, choir, and orchestra: 'Scène de la vie de Brigand' (IV); instrumental piece: 'Les Derniers Soupirs de la harpe — Souvenirs' (V).
23. Letter to Thomas Gounet, 14 June 1831: *Correspondance générale*, I, 429.
24. There are many examples of such concerts in Berlioz's reviews. For example, the first concert for 1833 of the Société des concerts du Conservatoire: Weber, Overture; Cherubini, Credo; Ries, *La Fiancée du brigand*; Reicha, Quintet; Weber, *Der Freichütz* (Agathe's monologue); Beethoven, Pastoral Symphony (*La Revue européenne*, 1833; repr. in *La Critique musicale*, I: 1823–1834 (1996), p. 85).
25. Hector Berlioz, 'Concerts de Richard Wagner, la musique de l'avenir', in *À travers chants* (1862) (Paris: Calmann-Lévy, 1927), p. 304.
26. Hector Berlioz, *Lélio ou le Retour à la vie* (Paris: Schlesinger, 1855), p. i.

CHAPTER 13

Literature as *Déjà vu?* The Third Movement of Gustav Mahler's First Symphony

Federico Celestini

Several of Gustav Mahler's contemporary critics accused him of a lack of originality, claiming him to be a 'Kapellmeister' composer, namely one who recycled pre-existent music instead of inventing and producing new works. Nowadays it is evident that Mahler's music demonstrated a new kind of creativity, where originality no longer lay in the novelty of thematic invention and in the development of the musical material, but in the expressive force emanating from the combination of music of differing styles and genres. This plurality of stylistic voices characterizes the Mahler symphonies, particularly as compared with works from an earlier symphonic tradition exclusively devoted to a sublime style, and it determines Mahler's very individual conception of polyphony, now no longer a moment of erudition, seriousness, and homage to tradition, but a powerful means of bringing together heterogeneous and disparate elements.

Numerous passages from Mahler's symphonies could be mentioned in this respect, but perhaps the most impressive example is to be found in the third movement of the First Symphony, where, at the beginning of the reprise, the famous canon *Frère Jacques*, a Bohemian melody, and self-quotation from the fourth of the *Lieder eines fahrenden Gesellen* are combined in an astonishing montage. Peter Ruzicka regards this movement as the first example of the split between the 'eigentliche' and 'uneigentliche' music in Mahler, that is, between music considered to be an authentic expression of original compositional subjectivity, and music that has been found and used by the composer.[1] The first kind of music represents the ideal of absolutely original and sublime music that the majority of the nineteenth-century public shared; the second kind, which already had a long tradition in lesser genres such as parody, pastiche, the grotesque, and satire, did not appear in the elevated genre of the symphony until Berlioz, followed many years later by Mahler, each time scandalizing public and critics alike. According to Ruzicka, 'uneigentliche' music breaks down the insularity of an autonomous invention, opening up a work to the world outside and activating its network of references, associations, and allusions.[2] Mahler's music becomes a world of its own — not an imitation of the real one — where sounds, pictures, and words are reminders of each other in a temporal structure in which fragments of the past, impressions of the present, and images of the future are merged through the narrative flow of the music.[3] This openness of music to extramusical references is a familiar characteristic of Mahler's works, and in so far as his symphonies are concerned, such references and the ways in which they are incorporated raise an aesthetic question. The aim of this chapter is to show that in the third movement of Mahler's First Symphony — that is, in the *Todtenmarsch in Callots Manier* — music and literature are interconnected in a manner that abolishes the traditional division between programme music and absolute music, establishing a new relationship between autonomy and heteronomy. A comparison with Hector Berlioz's *Symphonie fantastique*, the work that marks the origin of programme music, will show that there is a fundamental and far-reaching aesthetic difference between the works despite their many compositional similarities.

Berlioz and Mahler: Compositional Similarities and Aesthetic Differences

Throughout his life Gustav Mahler showed great interest in the music of Hector Berlioz. As a conductor he often included the *Symphonie fantastique* in concert programmes, as, for instance, in his first season with the Vienna Philharmonic Orchestra in 1898. It is not surprising, therefore, that numerous technical elements are common to both the *Songe d'une nuit du Sabbat*, the fifth and last movement of Berlioz' *Symphonie fantastique*, and the third movement of Mahler's First Symphony. Above all, it is worth noting the daring inclusion of a grotesque movement within the framework of a symphony. This was absolutely unheard of until the *Symphonie fantastique* was premiered in 1830, and was not attempted again until Mahler composed his First Symphony. However, the similarities extend far beyond this, from fundamental elements in the conception of both movements to the many compositional methods used in bringing these to fruition.

The foundation for the grotesque effect of both movements is the humorous distortion of a funeral: Mahler's parody of a funeral march corresponds to what Berlioz, in his 1830 programme for the *Symphonie fantastique*, terms a 'parodie burlesque du Dies Irae'.[4] Furthermore, a trivial trait is common to both, through Mahler's use of Bohemian-coloured street music[5] and Berlioz' distortion of the 'ideé fixe',[6] which he also addresses in the programme for his symphony. Several unusual instrumental effects occur in both movements, adding to the trivial flavour; for instance, the use of the E flat clarinet, which had originated in military music, and the *col legno* and broad *glissando* effects in the strings. Finally, as already mentioned, in the last section of his movement Mahler chose a procedure of polyphonic montage in which fragments of the *Frère Jacques* canon are heard simultaneously with the Bohemian melodies presented in the second section as well as self-quotations from the fourth song of the *Lieder eines fahrenden Gesellen*.[7] Berlioz used a similar device by juxtaposing the *Dies irae* and the *Ronde du Sabbat* melodies.[8]

Unusually for a symphony, Berlioz' *Symphonie fantastique* has five movements, corresponding to the five acts of a French *grand opéra*. In addition, several characteristics of the opera orchestra, for example bells and multiple timpani, were appropriated for the instrumentation.[9] Berlioz himself speaks of an instrumental drama and compares the programme to the 'spoken text of an opera'.[10] Wolfgang Dömling stressed that

FIG. 13.1. Moritz von Schwind, 1804–71 (Austrian),
Wie die Tiere den Jäger begraben. Woodcut, from *Münchner Bilderbogen* (1850)

FIG. 13.2. Jacques Callot, *c.* 1592–1635 (French), *Razullo e Cucuruccu*
Etching from *Balli di Sfessania* (1621)

the imagination of a scenic process is of great importance here.[11] Knowledge of the programmatic content helps the listener to understand the new developments that challenge his sense of musical logic, and enables him to conjure up an imaginary scene in his mind. Musical discontinuity, therefore, no longer hinders the comprehension of a movement; rather, it is an essential element in the convincing dramatic representation of the *Dream from a Sabbath Night*, for which no typical sonata form would be adequate.

The main difference between the finale of Berlioz's *Symphonie fantastique* and the third movement of Mahler's First Symphony is that Berlioz represents an imaginary scene in his music. The notes that Mahler prepared for the printed concert programme for the second performance of the symphony (Hamburg 1893) make no reference to a scenic event and provide no 'programme' as such. Rather, Mahler presents a discussion justifying the origins of the movement, explaining his 'external stimulation' as well as giving a clarification of the moods evoked to avoid any possible misunderstanding:

> The following may serve as an explanation for this movement: the author received an overt suggestion for it from *Des Jäger Leichenbegängnis* (*The Hunter's Funeral Procession*), a parodistic picture that is well-known to all Austrian children and is taken from an old book of children's fairy tales. The animals of the forest escort the coffin of a deceased hunter to the grave site. Rabbits carrying a banner follow a band of Bohemian musicians accompanied by music-making cats, toads, crows, and so on; stags, does, foxes, and other four-legged and feathered animals of the forest follow the procession in amusing poses. At that point the piece in some ways expresses an ironic, humorous mood and in other ways expresses an eerie, brooding mood, followed immediately by V. *Dall'inferno* (Allegro furioso) — as the sudden outburst of despair from a deeply wounded heart.[12]

Most commentators interpret this as a description of the woodcut *Wie die Thiere den Jäger begraben* by Moritz von Schwind, published in the *Münchener Bilderbogen* in 1850 (see Fig. 13.1).[13] However, the significance of the children's picture, the only element suggesting a possible scenic course of events in the movement, is played down by Mahler himself in a letter to the music critic Max Marschalk:

> As regards the third movement ('Marcia funebre'), I must admit that my inspiration came from the well-known nursery-picture (The Burial of the Huntsman). — But at this point in the work it is irrelevant — what matters is only the *mood* that has to be expressed [...] It is simply the outcry of a heart deeply wounded, a cry preceded by the uncannily and ironically brooding sultriness of the funeral march. 'Ironic' in the sense of the Aristotelian *eironeia*.[14]

Initially, the absence of a dramatic scene — even if only imaginary — to be portrayed in music resulted in the piece's unfavourable reception. For years the public lacked a sense of orientation towards the third movement of the First Symphony.[15] By contrast, although the earliest critics of the *Symphonie fantastique* were divided over the aesthetic question of such an instrumental drama as well as over its anti-classical forms and content, there were no problems of comprehension, as the imaginary plot was easily understandable on the basis of the given programme. The *Songe d'une nuit du Sabbat* is set in the abstract sphere of the fanciful. The narrative fiction of the opium delirium in the *Symphonie fantastique*'s programme allows the creation of a fantasy world of monsters through the elimination of reason. Late eighteenth-century painting had already contributed a number of famous examples of this, among them Heinrich Füssli's *Nightmare* and Francisco de Goya's *The Sleep of Reason Creates Monsters*. Mahler, however, conjures up no such fantasy world. He perceives reality as grotesque. However, this 'reality' is itself internalized through the memory, and is thus no longer objective. In the music of Mahler the subjective internal and objective external worlds meet through the memory. Here literature also plays an important role.

Structure and Function of References

The third movement of Mahler's First Symphony consists of three main sections: the *Frère Jacques* canon (bars 1–38); the 'Bohemian marching band' (bars 39–60), in which Bohemian folk tunes may be recognized; and the 'Lindenbaum episode' (bars 83–112), which acts as a trio and quotes the last strophe melody from the final song of the *Lieder eines fahrenden Gesellen* — 'Auf der Straße stand ein Lindenbaum, da hab' ich zum ersten Mal im Schlaf geruht! Unter dem Lindenbaum!'.[16] A markedly altered reprise of the first two sections closes the movement. Even if one were to attempt to find a 'programme' within the movement, the sequence of these sections is unsuitable for the musical representation of a dramatic scene. In particular, the Lindenbaum episode is dramatically incompatible with the preceding sections; Hans Heinrich Eggebrecht sees this episode as a representation of the 'Other'.[17] Constantin Floros establishes the semantics of 'tranquility' and of 'forgetfulness' through his consideration of the verse lines of the quoted poem.[18] Paul Bekker speaks of a 'symbol of liberation from pain through the dream'.[19]

In a letter to Josef Steiner in 1879 the young Mahler wrote of climbing a linden tree with a heavy heart, but then, at last, finding peace:

> But in the evening when I go out on to the heath and climb a lime tree that stands there all lonely, and when from the topmost branches of this friend of mine I see far out into the world: before my eyes the Danube winds her ancient way, her waves flickering with the glow of the setting sun; from the village behind me the chime of the eventide bells is wafted to me on a kindly breeze, and the branches sway in the wind, rocking me into a slumber like the daughters of the elfin king, and the leaves and blossoms of my favourite tree tenderly caress my cheeks. — Stillness everywhere! Most holy stillness![20]

This extract portrays the dissolution of the self into an idyllic world, whereby the linden tree, which Mahler describes as his favourite, appears to be the epicentre of this experience. The linden tree as a *locus amoenus*, as an idyllic place of forgetting and dreaminess, was a popular symbol in the literature of the German Romantic period. One is reminded of Wilhelm Müller's 'Lindenbaum', set by Franz Schubert in his *Winterreise*: 'Am Brunnen vor dem Tore da steht ein Lindenbaum; ich träumt in seinem Schatten so manchen süßen Traum'.[21] With his reference to the widely accepted symbol of the linden tree as an idyllic place, Mahler transforms the private experience reported in his letter into a universal one. Here literature serves as a symbolic order in which the subjective experience is integrated.

Ex. 13.1 Gustav Mahler, First Symphony, third movement, bars 80–86

The instruction 'very simple and straightforward like a folk tune'[22] is given in the score at the beginning of the Lindenbaum episode (see Ex. 13.1). This is, however, by no means a direct reference to the folk tradition in the sense of being a realistic imitation or quotation of folk music. Instead, as Mahler's choice of a self-quotation suggests, this sphere is evoked indirectly. There are clear indications to support this in Mahler's refined instrumentation, which produces a differentiated and constantly changing sound. Muted violins, first divided into three groups, then into four, are joined by two further unmuted solo violins. Cellos, flutes, and clarinets are also divided into groups. Chromatic figures like those in the first solo violin and in the oboe (bars 97–100) also demonstrate clearly that this is a retrospectively constructed impression of the folk tradition. The Lindenbaum episode does not represent a rural scene, but a psychological state in which consciousness of the self is dissolved ecstatically. The folk tradition is the medium through which this state is conveyed, rather than the subject itself. The idyllic state of painlessness and of forgetting is evoked through the suggestion of a folk atmosphere. Evidently, the Lindenbaum episode embodies a resonance of the utopian state, in which nature and culture, rather than contrasting, join in unclouded harmony, endowing mankind with happiness.

This episode is not connected with the preceding sections by way of logical, factual procedure, but through the principle of psychological association. The triviality and nastiness of the first section is followed by the escape into an idyllic 'other state'. In his analysis of the 'utopia of the moment' in modern literature, Karl Heinz Bohrer stresses the 'interdependence between idyll and satire, happiness and aggression'.[23] This observation applies astonishingly well to the third movement of Mahler's First Symphony, to the scherzos of the Second and Third Symphonies, as well as to the three middle movements of the Seventh Symphony. In the respective idyllic episodes Mahler gives musical shape to the German Romantic version of the literary *locus amoenus*, whose symbolic inventory is transformed into music: distant horn-calls in the forest, pure folk tunes, peace under the linden tree, evening walks, songs with lute and harp, the post-horn call, and so on. The reference to Arcadian felicity indicates a regression to the heavenly states of childhood and nature, in which the I and the World melt together in the oblivion of the Self.

A detailed consideration of the first two sections of the movement (the *Frère Jacques* canon and the Bohemian marching band) reveals that, while these sections are seemingly closer to describing a course of events than the Lindenbaum episode, a dramatic background is similarly lacking in each case. The *Frère Jacques* canon is introduced by the interval of a fourth in the timpani, repeated unchanged throughout the whole section (see Ex. 13.2). The heavy step of the funeral march is easily recognizable in this figure. But this pacing leads nowhere: the harmony remains absolutely static, a play around the D minor chord. This oppressive immobility becomes an obsession through the repeated entries of voices in every bar. Mahler's carefully considered instrumentation also contributes significantly to the stifling nature of the atmosphere, which is indeed disturbed by the 'spiky oboe melody' (bars 19–23, repeated in bars 29–33),[24] but not completely dissolved. The oboe melody is itself a rhythmic elaboration of the repeated interval of a fourth, A–D. The Bohemian band begins its scurrilous melody only after the canon has gradually faded away.

Ex. 13.2 Gustav Mahler, First Symphony, third movement, bars 1–23

Again, no dramatic event is portrayed — there is no 'intrusion' by a band, but a short 'dissolution' of six bars (33–38), which produces an aura of unreality. This fade-out leaves the listener somewhat puzzled: there is neither a satisfactory bridge to a new section, nor a sudden interruption of new material. Hence the relationship between the sections is neither realistically dramatic, nor is it associative as in the case of the Lindenbaum episode. We sense the echo of a genuine succession of events, yet in the psychological state of memory rather than in actuality or in a dreamworld. The mesmerizing oscillation between tonic and dominant in the canon, as regular as clockwork, is taken over by the Bohemian band and continued through into the Lindenbaum episode in the harp. Despite the pendulum-like regularity of this figure, the time flux here is not a linear one in a physical sense, but one as experienced in the consciousness, an 'internalized' time as described by Mahler's contemporary, the French philosopher Henri Bergson,[25] in which a succession of events may be perceived simultaneously, as in the reprise section already mentioned .

Literary References

A surprising range of artistic influences is apparent in the third movement of the First Symphony. Even the title, *Todtenmarsch in Callots Manier*, chosen by Mahler for the symphony's second performance in Hamburg, implies sound, word, and picture. He refers to the literary *Phantasiestücke in Callots Manier* published by E. T. A. Hoffmann in 1814, which themselves adopt the aesthetic of the grotesque paintings of the baroque artist Jacques Callot (see fig. 13.2). Ferdinand Pfohl, who had known Mahler since 1887 and met him often in Hamburg,[26] claimed in his memoirs to have given Mahler the idea of using a play on Hoffmann's book as the title for the funeral march. Mahler was initially hesitant, as he did not have a copy of the *Phantasiestücke*, but took up this suggestion after reading the book.[27] According to Pfohl, Mahler found points of contact between Hoffmann's work and his own movement retrospectively, rediscovering the atmosphere of his funeral march in the literary piece.

In a short foreword to his *Phantasiestücke* Hoffmann writes:

> The irony which sets the human in conflict with the animal and ridicules man with all his shabby actions and activities, exists solely in a great mind. In this manner, Callot's grotesque beings, comprising animal and human, reveal all the secret intimations hidden under the veil of absurdity to the deeply penetrating observer.[28]

The content of this section of Hoffmann's foreword reflects that of Mahler's own writings. In the letter to Marschalk quoted above, Mahler speaks of irony 'in the sense of Aristotelian *eironeia*', meaning pretence, mischief, or feigned innocence, that is, to think something else to that which one expresses openly.[29] In this case the pretence resides in the ironic representation of animals to mock human beings. Furthermore, the elite character of this irony, to which Hoffmann ascribes a 'great mind', is also asserted by Mahler, though mostly in the form of complaint: 'precisely the humour is understood the very least': he told Natalie Bauer-Lechner in relation to the fifth movement of the Third Symphony.[30] Mahler misses the 'deeply penetrating observer' referred to by Hoffmann. Only he can understand the 'secret intimations hidden under the veil of absurdity'. In the end, the 'grotesque beings, comprising animal and human' admired by Hoffmann in Callot's pictures, as well as the animals 'in amusing poses' in Mahler's children's picture, serve to mock 'man with all his shabby actions and activities'. It is important, however, to stress that this allusion to Hoffmann's *Phantasiestücke* is not intended to provide a programme for Mahler's piece, but acknowledges an aesthetic relationship based on grotesque distortion and scurrilous irony.

It is well known that Mahler's First Symphony was given the title 'Titan', named after Jean Paul's novel, for its Hamburg performance, as well as for the following performance in Weimar in 1894. But Natalie Bauer-Lechner, who was in close contact with Mahler in the 1890s, warned against taking Jean Paul's book as the 'programme' for the symphony. Mahler, she said, had 'a powerfully heroic individual, his life and suffering, struggles and defeat at the hands of fate' in mind.[31] Bruno Walter also considers that this title demonstrates Mahler's love for the work of Jean Paul rather than providing particular programmatic information. Walter recalls frequent conversations with Mahler about this novel and Mahler's identification with the 'wild humour' of the character Schoppe.[32] In chapters 46 and 47 of the novel, Schoppe's 'wild humour' is directed at the 'parade funeral' of a prince and the hypocrisy of those present. Schoppe turns to Sara, a doctor's wife who wishes to observe the funeral festivities from his window, and asks her sarcastically:

> 'Do you, also, take as much interest as I in the universal joy of the land, and the long-desired court-mourning? Your eyes indicate something like it, Mrs. Provincial Physician'. 'What interest do you mean?' said the medical lady, struck quite stupid. 'In the pleasure of the courtiers, who, in general, are distinguished from monkeys, as the orang-outangs are, by the fact that they seldom make leaps of joy; at least, like young performers on the piano-forte, they drum away, without the smallest emotion, their most mournful and their merriest pieces one after the other.'[33]

After a long tirade by Schoppe about the meaning of the mourning colours in different countries, in which this same sharp irony is maintained, the narrator takes over and comments:

> Schoppe generally began with *comic* humour, and ended with *tragic*; so also now did the empty mourning-chest, the crape of the horses, their emblazoned caparisons, the Prince's contempt of the heavy German Ceremonial; in short, the whole heartless mummery, lead him up to an eminence, to which the contemplation of a multitude of men at once always impelled him, and where, with an exaltation, indignation, and laughing bitterness hard to describe, he looked down upon the eternal, tyrannical, belittling, objectless and joyless, bewildered and oppressed frenzy of mankind, and his own too.[34]

The narrator stresses the hypocrisy of the participants once more, before Schoppe expresses his outrage at their false emotion unmistakably: 'What a masquerade for the sake of a mask! Rag and tag for a piece of rag-paper! Throw a man quietly into his hole, and call nobody to see'.[35] This theme converges with that of the children's picture discussed, and it may be assumed that this section of Jean Paul's novel also played an indirect role in the composition of Mahler's funeral march. In the letter to

Josef Steiner quoted above, the young Mahler writes of his disgust at the 'modern hypocrisy and mendacity'.[36] This is also the prevailing mood that shapes Schoppe's reaction to the 'parade funeral' of the prince, where his infuriation towards the 'belittling... frenzy of mankind' reminds us strongly of Mahler. Above all, it is the sudden transformation of Schoppe's 'comic humour' to 'tragic humour' that reminds us of Mahler's programme notes, where the movement is described as expressing 'an ironic, humorous mood and in other ways an eerie, brooding mood'. Another obvious similarity is the manner in which the nobility, described by Schoppe as 'orang-outangs', 'drum away, without the smallest emotion, their most mournful and their merriest pieces one after the other', just as the parodied funeral march and trivial street music alternate in the third movement of Mahler's First Symphony.

This proximity of tragic and trivial was the subject of a psychoanalytical conversation between Mahler and Sigmund Freud in Leyden in the summer of 1910. Freud himself reports:

> Mahler's father treated his wife very badly, and when Mahler was still a small boy an especially embarassing scene had taken place between them. It became unbearable for the little one, and he ran away from home. But just at that moment the well-known Viennese song *Ach Du lieber Augustin* rang out from a hurdy-gurdy. Mahler thought that from this moment on, deep tragedy and superficial entertainment were tied together indissolubly in his soul and that one mood was inevitably tied to the other.[37]

Natalie Bauer-Lechner's assertion that Mahler's first childhood composition was a Polka, 'for which he wrote a funeral march as introduction',[38] is difficult to prove one way or the other, but may well demonstrate a connection with this incident. In any case, it is important to note how deeply the insoluble combination of tragedy and triviality is rooted in Mahler's consciousness. This motif proves to be of central concern to Mahler in the composition of the movement, as well as being the common denominator to which all musical and extramusical references may be traced. The interweaving of tragic and trivial forms the connection between childhood experiences, literary and pictorial suggestions, and compositional activity. Literary and pictorial sources are involved in Mahler's compositional process on the basis of their reference to particular tragic–trivial experiences, as a kind of *déjà-vu*.

Conclusions

With Mahler, the psychological dimension does not remain hidden in the intimate folds of the compositional process, but emerges recognizably in the music. However, attempts to 'psychologize' Mahler's music are also inappropriate. To regard music as a 'symptom' of a composer's psychological profile is certainly legitimate, but would lead an analysis beyond the bounds of aesthetic relevance. A more appropriate approach is to consider the third movement of the First Symphony as a musical text. According to Raymond Monelle,

> one thing is certain: the text, whether literary or musical, is profoundly abstract. It is not the score, not a performance, not an intention. It is also — and this is vitally important — not the *work*. The musical work is something somebody has made; it

is *poiesis*, Nattiez might say. It is perfectly legitimate, therefore, in connection with the work, to enquire about the composer's intentions, her history, her psychology, her limitations. Such enquiries have little bearing on the musical text, though they are related to some part of the text. But the text does not merely occupy a space defined by the composer's work. Its space is chiefly defined by certain other factors: in particular, by the universe of texts, which is to say, by *intertextuality*.[39]

In this case, those details of Mahler's personal life intimated in the music should be considered only as intertextual links of a similar kind to the pictorial or literary references discussed. As Monelle observes, from this perspective 'the author is, in any case, another text — a historical, anecdotal, biographical text, of which a fortiori the author is not author'.[40] In this way, for instance, Freud's report of the psychoanalytical conversation with Mahler is by no means a possible explanation of the latter's music, but simply one of a collection of biographical texts (among them Mahler's letters and Natalie Bauer-Lechner's memoirs) drawn upon when a reference to the combination of tragic and trivial in the musical text becomes the object of an analysis. A musical text can neither be 'explained' through recourse to the real life of the composer, nor lead to a deeper comprehension of his or her personality. Nevertheless, a musical text can address the biography of the composer in the form of references, of intertextual links to that 'historical, anecdotal, biographical text' through which we construct an image of the composer. Therefore, the biographical text can occupy a part of the network of intertextual references activated by the musical text, which in this way loses some of its anonymity.

The movement discussed in this essay is a particularly good example of such a phenomenon. Indeed, Mahler's music is generally characterized by the use of intertextual references, including of the biographical kind. Paradoxically, this becomes evident if we attempt to analyse Mahler's music from a traditional perspective as a 'work'. In this case we have to make a hypothesis about compositional intentions, which, for its part, requires making a choice between a range of musical and extramusical references and ordering them according to interpretative codes. Such an analysis soon leads to the conclusion that one of the most acclaimed qualities of a musical work, its autonomy and self-evident unity, is challenged by a range of 'centrifugal forces'. 'Uneigentliche' music like the *Frère Jacques* canon, the Bohemian melody, as well as the folk tune in the Lindenbaum episode is certainly the most conspicuous example of such 'forces'. The numerous references to literary and pictorial sources discussed also contradict the traditional concept of the autonomy of a work of art. They are pertinent to a traditional 'work analysis' because they correspond to the intentions of the author, expressed in the form of programme notes, letters, and oral communication. Nevertheless, none of them can be interpreted as the 'actual' programme of this movement. The *Todtenmarsch in Callots Manier* is not a musical representation of literary or pictorial content, or of a psychological trauma. The literary and pictorial references are associated with Mahler's own experiences of the proximity of tragedy to triviality. Rather than bestowing semantic content on the 'indeterminate' medium of music, these references serve to dissolve Mahler's own subjectivity by providing a universal outlet for the expression of his personal experience. At the same time, they actively question the traditional view of the objectivity of an artistic work. Intertextuality, diffuse subjectivity, and openness are properties that we usually associate with the abstract theoretical construction of 'text'. Indeed, we could say that Mahler composed his works as texts. Perhaps this is a reason for his postmodern renaissance.

Notes to Chapter 13

1. Peter Ruzicka, 'Befragung des Materials. Gustav Mahler aus der Sicht aktueller Kompositionsästhetik', in *Erfundene und Gefundene Musik. Analysen, Portraits und Reflexionen*, ed. by Thomas Schäfer (Hofheim: Wolke, 1998), pp. 27–38 (p. 28).

2. Ruzicka, p. 28.

3. See Federico Celestini, 'Tra sinfonia e romanzo. Gustav Mahler e la totalità del mondo', *Il Territorio*, 10.2 (2002), pp. 61–72.

4. Hector Berlioz, 'Programme', in *Symphonie fantastique*, ed. by Nicolas Temperley, New Berlioz Edition, 16 (Kassel and London: Bärenreiter, 1972), n.p.

5. Mahler, 1st Symphony, 3rd mvt, bars 39–60.

6. Berlioz, *Symphonie fantastique*, 5th mvt, bars 40–64, anticipated in bars 21–28.

7. Mahler, 1st Symphony, 3rd mvt, bars 138–44.

8. Berlioz, *Symphonie fantastique*, 5th mvt, bars 414–34.

9. Wolfgang Dömling, *Hector Berlioz. Symphonie fantastique*, Meisterwerke der Musik, 19 (Munich: Fink, 1985), p. 59.

10. Dömling, p. 65.

11. Wolfgang Dömling, 'Szenerie im Imaginären. Über dramatisch-symphonische Werke von Hector Berlioz', *Neue Zeitschrift für Musik*, 3 (1977), pp. 195–203.

12. Quotation after Constantin Floros, *Gustav Mahler: The Symphonies*, trans. by Vernon Wicker (Aldershot: Scholar Press, 1994), p. 30. The version of the symphony performed in Hamburg in 1893 contained a second movement entitled 'Blumine', which was later cut. Thus, the third movement, with which the present essay is concerned, is referred to in the quotation as the fourth, and the finale, accordingly, as the fifth.

13. Ute Jung-Kayser, 'Die wahren Bilder und Chiffren "tragischer Ironie" in Mahlers "Erster"', in *Neue Mahleriana: Essays in Honor of Henry-Louis de La Grange on his Seventieth Birthday*, ed. by Günther Weiß (Berne: Lang, 1997), pp. 101–52 (p. 145). The animals described by Mahler can be found in this picture, although the Bohemian musicians are missing, as observed by Donald Mitchell in *Gustav Mahler: The Wunderhorn Years* (Berkeley and Los Angeles: University of California Press, 1980), p. 236.

14. Gustav Mahler, *Selected Letters of Gustav Mahler*, orig. edn selected by Alma Mahler, enlarged and ed. by Knud Martner, trans. by Eithne Wilkins, Ernst Kaiser, and Bill Hopkins (London: Faber, 1979), pp. 177–78.

15. Bernd Sponheuer, 'Dissonante Stimmigkeit. Eine rezeptionsgeschichtliche Studie zum dritten Satz der Mahlerschen Ersten', in *Gustav Mahler*, ed. by Hermann Danuser (Darmstadt: Wissenschaftliche Buchgesellschaft, 1992), pp. 165–71.

16. 'By the roadside stands a linden tree | Where I first found peace in sleep! Beneath the linden tree!' (transl. by Stewart Spencer). Incidentally, this section is not mentioned at all in Mahler's printed programme notes.

17. Hans Heinrich Eggebrecht, *Die Musik Gustav Mahlers* (Munich: Piper 1982), pp. 18–19.

18. Floros, pp. 41–42.

19. Paul Bekker, *Gustav Mahlers Sinfonien* (Berlin: Schuster & Loeffler, 1921), p. 53.

20. *Selected Letters of Gustav Mahler*, p. 55.

21. 'By the fountain at the gate there stands a linden tree; in its shadow I have dreamed many a sweet dream' (transl. by William Mann).

22. 'Sehr einfach und schlicht wie eine Volksweise'.

23. Karl Heinz Bohrer, 'Utopie des "Augenblicks" und Fiktionalität. Die Subjektivierung von Zeit in der modernen Literatur', in *Plötzlichkeit. Zum Augenblick des ästhetischen Scheins* (Frankfurt a.M.: Suhrkamp, 1981), pp. 180–218 (p. 188).

24. Theodor W. Adorno, *Mahler: A Musical Physiognomy*, trans. by Edmund Jephcott (Chicago: University of Chicago Press, 1992), p. 113.

25. Henri Bergson, *Essai sur les données immédiates de la conscience* (Paris: Alcan, 1889).

26. Mahler was Kapellmeister of the Hamburg Opera from 1891 until 1897.

27. Ferdinand Pfohl, *Gustav Mahler. Eindrücke und Erinnerungen aus den Hamburger Jahren*, ed. by Knud Martner (Hamburg: Wagner, 1973), p. 17.

28. Ernst Theodor Amadeus Hoffmann, 'Phantasiestücke in Callots Manier', in *E. T. A. Hoffmann. Werke in vier Bänden* (Vienna: Caesar Verlag, 1980), I, 39 (trans. by Stacey Bartsch).

29. Werner Keil, 'Von Quarten, *Tristan*-Akkorden und "Callots Manier". Bemerkungen zur Musik Mahlers und Debussys um 1900', in *1900 Musik zur Jahrhundertwende*, ed. by Werner Keil (Hildesheim: Olms 1995), pp. 75–97 (p. 89).

30. Natalie Bauer-Lechner, *Recollections of Gustav Mahler*, trans. by Dika Newlin, ed. by Peter Franklin (London: Faber, 1980), p. 60. Mahler uses 'irony' and 'humour' as synonyms. (Note here the reference to the five-movement version of the symphony, see note 12 above.)

31. Bauer-Lechner, *Recollections*, p. 157.

32. Bruno Walter, *Gustav Mahler: Ein Portrait*, ed. by Ekkehart Kroher (Wilhelmshaven: Florian Noetzl, 1981), p. 102.

33. Jean Paul (Johann Paul Friedrich Richter), *Titan: A Romance*, trans. by Charles T. Brooks, 2 vols (Boston, 1868), I, 271.

34. Jean Paul, I, 275–76 (italics are Jean Paul's).

35. Jean Paul, I, 276: 'Only courtiers or his father could have set down this tragic exultation to an adulatory rejoicing over the new regency'; Jean Paul, I, 277.

36. See also Eggebrecht, pp. 11–17.

37. Quotation after Floros, p. 40.

38. Natalie Bauer-Lechner, *Gustav Mahler in den Erinnerungen von Natalie Bauer-Lechner*, ed. by Herbert Killian (Hamburg: Wagner, 1984), p. 69. This passage is missing from the English version.

39. Raymond Monelle, 'Text and Subjectivity', in *The Sense of Music: Semiotic Essays* (Princeton, NJ: Princeton University Press, 2000), pp. 147–69 (p. 150).

40. Monelle, p. 158.

CHAPTER 14

Fugue or Music Drama? Symmetry, Counterpoint, and Leitmotif in Dostoevsky's *The Brothers Karamazov*

Rosamund Bartlett

The movement of the novel is an almost perfect spiral, with three as its golden number.

JACQUES CATTEAU[1]

CRAB: How do you do fugue in a Dialogue?

AUTHOR: The most important idea is that there should be a single theme which is stated by each different 'voice', or character, upon entering, just as in a musical fugue. Then they can branch off into freer conversation.

DOUGLAS R. HOFSTADTER[2]

Many critics have alluded to the musical properties of Dostoevsky's prose.[3] One of the first was the Russian Symbolist Vyacheslav Ivanov, who argued in his 1914 article 'Dostoevsky and the Novel-Tragedy' that the writer operated like a composer of symphonies in his methods of narrative construction. According to Ivanov, Dostoevsky 'applied to the novel a method corresponding to the development of themes and counterpoint in music — a development through whose variations and transformations the composer leads us to the perception and psychological experience of the whole work as a kind of unity'.[4] For Jacques Catteau, meanwhile, one of the more recent commentators on Dostoevsky, the 'composition of the great novels, with their sudden conflagrations and tempests of passion, slowly prepared by cunning gradations of tension, their vast orchestration in magnificent crescendos, is reminiscent of Beethoven, for whom Dostoevsky always had a great passion'.[5] This essay explores ways in which a reading of Dostoevsky's *The Brothers Karamzov* can be illuminated by formal parallels with the music of composers as disparate as Bach and Wagner.

Dostoevsky's knowledge of music was not particularly sophisticated, and neither was his fondness of it noticeably deep. Apart from his love of Beethoven, he liked Mozart, Rossini, Glinka, and Serov, according to his second wife Anna Snitkina. One contemporary was so scathing of his lack of musical discrimination that she alleged he could be moved by a barrel organ.[6] Despite the apparent superficiality of Dostoevsky's musical appreciation, there are nevertheless serious grounds for drawing parallels between the world of music and his methods of literary construction. Here, the critic and one-time diplomat Eugène-Melchior, vicomte de Vogüé (1848–1910) was a pioneer. De Vogüé, who served in the French Embassy in St Petersburg between 1876 and 1882 (during which time Dostoevsky published *The Brothers Karamazov* and died), went on to publish a book entitled *Le Roman russe* (Paris, 1886), in which he discusses Dostoevsky's tendency to develop two story lines simultaneously:

> It is tempting to think that Dostoevsky sought in this bifurcation a very subtle artistic device borrowed from the musical experts: the main drama prompts an echo in the distance; this melodic picture reproduces in the orchestra the voice of the chorus which resounds onstage. This might remind us of two indivisible romantic *fabulas* which are made up of two contrasting mirrors sending each other one and same image.[7]

De Vogüé, of course, is speaking about polyphony — the term used both to describe music consisting of more than one part, and the way in which a musical work's constituent parts develop independently of one another.[8] It was Mikhail Bakhtin who first explicitly used the term polyphony in connection with Dostoevsky. In his ground-breaking study of 1928 he asserted that 'a genuine polyphony of fully valid voices is in fact the chief characteristic of Dostoevsky's novels'. This polyphony, in his view, can be found 'in the interplay among characters, within a single character, among fragments of the plot, and, most importantly, through the many kinds of narrative in the novel'.[9] Dostoevsky's creation of 'polyphonic' novels of autonomous characters who seem to be completely free thus provides a striking contrast to the traditional 'monologic' European novel.[10] But polyphony was ultimately only a metaphor for Bakhtin. In his opinion the respective languages of music and the novel were too dissimilar for the analogy to be taken further.

Bakhtin's reservations have not stopped later critics from conducting further investigations. Leonid Grossman, for example, went on to explore the analogy with music in an important article in 1959 on Dostoevsky's artistic technique.[11] As he points out, Dostoevsky himself described his *Notes from Underground* as a work of three parts, each with different content, but all internally linked: the polemical monologue in the first part is followed by a dramatic episode in the second, which is a preparation for the catastrophe resulting in the third part. Furthermore, in a letter to his brother in 1864 prior to the work's publication in their journal *Time*, Dostoevsky explained that the work's second part introduced a change of tonality rather than a mechanical break, and explicitly likened its relationship to the first part in terms of the transition in music from one tonality to another: 'You understand what *transition* in music is. It's just the same here. In the first chapter apparently it is just idle chatter, but suddenly this idle chatter is resolved in the last two chapters by an unexpected catastrophe'.[12] As Grossman comments, the psychological torment suffered by the prostitute Liza in the second part echoes the insults suffered by her tormentor in the first part, but in its unanswerability is at the same time a contrast to his wounded vanity. Here Grossman introduces the musical term counterpoint (as he puts it, *punctum contra punctum*) in order to illustrate Dostoevsky's 'different voices singing in different ways on one theme'.[13]

Counterpoint denotes the 'combination of simultaneously sounding musical lines according to a system of rules', and has been in use since the fourteenth century.[14]

Although used almost interchangeably with the term 'polyphony', Theodor Adorno's argument that counterpoint 'denotes a composition in which parts are graduated according to rank', while polyphony is 'a melodic arrangement of parts of equal importance'[15] is persuasive. It is a distinction that becomes particularly important when considering the narrative structure of *The Brothers Karamazov*, which seems to have something in common with the complex contrapuntal music of Bach's fugues. Moreover, the religiously inspired formal design of Dostoevsky's novels also bears comparison with the music of Bach, whose works are similarly characterized by intricate symmetrical patterns and number symbolism linked to their creator's profound Christian faith. Bach only occasionally made explicit his aim to praise God with his musical compositions, such as with the dedication to his *Orgel-Büchlein* ('Dem Höchsten Gott allein zu Ehren'), but certain passages in his small corpus of writings, together with the obvious symbolism present in many of his musical works underline that Bach not only 'saw music as a fundamental tool of religion and essential to his religious life', as John Butt has shown, but also that he 'believed music to be an essential component of the religion itself, indeed one of its defining characteristics'.[16] During Bach's education, in fact, musical instruction was even subsidiary to theological instruction (which was regarded as the 'crown of all learning'),[17] and taught by the same person at his last school.[18]

The study of Bach's use of symmetry began in 1926 when Friedrich Smend published a pioneering article in which he revealed intricate chiastic structures in the *St John Passion*, particularly in the organization of the central section of the work's second part. Bach's use of chiastic structures (derived from the Greek letter *chi* (χ), the 'sign of the cross'), in which elements of a particular composition are arranged symmetrically on either side of a central constituent element, is particularly pronounced in vocal works dealing with the birth and death of Christ. Thus the so-called 'Herzstück' of the *St John Passion* features a symmetry of ABCDEDCBA, which has a visual equivalent in the shape of a cross, with E representing the central quasi-chorale and the letters A–D signifying choruses, recitatives, ariosos, and arias that variously duplicate words or musical material.[19] As Robin Leaver observes, Bach even wrote 'X-Stab' in the manuscript score of Cantata BWV 56, *Ich will dem Kreuzstab gerne tragen* ('I will gladly carry the cross-staff'), and 'Domin: I Advent Xti' in the heading of Cantata BWV 61, since *chi* is also the first letter of *Christos*, and used to signify Christ.[20]

In the Mass in B minor and numerous other works Bach also employs complex Trinitarian symbolism and numbers that have a theological significance. During the 1930s German musicologists began to investigate this number symbolism in detail, with the aim of tracing, as Ruth Tatlow puts it in her summary overview, a 'direct path from the musical scores into the heart and mind of the composer'.[21] By counting and then computing the numbers of notes, phrases, movements, bars, repetitions, or similar in a work or individual section, it becomes possible to translate them into biblical symbols (such as three, representing the Trinity), words that denote Christian faith (as in 'Credo', 'Christus'), specific numbers in the Bible (twelve disciples, for example), and names.

A similar use of symmetry for theological ends and Christian number symbolism may be seen in Dostoevsky's writings, and particularly in *The Brothers Karamazov*, his most 'constructed' novel. As Konstantin Mochulsky has observed, 'the architectonics of *The Brothers Karamazov* are distinguished by their unusual rigidity: the law of balance, of symmetry, of proportionality is observed by the author systematically'.[22] *The Brothers Karamazov* consists of four parts, each of which contains three books, adding up to twelve. In an echo of Bach's chiastic structures in his Passions, the central message of the novel is placed exactly halfway, at the end of the second part, which is significantly called 'Pro et Contra'. In his study of *The Brothers Karamazov* as trinitarian theology, David S. Cunningham argues that the mystical number three holds for Dostoevsky 'much more than aesthetic and literary value', and he shows how 'triads dominate the novel': there are three brothers, for example, three 'confessions of an ardent heart' (chapters 3–5 of book 3, in the first part of the novel), three 'torments of the soul' (chapters 3–5 of book 9, in the third part of the novel), and frequent references to the three temptations of Christ in the wilderness. Other instances of the number three appearing in the novel arise when we learn that Dmitry needs three thousand roubles, and that his father Fyodor is struck three times. Later on a *troika* is invoked at Dmitry's trial three times.[23] As Mochulsky has also pointed out, Ivan has three conversations with Smerdyakov, and Dmitry has three trials, as does Alyosha at the hands of Father Ferapont, Rakitin, and Grushenka.[24]

Dostoevsky seems also to echo Bach's compositional method in creating in *The Brothers Karamazov* almost the prose equivalent of a fugue, in which different parts or voices appear successively, the first voice entering with the subject in the tonic key, the second answering it in the dominant (a fifth higher or a fourth lower). It could be argued that the novel's epigraph from St John 12. 24 ('Verily, verily I say unto you, Except a corn of wheat fall into the ground and die, it abideth alone: but if it die, it bringeth forth much fruit')[25] fulfils the role of the subject or main theme. In prophesying his Passion and Resurrection, Christ uses this metaphor to argue that if a seed falls to earth and dies, it will, paradoxically, be fruitful, because new life comes only through death. The same idea of death and rebirth runs through Dostoevsky's novel, which, like the parable, is built on a pro and contra opposition between the possession or yearning for religious faith, and the absence or denial of it, the latter fulfilling the function of the countersubject, traditionally introduced in the initial exposition section of a fugue. The question of immortality is raised, for example, at the end of chapter 4 in book 1 of part 1, and then commented on in the following chapter by Alyosha. As an atheist and socialist, the landowner Pyotr Myusov first introduces the countersubject (which has already been hinted at in connection with the Karamazov family) in chapter 5 of book 1, and it is then explicitly addressed in chapter 8 of book 3 by Ivan's statement that God does not exist. In more general terms, the central ethical idea that 'everyone is responsible for everything', which runs throughout the novel and is closely related to the miracle of resurrection contained in the subject, is first adumbrated by the Elder Zosima in chapter 1 of book 4 of part two. It is countered by the amoral countersubject of 'everything is permitted' through references to Satan (such as in chapter 5 of book 2 of part 1), contemporary 'dead men' such as Ivan (described as a 'tomb' in chapter 4 of book 3 of part 1), and socialism, which is aligned with atheism, and the notion that the love of mankind professed to by its adherents invariably results in a hatred of individual human beings (chapter 4 of book 2 of part 1).

It could even be argued that Dostoevsky observes the rules of strict counterpoint, which is the hallmark of Bach's fugal writing, whereby new voices are set against a short cantus firmus according to rules that dictate whether they proceed at the same pace, or at different relative speeds. The voice of Christ, then, operates as the cantus firmus in *The Brothers Karamazov*, as Jostein Børtnes has suggested.[26] Diane Thompson rightly comments that Dostoevsky never conceived of polyphony as 'relativism', for 'he clearly acknowledged the authoritative primacy of Christ', who 'must crown the world of voices, must organise and subdue it', thus the narrator, the characters, and the author are located on a 'lower' level, and their voices are variations on Christ's voice: 'whether they are accepting it in the form of various imitations, or denying it through a range of inversions and perversions, they are all responding to Him'.[27] A further similarity with fugal construction may be found in the way in which new voices are introduced.

If key contrasts (in the form of alternation of subject in the tonic key and the 'answer' in the dominant) constitute an important element of a musical fugue, thematic contrasts, developed through consistent mirroring and doubling, are fundamental to Dostoevsky. Apart from the pro and contra opposition of faith and absence of faith in *The Brothers Karamazov* mentioned above, characters mirror each other. Examples of such pairings include Ivan and Kolya, Alyosha and Markel, and Dmitry and the young Zosima. Victor Terras's survey of the novel's storylines that echo or mirror each other includes the story of Father Zosima's youth and the Karamazov brothers' story; the Ilyusha story and Ivan's 'Rebellion' (containing the 'The Grand Inquisitor' legend); and Alyosha's vision in 'Cana of Galilee' (book 7 of part 3) and Ivan's nightmare 'vision' of the devil towards the end of the novel.[28]

In a fugue the main theme will be played 'in different voices and different keys, and occasionally at different speeds or upside down or backwards', as Douglas R. Hofstadter comments in his original exploration of music, mathematics, and art, *Gödel, Escher, Bach*, which contains several playful 'Dialogues' consciously fashioned in the form of a fugue (the book is styled on the cover as a 'metaphorical fugue on minds and machines in the spirit of Lewis Carroll').[29] In *The Brothers Karamazov*, the suffering of children that causes Ivan (in chapter 4 of book 5 in part 2) to 'return his ticket' and reject God — the novel's 'countersubject' — could be viewed as an 'inverted' or 'upside down' form of the 'subject' or main theme. And further resonances with elements of fugal structure may be seen both by examining the way in which the different voices interact in *The Brothers Karamazov*, and by taking into account the fact that the novel's many storylines (all of which are a meditation or variation on the main theme, as summarized in the epigraph) are narrated at different speeds. Take, for example, the chapter concerning Zosima's youth, located in the middle of book 6 in part 2, whose four stories contain the novel's central message in microcosm, and could be compared to 'diminution' in a fugue, when variation of the subject is provided by the time values of notes being shortened. In the first story there is the amoral life, last-minute religious conversion, and death of Zosima's brother Markel, a 'double' of all three Karamazov brothers. In the second there are references to Job's love of God in the face of the suffering of innocent children, and the need for a 'tiny seed' to be sown, which echoes the novel's epigraph. In the third Zosima discusses his early life in order to teach the lesson that each person is guilty for all creatures and all things; and in the fourth the novel's epigraph is voiced directly, having been echoed earlier by the idea of physical self-abasement before others (bowing). Ivan's narration of the Virgin's Descent into Hell at the beginning of the Legend of the Grand Inquisitor in book 5 of part 2, and Grushenka's story about hell in book 7 of part 3, meanwhile, might be regarded as more extreme examples of diminution. The onion that is the subject of Grushenka's tale becomes a symbol of the seed in the epigraph, and is connected to the restoration of faith for both her and Alyosha.

One should also consider the extended story of the children Ilyusha and Kolya: introduced in book 4 of part 2, it spans book 10 in its entirety, is returned to in the epilogue, and serves to provide a concrete illustration of the central theme of suffering children (itself echoing the main story of the Karamazov brothers), thus performing, as it were, the function of 'augmentation' in a fugue, whereby note values are lengthened to provide a variation on the subject. Another example is the story of Zosima's death in the novel, which provides yet another extended variation on the 'subject', since his 'falling to the ground' in the form of his burial ultimately leads to the bringing forth of much fruit. Alyosha's subsequent decision to leave the monastery and 'live in the world', as Zosima had wished, means that he is able to be far more effective in putting into practice his beliefs. A loose analogy may even be drawn between a 'stretto' in a fugue, when a new entry of the subject overlaps with an earlier entry, and the essentially contrapuntal way in which Dostoevsky introduces the variations on his main theme via the novel's many voices, and his sophisticated use of foreshadowing.

But Dostoevsky was a novelist writing in late nineteenth-century Russia, and polyphony and counterpoint are terms most frequently associated with music from the thirteenth to the eighteenth centuries. The overriding impression we gain from a first reading of *The Brothers Karamazov*, furthermore, is one of chaos and dissonance, which are qualities associated with late nineteenth-century European culture. Indeed, Dostoevsky's innovative use of myth, leitmotif, and symbol in his novels, coupled with the intensely dramatic qualities of his writing, suggest parallels with his contemporary Wagner, rather than with Bach. Although Dostoevsky and Wagner were largely uninterested in each other's existence, their creative careers were coterminous, and it is perhaps not surprising to find points of contact between the œuvres of these two great nineteenth-century artistic revolutionaries. If *The Brothers Karamazov* is explored through the prism of Wagnerian music drama, it becomes possible to see how much the novel also has in common, both structurally and thematically, with works such as *Der Ring des Nibelungen* and *Parsifal*.

To begin with, there are some striking biographical parallels. While Wagner (1813–83) was older than Dostoevsky (1821–81) by eight years and outlived him by two, their creative careers very largely coincided. *Rienzi*, Wagner's first success, was premiered in 1842, whilst Dostoevsky's first published work, *Poor Folk*, appeared in 1846. There is also a parallel where their last works are concerned: *The Brothers Karamazov* was first published as a book in 1881, while *Parsifal* was completed in 1882. Apart from the fact that both Wagner and Dostoevsky combined publicistic and creative careers, they also became embroiled in radical left-wing politics early on in their lives, with dire consequences. Dostoevsky was arrested and exiled in 1849 for his involvement with the subversive Petrashevsky circle, whilst Wagner fled Germany that same year to avoid arrest after the Dresden Uprising. The shock of these events caused a lengthy hiatus in the creative work of both artists, and both also eventually eschewed political radicalism in favour of decidedly reactionary views. Wagner was of the opinion that the *Ring* was the greatest thing that had ever been written, and appears to have remained oblivious of Dostoevsky's existence. Dostoevsky was only slightly acquainted with Wagner's works. In 1873 he claimed that Wagner's music was 'full of noble aims', but six years later had concluded that it was 'the most utterly boring German rubbish'. [30] Nevertheless, no other artist comes near Wagner in terms of the scope and ambition of his artistic works, with the possible exception of Tolstoy.

Despite the apparent lack of common ground between Wagner's mythological world of gods and dwarfs and the seemingly concrete nineteenth-century world of Dostoevsky's Russia, both are linked by the fact that their creators are far more interested in the psychology of their characters, and in the ideas they represent, than in their surroundings. The inner world of Dostoevsky's and Wagner's characters is in fact deliberately more convincing than the external world that they inhabit. Space and time are treated symbolically. Dostoevsky and Wagner are also linked by the central idea of redemption that runs through their work. In the third volume of *À la recherche du temps perdu* Proust suggests that *The Brothers Karamazov* can be interpreted as a re-enactment of the ancient myth of crime, vengeance, and expiation. [31] Like *Das Rheingold*, the first part of *The Brothers Karamazov* acts as a prologue to the main drama contained in the subsequent three parts. And as with the *Ring*, important events have taken place even before the action begins. The 'myth' in *The Brothers Karamazov* begins before the novel starts with the rape of an innocent Holy Fool, Lizaveta Smerdyashchaya. This in turn leads to the murder of the rapist (Fyodor Karamazov) by the son born of that union (Smerdyakov), and culminates in the innocent son Dmitry atoning for his father's sin through his suffering. His brother Alyosha is thus free of the curse. A similar progression can be seen in the *Ring*, where Siegfried ultimately sacrifices his life to atone for the initial crime of his forbear Wotan, ruler of the Gods. In *Götterdämmerung* we learn that Wotan broke a branch from the world ash tree — the source of life — in his quest for world domination (sacrificing an eye in order to gain wisdom). He is punished for his lust for power in a series of events that begins with the Nibelung Alberich's theft of the Rhinegold from the Rhinemaidens. Since these are works written during the rise of nineteenth-century capitalism, the corrupting power of money is central to both the crimes of the Ring and *The Brothers Karamazov*, but so is the regenerative power of love. Wagner was not a religious artist in the way that Dostoevsky was, although the life of Siegfried has unmistakably Christian overtones; but he ultimately preaches the same idea of regeneration through love. Compassion plays a crucial role here. Parsifal's rejection of Kundry's sexual advances and his compassion for her, for example, leads ultimately to her redemption, and to his ('Durch Mitleid wissend, der reine Tor'). A pivotal point comes in chapter 3 of book 7 in part 3 of *The Brothers Karamazov* when Alyosha (who is likened to a

'Holy Fool') comes face to face for the first time with the equally sultry Grushenka, who also attempts a seduction.[32] Here it is Grushenka who backs away first, and her compassion for Alyosha, grieving over the death of his spiritual father, and doubting his faith, leads to his redemption. His compassion for her, meanwhile, is responsible in turn for her own redemption.

The Brothers Karamazov is an intensely dramatic novel, consisting of what Lunacharsky termed 'brilliantly staged dialogues'.[33] This is also a key innovation in Wagner's music dramas, where he breaks sharply with operatic convention by creating texts in dialogue form set in an uninterrupted musical structure. As befits a drama rather than an opera, the separate acts of each part of the cycle are divided into scenes. In both the Ring and *The Brothers Karamazov* most of the dialogue consists of lengthy exchanges between pairs of characters in which various themes are developed, and it is perhaps here that we find the most interesting analogy with Wagnerian music drama, for Dostoevsky treats his themes very much like musical leitmotifs.[34]

Wagner did not introduce the term 'leitmotif', but the idea of employing thematic orchestral motifs is discussed in his treatise *Oper und Drama* (1851–52), where he first advocates the creation of a continuous musical structure to replace the conventional operatic format of discrete arias, choruses, and orchestral accompaniment.[35] The motifs in Wagner's music dramas designate both material objects and abstractions, with the main characters usually represented by more than one motif to allow for a greater degree of sophistication in the presentation of their psychological states. The purpose of this system of symphonic motifs was to create a network of specific emotional or conceptual associations that would evolve over the course of the work, accumulating, in Thomas S. Grey's definition, 'additional layers of significance through their modified reappearance in appropriate dramatic contexts throughout the drama, at the same time endowing the drama with a compelling sense of large structural unity'.[36] Leitmotifs were thus never intended to be 'visiting cards', as Debussy once jocularly referred to them, implying that they were static recurrent themes linked to certain characters and concepts. Instead, the themes metamorphose so that they sometimes become the opposite of what they originally represent: thus the Rhinegold theme is initially one of ascent and 'becoming', but ultimately one of descent, denoting the extinction of the Gods, as Werner Breig has shown.[37] Wagner also frequently combines motifs so that he can convey complex emotional ideas. As Carl Dahlhaus has commented, Wagner's themes and motifs are 'unceasingly varied, taken apart and merged with or transformed into each other', moving 'gradually closer together or further apart as they are modified'.[38]

The idea of thematic links is essentially literary, so it is perhaps not all that surprising to find an analogy in *The Brothers Karamazov*. The theme of the seed falling to the ground and bearing fruit, for example, recurs throughout the novel in different guises, as has been discussed earlier. The narration of the brief life of the Elder Zosima's brother Markel exemplifies the theme in microcosm as a story within a story, whilst the account of the death of the boy Ilyusha provides an echo of the miraculous results of the Elder Zosima's death. The idea of the seed is also used metaphorically. Zosima receives the seed of God as a young boy, then is spiritually 'reborn' as he is about to fight a duel (when we learn that all that is required is a 'tiny seed'). The Elder Zosima utters the words of the epigraph to Alyosha just before he dies, but the reader cannot at this point fully understand its implications. In chapter 4 of book 7 of part 3 Grushenka tells the story of an old woman whose only good deed in life was to give an onion, but who remains in hell by denying others the chance to be redeemed with her. When Grushenka discovers the Elder Zosima has died, she repents for wanting to have seduced Alyosha at a time when his faith is in doubt, and has deep compassion for him instead. This is her 'onion', and she goes on to play a vital role in Dmitry's redemption, thus doing the opposite of the old woman. Alyosha in turn forgives Grushenka, telling her he has only given her an onion, but it is this kind of charitable act that leads to redemption. The Elder Zosima's death also exemplifies the parable of the seed dying and bearing fruit, and Alyosha symbolically kisses the earth when he realizes this. At the very end of the novel we learn that Dr Herzenstube once gave Dmitry a bag of nuts. Twenty three years later that charitable act bears fruit: Dmitry thanks him, in an echo of the story of the onion. Even the godless Ivan does one good thing by saving a peasant in the blizzard. The leitmotif of the seed also metamorphoses into its opposite in an almost Wagnerian fashion. The Elder Zosima mentions the idea of an adult planting a bad seed in a child, and this is later developed by the devil who visits Ivan and talks of planting a seed in him. The symbol of the seed is thus the symbol of the structure of the novel as a whole. In Dostoevsky, as with Wagner, motifs are also symbols. Victor Terras briefly discusses Dostoevsky's use of 'leitmotifs' in the novel, and the way in which they appear in several variations, 'linked by a variety of syntagmatic as well as pradigmatic bonds', but makes the comparison only with 'symphonic composition', rather than going further to make the logical connection with Wagner.[39]

If one can ascribe nearly all the motifs in the *Ring* to two basic musical ideas, it is also possible to show the validity of each motif having its own individual character.[40] Something very similar could be said about *The Brothers Karamazov*, in which all the themes are at one level reducible to faith and lack of faith, but at the same time differ from each other. Each appearance of a leitmotif in Wagner and Dostoevsky, in fact, conveys 'different impressions of the same material' (in Dahlhaus' words), with each impression shedding light on a particular aspect of a situation.[41] As in Wagner also, the earliest form in which a motif appears in *The Brothers Karamazov* is not necessarily its primary form, 'from which all subsequent forms derive as secondary variations'.[42] To take an example of how this works in the novel, we could point to the idea that 'all things are lawful', which is a major counter-theme in the novel developed by Ivan, but it is expressed first by another character, Myusov. Similarly, the Elder Zosima's story of the man who loves mankind (in chapter 4 of book 2 in part 1) prefigures Ivan's renunciation of God through his supposed love of mankind (his unwillingness to pay the price of accepting that children must suffer in the world).

Wagner intended his motifs to be instruments of anticipation and recollection operating within a network of interrelated motifs within the orchestral score. Motifs of anticipation can be defined as a kind of musical foreshadowing, intimating what is to follow within the orchestral fabric, whilst motifs of remembrance perform a similar function with regard to what has gone before. A sophisticated system of narrative 'tenses' — past, present, and future — is thus created through motifs of anticipation and recollection or reminiscence.[43] Dostoevsky follows a similar practice in *The Brothers Karamazov*. The Elder Zosima bows to the ground at the beginning of the novel, anticipating Dmitry's future suffering. But the very act of bowing anticipates the main theme of the book, as conveyed in the epigraph from St John, and exemplified by Dmitry's fall and subsequent regeneration. And as Robin Feuer Miller puts it, Smerdyakov performs an important function by prefiguring 'in grotesque form the ideas that will shortly sound with complete seriousness'.[44] Mme Khokhlakova talks about Dmitry going to Siberia to work in gold mines; later in the novel he is exiled there.

In his discourses in chapter 3 of book 6 in part 2 the Elder Zosima speaks of everything being like an ocean: 'all flows and is contiguous, and if you touch it in one place it will reverberate at the other end of the world'.[45] It is a central idea in *The Brothers Karamazov*, and is reflected in the novel's complex organic structure of tightly interwoven themes. One cannot help but be reminded again of Wagner's 'network of leitmotifs in which, on one hand, everything is linked with everything else, and, on the other, each separate instance is unmistakably distinct', as Dahlhaus describes it.[46] Dostoevsky followed Glinka (one of his favourite composers) in believing that everything in life was counterpoint, that is, in opposition.[47] For him the central polarity was the dichotomy between faith and reason, but as an artist he shrank from simplistic binary oppositions. It is for this reason that we can perhaps at one and the same time see a work like *The Brothers Karamazov* as a fugue in the style of Bach, constructed on the basis of strict counterpoint, possessed of strict symmetries, and based on firm Christian belief, and as a Wagnerian music drama in which structural properties are far less clear-cut and whose foundations are based on ambivalence and doubt. The symbolic structure of Dostoevsky's theological ideal in *The Brothers Karamazov* may be perfectly symmetrical, since it represents perfection, but that of the fallen, and very human, world in which its characters move, is anything but.

Notes to Chapter 14

1. Jacques Catteau, *Dostoyevsky and the Process of Literary Creation*, trans. by Audrey Littlewood (Cambridge: Cambridge University Press, 1989), p. 360.
2. Douglas R. Hofstadter, *Gödel, Escher, Bach: An Eternal Golden Braid* (New York: Basic Books, 1979), p. 737.
3. For a useful overview see Malcolm Jones, *Dostoyevsky: The Novel as Discord* (London: Elek, 1976), pp. 63–65.
4. Vyacheslav Ivanov, 'Dostoevsky i roman-tragediya', *Russkaya mysl'*, 4 (1914), repr. in *Borozdy i mezhy* (Furrows and boundaries) (Moscow: Musaget, 1916), p. 20; cited in Leonid Grossman, 'Dostoevsky-khudozhnik', in *Tvorchestvo Dostoevskogo*, ed. by N. L. Stepanov (Moscow: Izdatel'stvo Akademii nauk, 1959), pp. 330–416 (p. 334). The English translation cited in Catteau (p. 504) is slightly inaccurate, being a translation from Catteau's French text rather than the original Russian.
5. Catteau, p. 30.
6. See Catteau, pp. 27–28.
7. E.-M. de Vogüé, *Le Roman russe* (Paris: Plon-Nourrit, 1886), cited in Grossman, p. 341.
8. See Wolf Frobenius, 'Polyphony, I', in *The New Grove Dictionary of Music and Musicians*, ed. by Stanley Sadie and John Tyrrell, 29 vols (London: Macmillan, 2001), xx, 74–78.
9. Mikhail Bakhtin, *Problems of Dostoevsky's Poetics* (1928), ed. and trans. by Caryl Emerson (Manchester: Manchester University Press, 1984), p. 30.
10. See Jostein Børtnes, 'Polyphony in *The Brothers Karamazov*: Variations on a Theme', *Canadian-American Slavic Studies*, 17 (1983), 402–11 (p. 409).

11. Grossman, pp. 341–42.

12. Letter to Mikhail Dostoevsky, cited in Grossman, p. 342.

13. Grossman, p. 342.

14. Klaus-Jürgen Sachs, 'Counterpoint, §§1–11', in *The New Grove*, VI, 551–61.

15. Theodor Adorno, 'Die Funktion des Kontrapunkts in der neuen Musik', in *Nervenpunkte der neuen Musik* (1969), cited in Carl Dahlhaus, 'Counterpoint, §17', in *The New Grove*, VI, 568–69.

16. John Butt, 'Bach's Metaphysics of Music', *The Cambridge Companion to Bach*, ed. by John Butt (Cambridge: Cambridge University Press, 1997), pp. 46–59 (p. 55).

17. Paul S. Minear, 'Bach and Today's Theologians', *Theology Today*, 202 (1985), 201–11 (p. 203).

18. Wilfrid Mellers, *Bach and the Dance of God* (London: Faber, 1980), p. 155.

19. F. Smend, 'Die Johannes-Passion von Bach. Auf ihren Bau untersucht', *Bach-Jahrbuch*, 23 (1926), 105–28.

20. Robin A. Leaver, 'The Mature Vocal Works', in *The Cambridge Companion to Bach*, pp. 86–122 (p. 101).

21. Ruth Tatlow, 'Number Symbolism', in *J. S. Bach*, ed. by Malcolm Boyd (Oxford: Oxford University Press, 1999), pp. 320–21.

22. Konstantin Mochulsky, *Dostoevsky: His Life and Work*, trans. by Michael A. Minihan (Princeton, NJ: Princeton University Press, 1967), p. 598.

23. See David Cunningham, 'Trinitarian Theology in The Brothers Karamazov', in *Dostoevsky and the Christian Tradition*, ed. by George Pattison and Diane Oenning Thompson (Cambridge: Cambridge University Press, 2001), pp. 134–55 (pp. 141–42). For a discussion of Dostoevsky's symbolism, see also Victor Terras, *A Karamazov Companion: Commentary on the Genesis, Language and Style of Dostoevsky's Novel* (Madison: University of Wisconsin Press, 1981), pp. 115–22.

24. Mochulsky, p. 607.

25. Citations are from Fyodor Dostoevsky, *The Brothers Karamazov*, trans. by David McDuff (Harmondsworth: Penguin, 1993).

26. Børtnes, p. 409.

27. Diane Oenning Thompson, *Dostoevsky and the Poetics of Memory* (Cambridge: Cambridge University Press, 1991), p. 70.

28. See Terras, pp. 104–06, 115–16.

29. Hofstadter, p. 9.

30. See Rosamund Bartlett, *Wagner and Russia* (Cambridge: Cambridge University Press, 1995), pp. 50–52. The present article reproduces and expands upon certain sections in these pages.

31. Cited in Terras, pp. 119–20.

32. *The Brothers Karamazov*, pp. 400–04.

33. Bakhtin, p. 33.

34. See Terras, pp. 102–04.

35. See Werner Breig, 'The Musical Works', in *Wagner Handbook*, ed. by Ulrich Müller and Peter Wapnewski, translation ed. by John Deathridge (Cambridge, MA: Harvard University Press, 1992), pp. 439–511.

36. Thomas S. Grey, 'A Wagnerian Glossary', in *The Wagner Compendium: A Guide to Wagner's Life and Music*, ed. by Barry Millington (London: Thames and Hudson, 1992; repr. with corrections, 2001), pp. 230–43 (p. 235).

37. Breig, p. 448.

38. Carl Dahlhaus, 'Style', in *The New Grove Wagner*, ed. by John Deathridge and Carl Dahlhaus (London: Macmillan, 1984), pp. 111–26 (p. 112).

39. Terras, pp. 103–04.

40. Dahlhaus, *The New Grove Wagner*, p. 113.

41. Dahlhaus, *The New Grove Wagner*, p. 112.

42. Dahlhaus, *The New Grove Wagner*, p. 112.

43. Grey, p. 231.

44. Robin Feuer Miller, *The Brothers Karamazov: Worlds of the Novel* (New York: Twayne, 1992), p. 56.

45. *The Brothers Karamazov*, p. 368.

46. Dahlhaus, *The New Grove Wagner*, p. 114.

47. Mikhail Ivanovich Glinka, Zapiski, cited in Grossman, p. 342.

CHAPTER 15

Benjamin Britten and Wilfred Owen: An Intertextual Reading of the *War Requiem*

David Crilly

In *The Anxiety of Influence* and *A Map of Misreading* Harold Bloom outlines a systematic procedure that attempts to account for the nature of influence in poetry. The question to which Bloom returns throughout his writings concerns the nature of poetic origins, and in so doing he recognizes that poets become poets only because of a love of someone else's poetry. Any poetic endeavour, therefore, is grounded in a tradition, and in a sense is reactionary rather than an original and autonomous creative impulse. 'Poetic history', he argues, 'is held to be indistinguishable from poetic influence, since strong poets make that history by misreading one another, so as to clear imaginative space for themselves.'[1] But poets resist the implications of influence, because of the desire to obtain and be recognized as having an individual voice. In *The Picture of Dorian Gray* Lord Henry Wooton tells Dorian that all influence is immoral:

> to influence a person is to give him one's own soul. He does not think his natural thoughts, or burn with his natural passion. His virtues are not real to him. His sins, if there are such things as sins, are borrowed. He becomes an echo of someone else's music, an actor of a part that has not been written for him.[2]

For Bloom, this rejection on the poet's part of the idea of influence creates an anxiety within the poet, who seeks to name things as though for the first time, because such an idea contains within it the implicit accusation of lack of originality. Influence becomes, as Kevin Korsyn says, 'something poets actively resist, rather than something they passively receive, and poetry becomes a psychic battlefield, an Oedipal struggle against one's poetic fathers, in which poems seek to repress and exclude other poems'.[3]

But, as with Hegelian dialectics, which outline a cyclic pattern of thesis and antithesis prior to synthesis, Bloom's conception of the anxiety of influence does not suggest an adoption or continuation of the aesthetic of a precursor. Rather, Bloom replaces the mimetic view of influence by the idea of antithetical completion, in which influence is regarded as the discontinuous relation between past and present texts, a kind of poetic misprision in which its elements become encoded anew, so that it retains the same terms whilst 'meaning' them in another sense. Indeed, this notion is so central to Bloom's writing that he was able to declare that the anxiety of influence is the true subject matter of all poetry, describing it as 'the story of intra-poetic relationships'.[4] This is the key distinction between Bloom's ideas and mere source study, since Bloom is not concerned with tracing the borrowing of external subject matter or quotation, or even with the adoption of stylistic norms between poets, but rather in the misprision of the precursor, in which the poet misreads or re-encodes the elements of the parent poem in order to generate an aesthetic object, the true subject of which is the anxiety of influence. Thus Bloom relegates the significance of the textual content of poetry. For Bloom, poetry itself is the true subject matter of the poem. But this is not to say that Bloom forgets what poems are about; rather, any poem's external subject matter is mediated through other poems via an anxiety of influence. He says:

> A poem can be *about* experience or emotion or whatever only by initially encountering another poem, which is to say a poem must handle experience and emotion as if they already were rival poems [...]. There is no unmediated vision, but only mediated revision, another name for which is anxiety.[5]

A consideration of Benjamin Britten's compositional style in the light of these Bloomian principles can be revealing: whilst it is possible to trace the anxiety of influence that is evident in his music, in so doing a clear and distinct compositional strategy emerges too. An intentional process can be discerned of the juxtaposition of diverse intertextual references and forms in order to subvert and disrupt their original meanings. This juxtaposition, I hope to show, resembles a cinematic montage, which in turn generates a narrative bred of the dialogic relation between the parts.

A student at the Royal College of Music during the early 1930s, under the instruction of John Ireland and Vaughan Williams, Britten was inevitably a product of the English Musical Renaissance, along with figures such as Parry, Holst, and Elgar. That said, apart from the occasional Lydian-dominant inflections to be found in the premeditated, pseudo-exoticism of Holst (see, for example, Holst's *Choral Hymns from the Rig Veda*), there is little in Britten's early music that overtly echoes the oppressive stylistic conservatism of the English Musical Renaissance. Rather, Britten allowed the modal ambiguity prevalent in the music of composers such as Fauré and Mahler to permeate his early work. Nevertheless, despite the tendency towards Europe, Britten could never fully circumnavigate the rather congenial tone of his contemporaries. The diatonic dissonance at the heart of the musical style of Vaughan Williams and Finzi, for example, and in particular the dissonance of the major second, made manifest in the music of the self-styled 'pastoral' school through the continued use of multiple suspensions, was to become a Britten fingerprint as his style matured. But, like Vaughan Williams (and Michael Tippett later on), Britten also became devoted to the English music of the seventeenth and eighteenth centuries, evidenced by the Purcell arrangements and the setting of *The Beggars' Opera*. Yet Purcell's influence on Britten lay mainly in economy of gesture; even though Mahler remained a more significant figure in Britten's early development, there is a sense in which Britten did not wish to show his hand too soon, for he managed to avoid the gushing emotional extravagance of the late nineteenth-century Romantic style in favour of a restrained and appropriately English linguistic register.

It is clear from Britten's diaries that the yearning to broaden his musical horizons intensified, and his initial enthusiasm for Vaughan Williams's music in particular soon turned to scorn. It is apparent, too, that Britten anticipated studying on the continent with Alban Berg, but that his well-mannered tutors at the Royal College of Music thought the Austrian to be a distinctly inappropriate influence for an English gentleman. Nevertheless, Britten's settings of the *Seven Sonnets of Michelangelo* and of Rimbaud's poems in *Les Illuminations* are indicative of an active desire to seek out and absorb a wider frame of stylistic reference. As Britten's style developed, however, a curious amalgam emerged, bringing together a range of disparate influences that went beyond the mere assimilation of other musical voices. The idea of conflict is central to his personal and musical life, and the coincidence that places this psychologically complex figure in England in the first half of the twentieth century, at a time when other English composers faced the dilemma of how to reconcile the oblique diatonicism central to the vernacular of the English Musical Renaissance with the iconoclasm of the Second Viennese School, is crucial to an understanding of the foundation of his aesthetic. Indeed, at the time when Britten's work focused on the reconciliation of these divergent artistic impulses there was both political and social turmoil in Europe, and despite Britten's strong sense of national identity, or, perhaps more significantly, his notion of community, he found himself marginalized by a society that criminalized his sexuality and condemned his pacifism to the extent that he felt it necessary to follow the example of others, like W. H. Auden and Christopher Isherwood, and seek temporary exile in the United States. Britten stayed in the US between 1939 and 1942, and it is both significant and poignant that his most English work, and his first full-scale operatic endeavour, *Peter Grimes*, should be begun during this period of self-imposed exclusion.

Whilst the seed of a compositional style which sought to combine the tonal conservatism of Britten's homeland with the modernity of Europe is evident in earlier compositions, it is clear that, following Britten's return from the United States in 1942, there emerges in his music a distinct compositional strategy that is concerned with isolation and subversion. These themes are represented in the operas by the solitary figures of Peter Grimes, The Governess in *The Turn of the Screw*, Billy in *Billy Budd*, and Aschenbach from *Death in Venice*. Subject matter such as the opposition of the individual and society, and the associations of innocence with youth contrasted with the corruption bred of experience are ever present (the attraction of the latter is evident most notably in Britten's setting of the poetry of William Blake). The music of the operas, and indeed all Britten's music from this time, contains elements of its own negation throughout, and the personal, political, and musical turmoil of Britten's life is expressed by and reflected in the development of a music–language game. This game, rather than solely reflecting Bloom's model of an anxiety of influence expressed via the misprision of a precursor, is founded in the generation of a guiding principle that seeks to foreground, then knowingly distort, the music-language-game of the precursor in order to invert or negate its traditional meaning.

Indeed, the compositional strategy evident in the *War Requiem* proves a particularly compelling example of this mode of thought, since the occasion for which it was written — the opening of the new Coventry Cathedral in 1962, in the shadow of the remains of the medieval cathedral, bombed during the Second World War

— immediately throws together the oppositions of modern and ancient. That Britten was alive to this polarity is clear. In discussing the *War Requiem* in his address 'On Receiving the First Aspen Award' he said, 'The best music to listen to in a great Gothic church is the polyphony which was written for it, and was calculated for its resonance: this was my approach in the War Requiem — I calculated it for a big, reverberant acoustic and that is where it sounds best'.[6]

The design of the new cathedral, and specifically the inclusion of the Chapel of Unity, reflected its ethos of absolution and reconciliation after conflict, with the desolate ruins of the old cathedral immovable, sentinel-like, alongside. Britten's decision, then, to compose a setting of the timeless *Missa pro defunctis*, interpolated by the relatively modern text of Wilfred Owen's war poems, whilst initially seeming quite radical to some, was entirely in keeping with this impulse. And, of course, its twofold message of warning and expression of the pity of war reflected the composer's own strong pacifist beliefs.

The *War Requiem* is divided into three distinct layers of musical activity. At the forefront are the two male soloists (representing the soldiers), who, together with the chamber orchestra, are concerned throughout with the poems of Wilfred Owen. They convey a highly emotive and personal vision of the immediacy of war and the grief of private loss. Beyond them range the large forces of the mass: soprano soloist, full chorus, and orchestra. They convey a more abstract and ritualized expression of mourning and the liturgical prayer for deliverance. Still more remote and inaccessible is the ethereal chorus of boys' voices and organ: a reflection of innocence and purity entirely at odds with the visceral world of the battlefield. Indeed, rarely in Britten's other work is the stratified layering of textural space more boldly delineated. In addition, the third level of musical activity sets the boys' choir and organ in isolation, not merely in their physical separation from the other performers, but also by virtue of the pseudo-archaic musical language that they adopt (evoking certain passages of Britten's *Missa brevis*, also composed around this time), which heightens the sense of remoteness and detachment from the raw emotive style of the soloists.

The juxtaposition of ancient and modern, sacred and secular may appear at first quite artificial, and indeed there are critics who have described the *War Requiem* as 'a paste job of past composers' creativity'.[7] However, a more considered examination of the intertextual aspects of the piece will highlight a work of considerable ingenuity and intricacy, and one that calls for a consideration of both medieval and baroque musical forms to generate a richer understanding of its essence. Laments for the dead are by no means restricted to the examples of the kind seen in the Owen settings in the *War Requiem*. The medieval planctus, for example, was a form of lament that reflected personal loss, often mourning the death of a nobleman lost in battle or sung by a mother as her son goes off to war. Whilst the main function of the medieval planctus was to lament the dead, the genre came to include a range of types from laments within a church ritual — such as those of Mary and others at the cross — to parodies of attitudes and beliefs — like Alan of Lille's medieval *Planctus naturae*. The term originally meant 'funeral lament', and it is significant that many planctus were sung in the vernacular to reinforce the communication between the listeners and the singer. By the twelfth century the planctus had a prominent role in the events of the Passion. The ability to reflect upon the anguish of the human drama of the mother allowed twelfth-century Christians a more intimate participation in a highly emotive and personalized dramatic language.

The intertextuality of the *War Requiem* establishes links with other composers and genres, including Bach and the Passion, which itself could be viewed as an extension of the planctus in its strategy of revealing doctrine through musical convention and symbols, and its ability to articulate spiritual concerns through emotional language. Throughout Bach's *St Matthew Passion*, for example, the tritone (the *diabolus in musica*, notably the interval that unifies the three musical levels of the *War Requiem*) is consistently and specifically associated with evil, and the tonal design of the piece is allegorical of spiritual concerns. In an overtly dramatic sense the Passion is presented by the Evangelist as a form of historical narrative, and Britten, in establishing this intertextual link, is alluding to both the planctus and the Passion; he also refers to the medieval Passion plays — folk dramas that supplemented the unchanging and impersonal liturgy with an intimate and immediate message.

In terms of its formal design and the moment-by-moment surface incident of the material, the *War Requiem* works on a number of intertextual levels simultaneously. Most notably, the opening of the piece, and indeed much of the rest of it, echoes Verdi's *Messa da Requiem* to such an extent that Robert Shaw described it as 'a personal paraphrase'. Throughout the *War Requiem* Britten makes use of Verdi's basic textual and formal groupings for the six movements, beginning with the pianissimo unison chanting of the *Requiem aeternam*, the brass fanfares of the *Dies irae*, the tempo, texture, and slow, plaintive lyricism of the *Lacrymosa*, the brisk fugato on 'Quam olim Abrahae', the slow, simple, hymn-like unison tone of the *Agnus dei*, and the dramatic *Libera me*, recalling the fanfares of the *Dies irae*. The following examples highlight just two instances where correlations between the works are explicit.

Ex. 15.1a

Ex. 15.1*b*

But what are we to make of this direct reference to the work of another composer? It would be simplistic to describe this response to Verdi as an unintentional anxiety of influence, and I would argue that Britten had a specific strategy in mind with this unequivocal reference to such a well-known work. *Requiem aeternam* opens clearly enough in D minor, but the tolling bells and choral incantation that are superimposed upon it oscillate between F sharp and C natural. This tritonal opposition is not merely significant because it corrupts the tonal clarity of the opening, but rather because the notes chosen essentially negate the music underneath, stressing as it does the cancellation of the modally defining minor third and major seventh of the D minor statement.

It would seem that this is not merely the misreading of a precursor in the Bloomian sense, but rather the desire to establish a music–language game and association for the express purpose of dismantling it. The choir prays for 'eternal rest', but unlike the Verdi, which is both hopeful and serene, the Britten is corrupted by these tonally negating elements, and contains a sourness that reflects the pity of mourning those who died needlessly. In this way the precursor is not negated, but rather we see its character anew, whilst Britten's music acquires a poignancy that is bred entirely of a correspondence defined by the intertextual subversion of the precursor.

The first statement of the boys' choir, supported by the organ playing simple major and minor triads, similarly creates a range of family resemblances. The melodic movement, almost entirely in fourths and fifths, evokes images of pre-tonal plainchant, but the choice of boys' voices with organ is reminiscent of the English parish church, the 'calling from sad shires' to which Owen's poetry refers. Despite the clear tonal allusions of the accompaniment and the movement in fourths and fifths of the line, the span of the melody is, once again, the tonally confounding tritone of the opening, and the nebulous, delicate quality of the 'Te decet hymnus' results from this loss of gravitational impulse through the predominance of inversional symmetry around the tritone. Symbolically, this reflects and differentiates between the heavenly and earthly planes, with the lilting duple to triple alternation of the boys' choir contrasted with the unsteady lurching quintuplets in the orchestra that open the movement.

In this passage Britten's intertextual strategy works on a subterranean as well as a surface level: whilst the foreground evokes a pseudo-archaic musical language with a melodic line moving almost entirely in fourths (here the 'playing out' of the fourth relationship in organum effects a clouding of melodic and harmonic function in the highly resonant acoustic of the cathedral), beneath it the organ's major and minor triads construct a clear tonal allusion. However, descending to a still deeper level we can see an intertextual reference that is fixed in the twentieth century, and reflects Britten's interest in Berg's serial technique. Ex.2*a* shows the melodic and harmonic content of 'Te decet hymnus', sung by the boys' choir with organ. Ex.2*b* draws attention to the fact that the root of each of these chords articulates a twelve-note row, an association that belies the nature of this music. Furthermore, the row itself, in its palindromic construction around fourths and tritones, reflects (paradoxically) the tonal opposition of the music around it. This constitutes a particularly ironic synthesis of ancient and modern, the point being in this music that nothing is what it appears to be.

Ex. 15.2*a* and *b*

Following 'Te decet hymnus' Britten's perspective changes considerably in the setting of Wilfred Owen's 'Anthem for Doomed Youth'. The textural shift from orchestra and chorus, and boys' choir with organ, to the disjunct and angular style presented by tenor soloist and chamber orchestra, now more reminiscent of Stravinsky than Verdi, places the solemnity of the Introit into stark relief. But the poem itself merits further scrutiny, not merely in terms of its content, which is significant, but also in terms of its style, which mirrors Britten's compositional strategy exactly. 'Anthem for Doomed Youth' is an elegy in sonnet form:

> What passing-bells for these who die as cattle?
> Only the monstrous anger of the guns.
> Only the stuttering rifles rapid rattle
> Can patter out their hasty orisons.
> No mockeries for them from prayers or bells,
> Nor any voice of mourning save the choirs, —
> The shrill, demented choirs of wailing shells;
> And bugles calling for them from sad shires.

What candles may be held to speed them all?
Not in the hands of boys, but in their eyes
Shall shine the holy glimmers of good-byes.
The pallor of girls' brows shall be their pall;
Their flowers the tenderness of silent minds,
And each slow dusk a drawing down of blinds.

Owen's style, like that of Britten, was criticized in this piece for being retrospective and relying too heavily upon established models. Jon Silkin, for example, described it as a relapse into a youthful Romanticism and an unintentional glorification of war.[8] The poem's language is certainly Keatsian (we are particularly reminded of lines like 'Then in a *wailful choir* the small gnats *mourn*' from 'To Autumn', which contains a number of similar images). Indeed, Owen encountered the Romantic poets at school, and he became particularly aware of Keats's vocabulary and the use of slow rhythmic effects. Consider, for example, the final line of 'Anthem for Doomed Youth' — 'And each slow dusk a drawing down of blinds' — which owes everything to the discipline instilled by Keats in 'On the Sonnet':

Let us inspect the Lyre, and weigh the stress
Of every chord, and see what may be gain'd
By ear industrious and attention meet;
Misers of sound and syllable, no less
Than Midas of his coinage, let us be
Jealous of dead leaves in the bay wreath crown;

Owen's anthem, then, is a Romantic sonnet, and positions itself in relation to (among other voices) Siegfried Sassoon and Laurence Binyon, Keats and Housman, and the classical elegists (in the same way that Britten's work positions itself with those of Bach, Mozart, and Verdi). But whilst these intertextual links between Owen and Keats are palpable, it should be recognized, too, that these allusions are meant to be noticed, rather than merely being an unintentional anxiety of influence, and as such reveal the battlefield in Owen's work as a demented parody of the Romantic landscape. In *Wilfred Owen's Voices* Douglas Kerr has applied a Bakhtinian analysis to Owen's parodic use of the elegy and dramatic monologue. Kerr demonstrates how Owen mixes the discourses of the military with those of Victorian Romantic poetry and the church (both scripture and ritual) to express the inadequacy of traditional genres of poetry and religions for responding to warfare. Owen confronts a genre, the elegy, of one discourse, poetry, with the experiences of another, the military, and 'creates a grim, covert, antagonistic dialogue with the genre'.[9] In the juxtaposition of the incongruous Owen thus subverts the traditional *raison d'être* of the sonnet and the elegy.

Both the octave and the sestet begin with questions. What burial ceremonies could be appropriate for those who die so needlessly at the front? The only appropriate 'passing bells' for those who 'die as cattle' are the guns with their 'monstrous anger'; the only suitable prayers are the 'hasty orisons' of the 'stuttering rifles' with their 'rapid rattle'; and the only music that could accompany their death would be 'the shrill demented choirs of wailing shells'. The sounds and music of traditional burials would be mere 'mockeries'. The only sound that might express the overwhelming pity of this kind of death would be the sound of 'bugles calling for them from sad shires'. The final line of the octave serves as transition to the sestet, where a similar question is asked, but this time answered using images of light: 'what candles may be held ...', '... in their eyes shall shine ...', and '... each slow dusk a drawing down of blinds'. The dynamic of the piece is generated by translating the speech and imagery of one environment into that of another. From the opening brutal depictions of the battlefield and the juxtaposition of Owen's references to a number of ecclesiastical details — passing-bells, orisons, prayers, choirs, candles, and flowers — Owen moves, in the sestet, to the private mourning of those who have lost loved ones. As Kerr suggests, the poem, 'reaches into silence on the eloquent sign of a family in mourning, the house with drawn blinds, beautifully naturalised as a figure for dusk'.[10]

In so doing, it is worth pointing out, the dramatic tension of all we have heard so far is inverted. The *War Requiem* begins with the introspection and prayer for eternal rest, followed by the disembodied sounds of the boys' choir. The setting of Owen's poem sets up a harsh intrusion, but as we move through the piece the visceral and physical descriptions of war give way to the internalization of feeling. The scene of the sestet is almost entirely interior, psychological, within the heads of the characters: 'in their eyes', in the soldiers, who are — like the acolytes at a funeral — just boys; in the 'brows' of the girls who mourn them, in 'the tenderness of silent minds'. The private grief behind the 'blinds' in the last line is really the focus of the sestet. Though the whole poem refers to the materials of ritual, the sestet moves the poem from the horror of the guns to the interior being of individuals who mourn the dead, to the 'glimmer of holiness'.

As well as the Keatsian lyricism of the lines and the dramatic juxtaposition of themes, the rhythmic drive of the poem, to which Britten responds so appropriately in the chamber orchestra's agitated accompaniment, is propelled through the use of half-rhyme and pararhymes, together with a network of alliteration and assonance that serve to emphasize the musical nature of the poem. This piece is particularly rich in these internal echo effects. For example, '*mons*(trous)' is echoed by '*guns*' in line 2; '*stutter*(ing)' by '*patter*' in lines 3 and 4; '*shrill*' by '*shell*(s)' and '*call*(ing)' in lines 7 and 8; '*boys*' by '*eyes*' in line 10; and'*pall*(or) and '*pall*' in line 12. Owen also skilfully uses onomatopoetic effects in the first half of the octave. In the two key words in the phrase 'monstrous *a*nger of the g*u*ns', the words have their vowels echoed in a series of assonances ('r*a*ttle, st*u*ttering ... r*a*pid, r*a*ttle, p*a*tter) that reflect the debilitating cacophony of irregular artillery and rifle fire.

It is clear that the use of such a provocative text at this point in the *War Requiem* serves to subvert the nature of the opening material, with the heavy intoning tritone of the choir and bells transformed into the uneasy and restless tremolo figure played by harp, itself underpinned by the sprightly and rhythmically dislocated bass line that offers a sharp contrast to the conjunct and uniform gestures preceding it. It is notable, too, that the chamber orchestra enters before the choir and orchestra have ended, creating a blurring or dovetailing effect that is accentuated not only in the timbral contrasts, but also in pitch clashes between the F natural woodwind and the F sharp bells, choir, and harp. This quasi-cinematic cross-fading is once again emphasized by the highly resonant acoustic of the cathedral setting.

The process of cross-fading between orchestral groups and formal sections can, in fact, be explored in terms of the principles of cinematic montage, and a consideration of the nature of montage itself provides a revealing perspective in an examination of the music–language game that Britten plays in this piece. In cinematography our perception of movement and the illusion of continuity are created by the juxtaposition of a series of discrete images resulting in a composite image — an internal representation — that may give the impression of movement or, more generally, the impression of being 'in' a particular environment. This internal representation is the result, on the perceiver's part, of an association of ideas and images presented in sequential succession. The film theorist Christian Metz describes montage as

> in a sense, an analysis, a sort of articulation of the reality shown on the screen. Instead of showing us an entire landscape, a filmmaker will show us successively a number of partial views, which are broken down and ordered according to a very precise intention.[11]

Both musically and dramatically Britten had already gained insight and experience of dramatic montage and cross-fading through his work with the Post Office Film Unit in London in the 1930s, and had employed aspects of montage in *Peter Grimes* and *The Turn of the Screw*.

In Act II, scene 1 of *Peter Grimes* the Lydian-inflected D major material of the 'Sunday morning interlude' is resisted by the B flat–E flat oscillation of bells from inside the church. Even more cinematic in style is the ensuing cross-fading between Ellen's questioning of the boy and the ritualistic incantation of the service within. Against the sureness and conviction of the Borough folk we hear Ellen's doubts and misgivings until, finally realizing the implications of the boy's torn coat (that is, that Grimes is once again mistreating the boy), she undoes the collar of his shirt and comments 'A bruise, well, it's begun' at the same moment that the Rector ends with the assurance, full of tragic irony, 'As it was in the beginning, is now ...' (and, presumably, ever shall be).

In Act II, scene 2 of *The Turn of the Screw*, the children (Flora and Miles) are waiting to go into church with Mrs Grose (the housekeeper) and the Governess. Initially all appears well, with the chiming F sharp bell reflected in the open, triadic nature of the children's melody as they sing 'O sing unto them a new song' and 'Let the congregation praise him'. But even at this point the word 'Bless' is sung to E natural (the flattened seventh of the mixolydian mode), suggesting perhaps that all may not be what it seems. The ever-optimistic Mrs Grose enters in B major, thus rendering the E natural diatonic again, but her enthusiasm for papering over the cracks that appears in their pastoral idyll is short-lived, and by her third phrase she too has cadenced in F sharp mixolydian. But the lack of dramatic resolution is underpinned by her final F sharp being read as the fifth of the diminished seventh on B sharp at this point. The darkness of the scene develops, with the children's 'Praise ye the Lord' giving way to 'O ye paths and woods' (echoing Quint's incantation at the end of Act I) and the pagan 'O ye dragons and snakes, worms and feathered fowl', now more witches' spell than Christian prayer. Ironically, Mrs Grose's encouraging 'They're so happy with you' in a clear F sharp major is negated by the tritonally opposed C major of the orchestra. This treatment of the material sets up a montage of three dramatic elements:

the children's incantation beginning on F sharp, the Governess's assertion that the children are 'talking horrors' and are under the sway of the ghosts, whilst Mrs Grose tries in vain to act as if nothing is amiss. Apart from the modal shifts and chromatic inflections that colour the text in this passage, the music lurches within just a few bars from F sharp mixolydian, A sharp minor, C major, and back to F sharp mixolydian. All this takes place with the ostinato-like offstage church bells calling attention to the pedal F sharp that underpins most of the scene.

The presentation of these spatially separated ensembles, unfolding simultaneously, underscores the notion of resistance and negation at the heart of Britten's aesthetic, and the conflict of sacred and secular realms in these examples strongly prefigures the scenario of the *War Requiem*. Of course, nearly a decade after the *War Requiem*, Britten's interest in cinematic technique resulted in *Owen Wingrave*, the opera composed in 1971 specifically for BBC television. In Act 1, sc.2, for example, the action cuts between characters and places: Owen at Hyde Park, and Miss Wingrave at her Baker Street address, a scene in which a single event is witnessed by both characters from radically opposing viewpoints.

Indeed, for the film director and theorist Sergei Eisenstein, the element of opposition and conflict is central to the idea of montage. He asks: 'By what, then, are montage and its embryo — the frame — characterised? By collision, by the conflict of two fragments placed side by side. By conflict. By collision', whilst Christian Metz defined montage as 'the structuring of intelligible coherence by means of various conjunctures.[12] The implication here is that montage becomes a principle of narrative, a means of communicating concepts through the collision of two or more frames that are seemingly independent of one another. An example of this notion in action can be seen in Japanese hieroglyphs in which two independent characters (or frames) are juxtaposed and 'explode' into a concept. So, for example:

eye + water	=	crying
door + ear	=	eavesdropping
child + mouth	=	screaming

In Britten's setting of the Requiem we might represent the relationship between the parts, and the image they create, as:

Requiem +	**Intrusion**	=	**Subversion**
hope	violence		turmoil
rest	interruption		upheaval
peace	inversion		optimism

The effect might be compared to the moment in a wedding service when the priest asks if anyone in the congregation knows of any reason why the couple should not be married. Although the wedding is a celebration, the moment is always a slightly uncomfortable one, since the clergyman is inviting intrusion, and indeed inversion, of the predominant imagery: that of integrity, fidelity, and truth. The difference in the *War Requiem* is that we actually witness a dramatic lurch from the formal, almost abstract ritualistic expression of mourning to an immediate and visceral world of here and now — the battlefield where we hear of those who 'die as cattle'.

But it is important to recognize that the image created in the *War Requiem* does not come about simply through the unapologetic juxtaposition of unlike material. The nature of a dramatic 'frame' is that it is defined in terms of its interpretation as an element of discourse, defined by its total relationship with other frames that precede and follow it. Indeed, it could be argued that the frame does not have meaning outside this system of dialogic relations. Moreover, the frame will carry with it a number of codes that may operate outside its normal sphere of reference, and the combination of frames and the 'image' they create will be determined by the reading of a range of cultural codes, and not just by an understanding of the highly coded structure and syntax of musical signification. For Eisenstein, an image is a selection and combination of representations: at midnight the hands of a clock form a representation of 12.00 pm; but the image of midnight consists of all the representations associated with that hour (whether that means contemplating the arrival of the witching hour or catching the 'midnight train to Georgia'). A montage, then, becomes a sequence of representations that when combined together create a dynamic image, a narrative that can be called a 'mode of knowing or comprehending', not so much of a story or chain of events, but rather of a complex of meanings, values, attentions, and emotions.

In the *War Requiem* the instrumental and vocal forces themselves signify as much as the purely musical rhetoric they articulate. In the same way that the combination of the frames 'eye' + 'water' can signify 'crying', and the tritonal opposition of the musical material can signify corruption, so, too, the three strata of the *War Requiem* signify through the cultural associations of their respective sound worlds. The full chorus and orchestra characterize the establishment, the formal and traditional mode of expression of the many, in an idiom removed from our everyday language of discourse. This is the sound world of Britten's heritage, the empire building of Elgar, Parry, and the English choral tradition. If this association with convention is not specific enough, then the self-conscious and unashamed echoes of Verdi serve to underscore it. The children's chorus with organ connotes innocence, purity, and a distance from corruption bred of experience. The image of the parish church, King's College Chapel on Christmas Eve, schooldays, and play all inform our reading of these sounds, irrespective of the musical material itself, even though, as we have seen, the impressions of simplicity and antiquity are merely a trick of the light, where the surface incident of this music conceals a deliberately modernistic scheme, and the transparently tonal references are ironically subverted by the constant insinuation of tritonal opposition.

By contrast, the solo tenor with chamber orchestra passages — the stop–start rhythmic dislocation of the orchestral lines and the personal and highly emotive English text — reveal modern images of resentment, bitterness, and pity, but also (and most significantly) further shade the cultural readings of the more 'traditional' setting of the requiem that preceded them, with what Britten, the atheist and pacifist, would have seen as the hypocrisy and moral bankruptcy of the establishment laid bare; a system which condones the corruption of innocence by allowing the church to sanction and bless wars they themselves never have to fight. We might express this equation in cinematic terms by saying that 'shot' A (chorus and orchestra) is 'read' both in terms of its individual significance and in terms of its dialogic significance to shot B (children's chorus and organ), but that shot C (tenor solo and chamber orchestra) also serves to 're-frame' shots A and B, resulting in a kind of 'seeing-after-the-event', or what Wittgenstein described as 'aspect change': our ability to perceive a single stimulus from completely differing perspectives (indeed, exactly the kind of dramatic montage that Britten was to use so effectively in *Owen Wingrave*).

Throughout the *War Requiem* Britten presents a complex blend of shifting per-spectives — from churchyard to battlefield, from public mourning to individual anger. In calculating the composition for a cathedral space, Britten also exploits the available acoustic to enhance a feeling of the simultaneous presence of diverse musics. This is appropriate in a setting that combines and contrasts the architecture of the Gothic with the modern, the ancient text of the *Missa pro defunctis* with Owen's war poetry, and the sacred with the secular. The antiphonal effect produced by the different orchestral groups, and the stylistic allusions associated with each underpin the intertextual subversion at the heart of Britten's compositional process. Through the collision of these musico-dramatic frames, the differing elements of the *War Requiem* serve to articulate one another more fully by placing each nuance of style in high relief. We hear, for example, the Latin texts bound into a traditional rhythm and phraseology, whilst the settings of Owen have sometimes a suspended motion, sometimes a vacillating rhythmic pulse that clearly establishes a 'modern' reference. By juxtaposing diverse literary and musical elements, Britten was interested in focusing attention explicitly on contrast and ambiguity, which play an important role in defining musical processes at all levels. We see, therefore, the development of a music–language game that takes as its main strategic impulse an aesthetic of intertextual subversion that goes beyond Bloom's notion of 'antithetical completion'. Britten neither imitates nor alludes to other settings solely through an unintentional anxiety of influence. His imitations and allusions are part of an intentional rhetoric of intertextuality that seeks to redefine, analyse, and re-present. Through the processes of intertextual subversion and montage Britten 'decodes' or interprets the text that he seeks to subvert, whether musical or literary, and then 'encodes' it for his own use, creating a dialogic chain of musical and cultural references that results in a dynamic and multi-faceted narrative.

Notes to Chapter 15

1. Harold Bloom, *The Anxiety of Influence: A Theory of Poetry* (London: Oxford University Press, 1973), p. 5.
2. Bloom, p. 6.
3. Kevin Ernest Korsyn, 'Towards a New Poetics of Musical Influence', *Music Analysis*, 10 (1991), 3–72 (p. 8).
4. Bloom, p. 5.
5. Bloom, quoted by Korsyn, p. 8.
6. Benjamin Britten, *On Receiving the First Aspen Award* (London: Faber & Faber, 1964), p. 11; repr. in *Britten on Music*, ed. by Paul Kildea (Oxford: Oxford University Press, 2003), pp. 255–63 (p. 256).
7. Robert Shaw, 'The Text of Britten's War Requiem', in *Five Centuries of Choral Music: Essays*, ed. by Gordon Paine (Stuyvesant, NY: Pendragon, 1988), pp. 357–83 (p. 360).
8. Jon Silkin, *Out of Battle: The Poetry of the Great War* (London: Oxford University Press, 1972), pp. 210–11.
9. Douglas Kerr, *Wilfred Owen's Voices* (New York: Oxford University Press, 1993), p. 290.

10. Kerr, p. 82.

11. Christian Metz, 'Film Language: A Semiotics of the Cinema' (1968), repr. in *Narrative, Apparatus, Ideology: A Film Theory Reader*, ed. by Philip Rosen (New York: Columbia University Press, 1986), pp. 31–91 (p. 40).

12. Sergei Eisenstein, quoted by Metz, p. 51.

BIBLIOGRAPHY

ABBATE, CAROLYN, *Unsung Voices: Opera and Musical Narrative in the Nineteenth Century* (Princeton, NJ: Princeton University Press, 1991)

ADAMS, STEPHEN J., 'Ezra Pound and Music' (unpublished doctoral thesis, University of Toronto, 1974)

ADORNO, THEODOR W., *Mahler: A Musical Physiognomy*, trans. by Edmund Jephcott (Chicago: University of Chicago Press, 1992)

AHREND, THOMAS, 'Das Verhältnis von Musik und Sprache bei Nietzsche', *Nietzscheforschung*, 2 (1995), 153–66

ALBRIGHT, DANIEL, *Representation and the Imagination: Beckett, Kafka, Nabokov, and Schoenberg* (Chicago: University of Chicago Press, 1981)

—— *Untwisting the Serpent: Modernism in Music, Literature, and Other Arts* (Chicago: University of Chicago Press, 2000)

ALLISON, DAVID B., 'Some Remarks on Nietzsche's Draft of 1871 "On Music and Words"', *New Nietzsche Studies*, 1 (1996), 15–41

ANON., 'The Education of Women', *Nature*, 10 (17 September 1874), 395–96

AYREY, CRAIG, 'Universe of Particulars: Subotnik, Deconstruction, and Chopin', *Music Analysis*, 17 (1998), 339–81

BAILEY, DEREK, *Improvisation* (Ashbourne: Moorland, 1980)

BAIR, DEIRDRE, *Samuel Beckett: A Biography* (London: Vintage, 1990)

BAKHTIN, MIKHAIL, *Problems of Dostoevsky's Poetics* (1928), ed. and trans. by Caryl Emerson (Manchester: Manchester University Press, 1984)

—— 'Toward a Methodology for the Human Sciences', in *Speech Genres and Other Late Essays*, trans. by Vern McGee (Austin: University of Texas Press, 1986), pp. 159–72

—— 'Author and Hero in Aesthetic Activity', in *Art and Answerability: Early Philosophical Essays*, trans. by Vadim Liapunov (Austin: University of Texas Press, 1990), pp. 4–256

—— 'The Problem of Content, Material, and Form in Verbal Art', in *Art and Answerability* (see previous), pp. 257–325

—— *Toward a Philosophy of the Act*, trans. by Vadim Liapunov (Austin: University of Texas Press, 1993)

BALAYÉ, SIMONE, *Les Carnets de voyage de Madame de Staël* (Geneva: Droz, 1971)

—— 'Fonction romanesque de la musique et des sons dans *Corinne*', *Romantisme*, 3 (1972), 2–32

BARLOW, GEORGE, 'White', in *The Poetical Works*, 11 vols (London: Henry T. Glaisher, 1902–14), II, 119

BARRELL, JOHN, *English Literature in History, 1730–80: An Equal, Wide Survey* (Hutchinson: London, 1983)

—— *The Birth of Pandora and the Division of Knowledge* (London: Macmillan, 1992)

BARTHES, ROLAND, *Image, Music, Text*, ed. and trans. by Stephen Heath (New York: Hill and Wang, 1977)

BARTLETT, ROSAMUND, *Wagner and Russia* (Cambridge: Cambridge University Press, 1995)

BARTOLI, JEAN-PIERRE, 'Symphonie fantastique', in *Dictionnaire Berlioz*, ed. by Pierre Citron and Cécile Reynaud (Paris: Fayard, 2003), pp. 537–41

BARZUN, JACQUES, *Berlioz and the Romantic Century* (New York: Columbia University Press, 1950)

BATTEUX, CHARLES, *Les Beaux-Arts réduits à un même principe* (Paris: Durand, 1746)

BAUER-LECHNER, NATALIE, *Gustav Mahler in den Erinnerungen von Natalie Bauer-Lechner* (1923), ed. by Herbert Killian (Hamburg: Wagner, 1984); Eng. trans. as *Recollections of Gustav Mahler*, trans. by Dika Newlin, ed. by Peter Franklin (London: Faber, 1980)

BECKETT, SAMUEL, 'Dante... Bruno. Vico.. Joyce', in *Our Exagmination Round his Factification for Incamination of Work in Progress* (1929) (London: Faber, 1972), pp. 3–22

—— *Watt* (1953) (New York: Grove, 1959)

—— *Collected Poems, 1930–1978* (London: Calder, 1984)

BEKKER, PAUL, *Gustav Mahlers Sinfonien* (Berlin: Schuster & Loeffler, 1921)

BENDER, BERT, 'The Teeth of Desire: *The Awakening* and *The Descent of Man*', *American Literature*, 63 (1991), 459–73

BENJAMIN, ANDREW, ed., *Judging Lyotard* (London: Routledge, 1992)

BENJAMIN, WALTER, *Illuminations*, trans. by Harry Zohn, ed. by Hannah Arendt (New York: Schocken, 1969)

BENNINGTON, GEOFFREY, 'Is It Time?', in *Interrupting Derrida* (London: Routledge, 2000), pp. 128–40

—— and JACQUES DERRIDA, *Jacques Derrida* (Paris, Seuil: 1991)

BERGSON, HENRI, *Essai sur les données immédiates de la conscience* (Paris: Alcan, 1889)

BERLIOZ, HECTOR, 'Aperçu sur la musique classique et la musique romantique', *Le Correspondant*, 22 October 1830

—— *Le Retour à la vie. Mélologue, faisant suite à la Symphonie fantastique* (Paris, Schlesinger, 1832)

—— *Symphonie fantastique* (Paris: Schlesinger, 1855)

—— *À travers chants* (1862) (Paris: Calmann-Lévy, 1927)

—— *Symphonie fantastique*, ed. by Nicholas Temperley, New Berlioz Edition, 16 (Kassel and London: Bärenreiter, 1972)

—— *Correspondance générale*, ed. by Pierre Citron, 8 vols (Paris: Flammarion, 1972–2003)

—— *Mémoires* (1870), ed. by Pierre Citron (Paris: Flammarion, 1991)

—— *Lélio, ou Le retour à la vie*, ed. by Peter Bloom, New Berlioz Edition, 7 (Kassel and London: Bärenreiter, 1992)

—— *La Critique musicale, 1823–1863*, ed. by H. Robert Cohen and Yves Gérard (Paris: Buchet-Chastel, 1996–), I: *1823–1834* (1996); II: *1835–1836* (1998)

BERNSTEIN, SUSAN, *Virtuosity of the Nineteenth Century: Performing Music and Language in Heine, Liszt, and Baudelaire* (Stanford, CA: Stanford University Press, 1998)

BIELIK-ROBSON, AGATA, 'Bad Timing: The Subject as a Work of Time', *Angelaki*, 5.3 (2000), 71–91

BLOOM, HAROLD, *The Anxiety of Influence: A Theory of Poetry* (London: Oxford University Press, 1973)

—— *A Map of Misreading* (Oxford: Oxford University Press, 1975)

BOHRER, KARL HEINZ, 'Utopie des "Augenblicks" und Fiktionalität. Die Subjektivierung von Zeit in der modernen Literatur', in *Plötzlichkeit. Zum Augenblick des ästhetischen Scheins* (Frankfurt a.M.: Suhrkamp, 1981), pp. 180–218

BORGES, JORGE LUIS, 'Tlön, Uqbar, Orbis Tertius' (1947), in *Labyrinths: Selected Stories and Other Writings*, ed. by Donald A. Yates and James E. Irby (Harmondsworth: Penguin, 1970), pp. 32–33

BØRTNES, JOSTEIN, 'Polyphony in *The Brothers Karamazov*: Variations on a Theme', *Canadian-American Slavic Studies*, 17 (1983), 402–11

BOSSE, MONIKA, '"Ce hasard qui m'entraîna dans la carrière littéraire": *Les Lettres sur les ouvrages et le caractère de J.-J. Rousseau* (1788)', *Cahiers staëliens*, 42 (1990–91), 29–47

BOURDILLON, FRANCIS WILLIAM, 'The Spinet', in *Young Maids and Old China* (London: Marcus Ward, 1888), n.p.

BOWEN, JOSÉ, 'Finding the Music in Musicology: Performance History and Musical Works', in *Rethinking Music* (see Cook and Everist, below), pp. 424–51

BOWMAN, FRANK P., 'Communication and Power in Germaine de Staël: Transparency and Obstacle', in *Germaine de Staël: Crossing the Borders*, ed. by Madelyn Gutwirth, Avriel Goldberger, and Karyna Szmurlo (New Brunswick, NJ: Rutgers University Press, 1991), pp. 55–68

BREIG, WERNER, 'The Musical Works', in *Wagner Handbook*, ed. by Ulrich Müller and Peter Wapnewski, translation ed. by John Deathridge (Cambridge, MA: Harvard University Press, 1992), pp. 439–51

BRITTEN, BENJAMIN, *On Receiving the First Aspen Award* (London: Faber & Faber, 1964); repr. in *Britten on Music*, ed. by Paul Kildea (Oxford: Oxford University Press, 2003), pp. 255–63

BROOKS, PETER, *Reading for the Plot: Design and Intention in Narrative* (New York: Knopf, 1984; repr. Cambridge, MA: Harvard University Press, 1992)

BROWN, CALVIN S., *Music and Literature: A Comparison of the Arts* (Athens, GA: University of Georgia Press, 1948)

BROWN, JOHN, *An Estimate of the Manners and Principles of the Times* (London, 1757)

—— *Letters upon the Poetry and Music of the Italian Opera Addressed to a Friend by the Late John Brown* (London, 1789)

BROWN, THOMAS EDWARD, 'Preparation', in *Poems*, 2 vols (Liverpool: University Press of Liverpool, 1952), II, 380–81

BUELOW, GEORGE J., 'Rhetoric and Music: Musical Figures', in *The New Grove Dictionary of Music and Musicians*, ed. by Stanley Sadie and John Tyrrell, 29 vols (London: Macmillan, 2001), XXI, 236

BURTT, SHELLEY, *Virtue Transformed: Political Argument in England, 1688–1740* (Cambridge: Cambridge University Press, 1992)

BUSH, RONALD, '"Quiet, Not Scornful"? The Composition of *The Pisan Cantos*', in *A Poem Containing History: Textual Studies in 'The Cantos'*, ed. by Lawrence S. Rainey (Ann Arbor: University of Michigan Press, 1997), pp. 169–211

BUTT, JOHN, 'Bach's Metaphysics of Music', in *The Cambridge Companion to Bach*, ed. by John Butt (Cambridge: Cambridge University Press, 1997), pp. 46–59

CADUFF, CORINA, 'Vom "Urgrund" zum Supplement. Musik in den Sprachtheorien von Rousseau, Nietzsche und Kristeva', *Musik & Ästhetik*, 1.3 (1997), 37–54

CAMPIONI, GIULIANO, 'Wohin man reisen muß', *Nietzsche-Studien*, 16 (1987), 209–26

CARPENTER, HUMPHREY, *A Serious Character: The Life of Ezra Pound* (New York: Delta, 1988)

CATTEAU, JACQUES, *Dostoyevsky and the Process of Literary Creation*, trans. by Audrey Littlewood (Cambridge: Cambridge University Press, 1989)

CELESTINI, FEDERICO, 'Tra sinfonia e romanzo. Gustav Mahler e la totalità del mondo', *Il Territorio*, 10.2 (2002), 61–72

CHEYNE, GEORGE, *The English Malady* (London, 1733)

CHOPIN, KATE, *The Awakening; and Other Stories*, ed. by Pamela Knights (Oxford: Oxford University Press, 2000)

CIXOUS, HÉLÈNE, 'Le Rire de la Méduse', *L'Arc*, 61 (1975), 39–54

CLARKE, ERIC, 'Generative Principles in Musical Performance', in *Generative Processes in Music: The Psychology of Performance, Improvisation, and Composition*, ed. by John Sloboda (Oxford: Oxford University Press, 1988), pp. 1–26

—— 'Mind the Gap: Formal Structures and Psychological Processes in Music', *Contemporary Music Review*, 3 (1989), 1–13

COLERIDGE, MARY ELIZABETH, *The Lady on the Drawing-Room Floor* (London: Edward Arnold, 1906)

——'To a Piano', in *Poems* (London: Elkin Mathews, 1908), p. 58

COLVILL, ROBERT, 'To the Elegant Seraphina, Performing on the Piano forte, at a Private Concert', in *The Poetical Works* (London: Dodsley, 1789), pp. 97–99

CONRAD, PETER, *Romantic Opera and Literary Form* (Berkeley: University of California Press, 1977)

COOK, NICHOLAS, *Music, Imagination, and Culture* (Oxford: Oxford University Press, 1990)

——'Perception: A Perspective from Music Theory', in *Musical Perceptions*, ed. by Rita Aiello (Oxford: Oxford University Press, 1994), pp. 64–95

——*Music: A Very Short Introduction* (Oxford: Oxford University Press, 1998)

——'Between Process and Product: Music and/as Performance', *Music Theory Online*, 7.2 (2001) <http://www.societymusictheory.org/mto/issues/mto.01.7.2.cook.html> [accessed 19 October 2005]; repr. in condensed form as 'Music as Performance', in *The Cultural Study of Music: A Critical Introduction*, ed. by Martin Clayton, Trevor Herbert, and Richard Middleton (New York: Routledge, 2003), pp. 204–14

——and Mark Everist, eds., *Rethinking Music* (Oxford: Oxford University Press, 1999)

[C.R.], *Danger of Masquerades* (London, 1718)

CUILLÉ, TILI BOON, 'Women Performing Music: Staging a Social Protest', *Women in French Studies*, 8 (2000), 40–54

CUNNINGHAM, DAVID, 'Trinitarian Theology in *The Brothers Karamazov*', in *Dostoevsky and the Christian Tradition*, ed. by George Pattison and Diane Oenning Thompson (Cambridge: Cambridge University Press, 2001), pp. 134–55

DA SOUSA CORREA, DELIA, *George Eliot, Music and Victorian Culture* (Basingstoke: Palgrave, 2002)

DAHLHAUS, CARL, 'Style', in *The New Grove Wagner*, ed. by John Deathridge and Carl Dahlhaus (London: Macmillan, 1984), pp. 111–26

——'Counterpoint, §17', in *The New Grove Dictionary of Music and Musicians*, ed. by Stanley Sadie and John Tyrrell, 29 vols (London: Macmillan, 2001), VI, 568–69

DARWIN, CHARLES, *The Descent of Man, and Selection in Relation to Sex*, 2 vols (London: John Murray, 1871)

DAVIES, STEPHEN, 'Authenticity in Musical Performance', *British Journal of Aesthetics*, 27 (1987), 39–50

——'Transcription, Authenticity and Performance', *British Journal of Aesthetics*, 28 (1988), 216–27

DEHON, CLAIRE L., 'Corinne: Une artiste héroïne de roman', *Nineteenth-Century French Studies*, 9 (1980–81), 1–9

DELEUZE, GILLES, and FELIX GUATTARI, *Anti-Oedipus*, I: *Capitalism and Schizophrenia*, trans. by Robert Hurley and others (Minneapolis: University of Minnesota Press, 1977)

DENEYS-TUNNEY, ANNE, 'Corinne by Madame de Staël: The Utopia of Feminine Voice as Music within the Novel', *Dalhousie French Studies*, 28 (1944), 55–63

DENORA, TIA, *Music in Everyday Life* (London: Routledge, 2000)

DERRIDA, JACQUES, 'Tympan', in *Marges de la philosophie* (Paris: Minuit, 1972), pp. i–xxv; Eng. trans. in *A Derrida Reader: Between the Blinds*, ed. by Peggy Kamuf (New York: Harvester Wheatsheaf, 1991), pp. 148–68

——*Glas* (Paris: Galilée, 1974); Eng. trans. by John P. Leavey and Richard Rand (Lincoln: University of Nebraska Press, 1986)

——*La Carte postale, de Socrate à Freud et au-delà* (Paris: Flammarion, 1980); Eng. trans. by Alan Bass (Chicago: University of Chicago Press, 1987)

——*Psyché. Inventions de l'autre* (Paris: Galilée, 1987)

——'The Deaths of Roland Barthes', trans. by Pascale-Anne Brault and Michael Naas, in *Philosophy and Non-Philosophy since Merleau-Ponty*, ed. by Hugh J. Silberman (London: Routledge, 1988), pp. 259–96

——'Signature Event Context', in *Limited Inc*, trans. by Samuel Weber and Jeffrey Mehlman (Evanston, IL: Northwestern University Press, 1988), pp. 1–23

——*Donner le temps 1. La fausse monnaie* (Paris: Galilée, 1991); Eng. trans. by Peggy Kamuf (Chicago: University of Chicago Press, 1992)

——*Acts of Literature*, ed. by Derek Attridge (London: Routledge, 1992)

——'Demeure. Fiction et témoignage', in *Passions de la littérature*, ed. by Michel Lisse (Paris: Galilée, 1996), pp. 13–74

——'La Langue de l'autre', *Les Inrockuptibles*, 115 (20 August–2 September 1997), 36–43

——(unsigned) 'Le Musicien, le philosophe et les fanatiques', *Jazz Magazine*, 473 (1997), 26–28

——'La Langue de l'étranger, discours de réception du prix Adorno à Francfort', *Le Monde diplomatique* (January 2002), 24–27

DICKENS, CHARLES, *Dealings with the Firm of Dombey and Son, Wholesale, Retail and for Exportation* (Oxford: Clarendon Press, 1974)

DOBSON, AUSTIN, 'Gentlewoman of the Old School', in *Collected Poems*, 9th edn (London: Kegan Paul, Trench, Trübner, 1913), pp. 14–18

DÖMLING, WOLFGANG, 'Szenerie im Imaginären. Über dramatisch-symphonische Werke von Hector Berlioz', *Neue Zeitschrift für Musik*, 3 (1977), 195–203

——*Hector Berlioz. Symphonie fantastique*, Meisterwerke der Musik, 19 (Munich: Fink, 1985)

DOSTOEVSKY, FYODOR, *The Brothers Karamazov*, trans. by David McDuff (Harmondsworth: Penguin, 1993)

DREW, ELIZABETH, *The Modern Novel: Some Aspects of Contemporary Fiction* (London: Jonathan Cape, 1926)

DUBOS, JEAN-BAPTISTE, *Réflexions critiques sur la poésie et sur la peinture* (Paris: Mariette, 1719)

DUNSBY, JONATHAN, 'The Multi-Piece in Brahms: *Fantasien* Op. 116', in *Brahms: Biographical, Documentary and Analytical Studies*, ed. by Robert Pascall (Cambridge: Cambridge University Press, 1983), pp. 163–89

——*Performing Music: Shared Concerns* (Oxford: Oxford University Press, 1995)

EGGEBRECHT, HANS HEINRICH, *Die Musik Gustav Mahlers* (Munich: Piper 1982)

ELIOT, GEORGE, *Felix Holt, the Radical* (Oxford: Clarendon Press, 1980)

FLOROS, CONSTANTIN, *Gustav Mahler: The Symphonies*, trans. by Vernon Wicker (Aldershot: Scholar Press, 1994)

FORSTER, E. M., 'Word-Making and Sound-Taking', *Abinger Harvest* (London: Edward Arnold, 1936), 100–04

FREUD, SIGMUND, *Art and Literature: Jensen's 'Gravida', Leonardo da Vinci and Other Works*, The Pelican Freud Library, 14, ed. by Albert Dickenson (London: Penguin, 1985)

FROBENIUS, WOLF, 'Polyphony, I', in *The New Grove Dictionary of Music and Musicians*, ed. by Stanley Sadie and John Tyrrell, 29 vols (London: Macmillan, 2001), xx, 74–78

GALE, NORMAN ROWLAND, 'The Old Piano', in *Song in September* (London: Constable, 1912), pp. 78–80

GIBBON, EDWARD, *The History of the Decline and Fall of the Roman Empire*, ed. by J. B. Bury, 7 vols (London: Methuen, 1896–1900)

GOEHR, LYDIA, 'Being True to the Work', *Journal of Aesthetics and Art Criticism*, 47 (1989), 55–67

——*The Quest for Voice: Music, Politics, and the Limits of Philosophy* (Oxford: Oxford University Press, 1998)

GOETHE, JOHANN WOLFGANG VON, *Selected Poems*, ed. by Christopher Middleton, trans. by Michael Hamburger and others (Princeton, NJ: Princeton University Press, 1994)

GREGORY, JOHN, *A Comparative View of the State and Faculties of Man with Those of the Animal World* (London, 1766)

GREY, THOMAS S., 'A Wagnerian Glossary', in *The Wagner Compendium: A Guide to Wagner's Life and Music*, ed. by Barry Millington (London: Thames and Hudson, 1992; repr. with corrections, 2001), pp. 230–43

GROSSMAN, LEONID, 'Dostoevsky-khudozhnik', in *Tvorchestvo Dostoevskogo*, ed. by N. L. Stepanov (Moscow: Izdatel'stvo Akademii nauk, 1959), pp. 330–416

GROSSMAN, MORRIS, 'Performance and Obligation', in *What is Music? An Introduction to the Philosophy of Music*, ed. by Philip Alperson (New York: Haven, 1987; repr. with updated bibliography, University Park, PA: Pennsylvania State University Press, 1994), pp. 257–81

GUREVITCH, ZALI, 'Plurality in Dialogue: A Comment on Bakhtin', *Sociology*, 34 (2000), 243–63

GUTWIRTH, MADELYN, 'Madame de Staël, Rousseau and the Woman Question', *PMLA*, 86 (1971), 100–09

——'Woman as Mediatrix: From Jean-Jacques Rousseau to Germaine de Staël', in *Woman as Mediatrix: Essays on Nineteenth-Century Women Writers*, ed. by Avriel H. Goldberger (Westport, CT: Greenwood, 1987), pp. 13–29

HALLMARK, RUFUS E., *The Genesis of Schumann's Dichterliebe: A Source Study* (Ann Arbor: University of Michigan Press, 1979)

HAMILTON, JAMES, 'Musical Noise', *British Journal of Aesthetics*, 39 (1999), 350–63

HARDY, THOMAS, *The Complete Poetical Works of Thomas Hardy*, ed. by Samuel Hynes, 5 vols (Oxford, Clarendon Press, 1982–95), I (1982); II (1984); III (1985)

HARVEY, LAWRENCE E., *Samuel Beckett: Poet and Critic* (Princeton, NJ: Princeton University Press, 1970)

HAVERGAL, FRANCES RIDLEY, 'The Moonlight Sonata', in *The Poetical Works*, 2 vols (London: James Nisbet, 1884), II, 14–31

HEGEL, GEORG WILHELM FRIEDRICH, *The Phenomenology of Spirit*, trans. by A.V. Miller (Oxford: Oxford University Press, 1977)

HEIDEGGER, MARTIN, *Poetry, Language, Thought*, trans. by Albert Hofstadter (New York: Harper, 1975)

HELLER, PETER, *'Von den ersten und letzten Dingen'. Studien und Kommentar zu einer Aphorismenreihe von Friedrich Nietzsche,* Monographien und Texte zur Nietzsche-Forschung, 1 (Berlin: de Gruyter, 1972)

HOFFMANN, E. T. A., 'Phantasiestücke in Callots Manier', in *E. T. A. Hoffmann. Werke in vier Bänden* (Vienna: Caesar Verlag, 1980), I, pp. 37–331

—— *Tales of Hoffmann*, trans. by R. J. Hollindale, with Stella and Vernon Humphries and Sally Hayward (London: Penguin, 1982)

—— *E. T. A. Hoffmann's Musical Writings: Kreisleriana, The Poet and the Composer, Music Criticism,* ed. by David Charlton, trans. by Martyn Clarke (Cambridge: Cambridge University Press, 1989)

HOFSTADTER, DOUGLAS R., *Gödel, Escher, Bach: An Eternal Golden Braid* (New York: Basic Books, 1979)

HÖLDERLIN, FRIEDRICH, and EDUARD MÖRIKE, *Selected Poems*, ed. and trans. by Christopher Middleton (Chicago: University of Chicago Press, 1972)

HORNER, AVRIL, and SUE ZLOSNIK, *Landscapes of Desire* (London: Harvester Wheatsheaf, 1990)

HUNT, LEIGH, 'The Lover of Music to his Piano-forte', in *The Poetical Works of Leigh Hunt*, ed. by Humphrey Milford (Oxford: Oxford University Press, 1923), p. 355

INGOLDSBY, THOMAS (The Revd Richard H. Barham), 'Nell Cook', *The Ingoldsby Legends, or, Mirth and Marvels*, 3 vols (London: Richard Bentley, 1840), II, 91–99, in *Literature Online* <http://lion.Chadwyck.co.uk> [accessed 27th April 2006]

IVANOV, VYACHESLAV, *Borozdy i mezhy* (Furrows and boundaries) (Moscow: Musaget, 1916)

JANZ, CURT PAUL, 'Die Musik im Leben Friedrich Nietzsches', *Nietzsche-Studien*, 26 (1997–98), 72–86

JEAN PAUL (Johann Paul Friedrich Richter), *Titan: A Romance*, trans. by Charles T. Brooks, 2 vols (Boston, 1868)

JONES, MALCOLM, *Dostoyevsky: The Novel as Discord* (London: Elek, 1976)

JOYCE, JAMES, 'Chamber Music', in *Poems and Shorter Writings* (London: Faber, 1991), p. 14

JUNG-KAYSER, UTE, 'Die wahren Bilder und Chiffren "tragischer Ironie" in Mahlers "Erster"', in *Neue Mahleriana: Essays in Honor of Henry-Louis de La Grange on his Seventieth Birthday*, ed. by Günther Weiß (Berne: Lang, 1997), pp. 101–52

KALLBERG, JEFFERY, *Chopin at the Boundaries: Sex, History and Musical Genre* (Cambridge, MA and London: Harvard University Press, 1996)

KANT, IMMANUEL, *The Moral Law, or Kant's Groundwork of the Metaphysic of Morals*, trans. and ed. by H. J. Paton (London: Hutchinson, 1948; repr. London: Routledge, 1991)

—— *Critique of Practical Reason*, trans. by Lewis White Beck (New York: Bobbs-Merrill, 1956)

—— *Critique of Judgment*, trans. by Werner S. Pluhar (Indianapolis: Hackett, 1987)

—— *Raising the Tone of Philosophy: Late Essays by Immanuel Kant, Transformative Critique by Jacques Derrida*, ed. by Peter Fenves (Baltimore, MD: Johns Hopkins University Press, 1993)

—— *The Metaphysics of Morals*, trans. by Mary Gregor (Cambridge: Cambridge University Press, 1996)

KEATS, JOHN, *Selected Poems and Letters*, ed. by Douglas Bush (Boston: Houghton Mifflin, [1959])

KEIL, WERNER, 'Von Quarten, *Tristan*-Akkorden und "Callots Manier". Bemerkungen zur Musik Mahlers und Debussys um 1900', in *1900 Musik zur Jahrhundertwende*, ed. by Werner Keil (Hildesheim: Olms 1995), pp. 75–97

KENNEDY, SIGHLE, '"Astride of the Grave and a Difficult Birth": Samuel Beckett's *Watt* Struggles to Life', *Dalhousie French Studies*, 42 (1998), 115–47

KERMAN, JOSEPH, *Opera as Drama* (London: Cambridge University Press, 1957 [c. 1956])

KERR, DOUGLAS, *Wilfred Owen's Voices* (New York: Oxford University Press, 1993)

KIPLING, RUDYARD, 'The Song of the Banjo', *The Complete Verse* (London: Kyle Cathie, 1990), pp. 82–84

KIVY, PETER, *Fine Art of Repetition: Essays in the Philosophy of Music* (Rochester, NY: University of Rochester Press, 1992)

KNOWLSON, JAMES, *Damned to Fame: The Life of Samuel Beckett* (London: Bloomsbury, 1996)

KOMAR, ARTHUR, ed., *Robert Schumann: Dichterliebe* (New York: Norton, 1971)

KORSYN, KEVIN ERNEST, 'Towards a New Poetics of Musical Influence', *Music Analysis*, 10 (1991), 3–72

KRAMER, LAWRENCE, *Music and Poetry: The Nineteenth-Century and after* (Berkeley: University of California Press, 1984)

—— *Music as Cultural Practice, 1800–1900* (Berkeley: University of California Press, 1990)

—— *Classical Music and Postmodern Knowledge* (Berkeley: University of California Press, 1995)

—— *After the Lovedeath: Sexual Violence and the Making of Culture* (Berkeley: University of California Press, 1997)

—— *Franz Schubert: Sexuality, Subjectivity, Song*, Cambridge Studies in Music Theory and Analysis, 13 (Cambridge: Cambridge University Press, 1998)

—— *Musical Meaning: Toward a Critical History* (Berkeley: University of California Press, 2001)

—— 'Analysis Worldly and Unworldly', *Musical Quarterly*, 87 (2004), 119–39

KURTH, RICHARD, 'Music and Poetry, a Wilderness of Doubles: Heine – Nietzsche – Schubert – Derrida', *19th-Century Music*, 21 (1997), 3–37

KWASS, MICHAEL, 'Ordering the World of Goods: Consumer Revolution and the Classification of Objects in Eighteenth-Century France', *Representations*, 82 (2003), 87–116

LAMB, JONATHAN, 'Modern Metamorphoses and Disgraceful Tales', *Critical Inquiry*, 28 (2001), 133–66

LANG, ANDREW, 'The Spinet', in *Poetical Works*, 4 vols (London: Longmans, Green, 1923), II, 25

LANGER, SUSANNE K., *Philosophy in a New Key: A Study in the Symbolism of Reason, Rite and Art* (Cambridge, MA: Harvard University Press, 1942)

LAWRENCE, D. H., 'Piano', in *Complete Poems*, ed. by Vivian de Sola Pinto and Warren Roberts, 2 vols (London: Heinemann, 1972), I, 148

LEAVER, ROBIN A., 'The Mature Vocal Works', in *The Cambridge Companion to Bach*, ed. by John Butt (Cambridge: Cambridge University Press, 1997), pp. 86–122

LEAVIS, F. R., *The Living Principle: 'English' as a Discipline of Thought* (London: Chatto and Windus, 1977)

LEPPERT, RICHARD, *The Sight of Sound: Music, Representation and the History of the Body* (Berkeley: University of California Press, 1993)

LESSING, GOTTHOLD, *Laocoön, Nathan the Wise, Minna von Barnhelm*, ed. by William A. Steel (London: Dent, 1930)

LETZTER, JACQUELINE, 'Isabelle de Charrière versus Germaine de Staël: Textual Tactics in the Debate about Rousseau', *Studies on Voltaire and the Eighteenth Century*, 362 (1998), 27–40

LEVIN, DAVID MICHAEL, *The Listening Self: Personal Growth, Social Change and the Closure of Metaphysics* (London: Routledge, 1989)

LEVINAS, EMMANUEL, *Totality and Infinity: An Essay on Exteriority*, trans. by Alphonso Lingis (Pittsburgh, PA: Duquesne University Press, 1969)

—— *Otherwise than Being or Beyond Essence*, trans. by Alphonso Lingis (Pittsburgh, PA: Duquesne University Press, 1981)

——'Language and Proximity', in *Collected Philosophical Papers*, trans. by Alphonso Lingis (Dordrecht: Kluwer, 1987), pp. 109–26

—— *Existence and Existents*, trans. by Alphonso Lingis (Dordrecht: Kluwer, 1988)

LEVINSON, JERROLD, 'Evaluating Musical Performance', in *Music, Art, and Metaphysics: Essays in Philosophical Aesthetics* (Ithaca, NY: Cornell University Press, 1990), pp. 376–92

LINGIS, ALPHONSO, *The Imperative* (Bloomington: Indiana University Press, 1998)

LUCAS, JOHN, *Modern English Poetry from Hardy to Hughes* (London: Batsford, 1986)

LYOTARD, JEAN-FRANÇOIS, *Discours, Figure* (Paris: Klincksieck, 1971)

——'Judiciousness in Dispute, or Kant after Marx', in *The Aims of Representation: Subject / Text / History*, ed. by Murray Krieger (Stanford, CA: Stanford University Press, 1987), pp. 23–67

—— *The Differend: Phrases in Dispute*, trans. by Georges Van Den Abbeele (Minneapolis: University of Minnesota Press, 1988)

—— *Peregrinations: Law, Form, Event* (New York: Columbia University Press, 1988)

—— *The Inhuman: Reflections on Time*, trans. by Geoffrey Bennington and Rachel Bowlby (London: Polity, 1991)

—— *Lessons on the Analytic of the Sublime*, trans. by Elizabeth Rottenberg (Stanford, CA: Stanford University Press, 1994)

MAHLER, GUSTAV, *Selected Letters of Gustav Mahler*, orig. edn selected by Alma Mahler, enlarged and ed. by Knud Martner, trans. by Eithne Wilkins, Ernst Kaiser, and Bill Hopkins (London: Faber, 1979)

MAN, PAUL DE, *Allegories of Reading: Figural Language in Rousseau, Nietzsche, Rilke and Proust* (New Haven, CT: Yale University Press, 1979)

MARCELLO, BENEDETTO GIACOMO, *Il teatro alla moda, o sia metodo securo, e facile per ben comporre, eseguire l'opera italiane in musica all'uso moderno* (Venice, [1720])

MARSO, LORI JO, *(Un)Manly Citizens: Jean-Jacques Rousseau's and Germaine de Staël's Subversive Women* (Baltimore, MD: Johns Hopkins University Press, 1999)

MARSTON, PHILIP BOURKE, 'A Remembered Tune', in *The Collected Poems of Philip Bourke Marston* (London and Melbourne: Ward, Lock, Bowden, 1892), p. 348

MELLERS, WILFRID, *Bach and the Dance of God* (London: Faber, 1980)

MERLEAU-PONTY, MAURICE, 'What is Phenomenology', *Phenomenology of Perception*, trans. by Colin Smith (London: Routledge & Kegan Paul, 1962), pp. vii–xxi

METZ, CHRISTIAN, 'Film Language: A Semiotics of the Cinema' (1968), repr. in *Narrative, Apparatus, Ideology: A Film Theory Reader*, ed. by Philip Rosen (New York: Columbia University Press, 1986), pp. 31–91

MILLER, ROBIN FEUER, *The Brothers Karamazov: Worlds of the Novel* (New York: Twayne, 1992)

MINEAR, PAUL S., 'Bach and Today's Theologians', *Theology Today*, 202 (1985), 201–10

MITCHELL, DONALD, *Gustav Mahler: The Wunderhorn Years* (Berkeley and Los Angeles: University of California Press, 1980)

MOCHULSKY, KONSTANTIN, *Dostoevsky: His Life and Work*, trans. by Michael A. Minihan (Princeton, NJ: Princeton University Press, 1967)

MONCRIEFF, WILLIAM THOMAS, 'The Good Old English Gentlewoman', in *An Original Collection of Songs* (London: John Duncombe, 1850), pp. 150–51

MONELLE, RAYMOND, 'Text and Subjectivity', in *The Sense of Music: Semiotic Essays* (Princeton, NJ: Princeton University Press, 2000), 147–69

MORRIS, CHRISTOPHER, Review article, 'Songs of the Living Dead', *19th-Century Music*, 27 (2003), 74–93

MORSON, GARY SAUL, and CARYL EMERSON, 'Introduction: Rethinking Bakhtin', in *Rethinking Bakhtin: Extensions and Challenges*, ed. by Gary Saul Morson and Caryl Emerson (Evanston, IL: Northwestern University Press, 1989), pp. 1–60

—— *Mikhail Bakhtin: Creation of a Prosaics* (Stanford, CA: Stanford University Press, 1990)

MÜLLER-LAUTER, WOLFGANG, *Nietzsche: His Philosophy of Contradictions and the Contradictions of his Philosophy*, trans. by David J. Parent (Urbana: University of Illinois, 1999)

NANCY, JEAN-LUC, *The Experience of Freedom*, trans. by Bridget McDonald (Stanford, CA: Stanford University Press, 1993)

—— 'The Surprise of the Event', in *Being Singular Plural*, trans. by Robert Richardson and Anne O'Byrne (Stanford, CA: Stanford University Press, 2000), pp. 159–76

NATTIEZ, JEAN-JACQUES, *Music and Discourse: Toward a Semiology of Music*, trans. by Carolyn Abbate (Princeton, NJ: Princeton University Press, 1990)

NAUDIN, MARIE, 'Mme de Staël précurseur de l'esthétique musicale romantique', *Revue des sciences humaines*, 35, no. 139 (1970), 391–400

NEWMAN, GERALD, *The Rise of English Nationalism* (London: Weidenfeld & Nicolson, 1987)

NICHOLSON, JOHN, 'The Dying Lover', in *The Poetical Works* (Bradford: Thomas Brear, 1876), p. 243

FRIEDRICH NIETZSCHE, *The Birth of Tragedy; and, The Case of Wagner*, trans. by Walter Kaufmann (New York: Vintage books, 1967)

—— 'On Music and Words', trans. by Walter Kaufmann, in *Between Romanticism and Modernism: Four Studies in the Music of the Later 19th Century*, ed. by Carl Dahlhaus (Berkeley: University of California Press, 1980), pp. 106–19

—— *Human, All Too Human: A Book for Free Spirits*, trans. by R. J. Hollingdale (Cambridge: Cambridge University Press, 1986)

—— 'Description of Ancient Rhetoric (1872–73)', trans. by R. J. Hollingdale, in *Friedrich Nietzsche on Rhetoric and Language*, ed. by Sander Gilman, Carole Blair, and David J. Parent (Oxford: Oxford University Press, 1989), pp. 2–193

—— *Ecce Homo: How One Becomes What One Is*, trans. by R. J. Hollingdale (New York: Penguin, 1993)

—— *Beyond Good and Evil: Prelude to a Philosophy of the Future*, trans. by Judith Norman (Cambridge: Cambridge University Press, 2001)

NOVALIS (Friedrich Leopold von Hardenberg), 'On Goethe', in *German Aesthetic and Literary Criticism: The Romantic Ironists and Goethe*, ed. by Kathleen Wheeler (Cambridge: Cambridge University Press, 1984), pp. 102–08

O'SHAUGHNESSY, ARTHUR EDWARD WILLIAM, 'Music and Moonlight', in *Music and Moonlight: Poems and Songs* (London: Chatto and Windus, 1874), pp. 7–37

OTTO, DETLEF, 'Die Version der Metapher zwischen Musik und Begriff', in *'Centauren-Geburten': Wissenschaft, Kunst und Philosophie beim jungen Nietzsche*, ed. by Tilmann Borsche, Federico Gerratana, and Aldo Venturelli, Monographien und Texte zur Nietzsche-Forschung, 27 (Berlin: de Gruyter, 1994), pp. 167–90

PASTERNAK, LAWRENCE, ed., *Immanuel Kant: 'Groundwork of the Metaphysic of Morals' in Focus* (London: Routledge, 2002)

PAYNE, JOHN, 'At the Piano', in *Vigil and Vision: New Sonnets* (London: Villon Society, 1903), p. 48

PEARSALL, ROLAND, *Victorian Popular Music* (Newton Abbot: David and Charles, 1973)

PERLOFF, MARJORIE, *The Poetics of Indeterminacy: Rimbaud to Cage* (Princeton, NJ: Princeton University Press, 1981)

PFOHL, FERDINAND, *Gustav Mahler. Eindrücke und Erinnerungen aus den Hamburger Jahren*, ed. by Knud Martner (Hamburg: Wagner, 1973)

POCOCK, J. G. A., *The Machiavellian Moment: Florentine Political Thought and the Atlantic Republican Tradition* (Princeton, NJ: Princeton University Press, 1975)

——'The Myth of John Locke and the Obsession with Liberalism', in *John Locke: Papers Read at a Clark Library Seminar, 10 December 1977*, ed. by J. G. A. Pocock and Richard Ashcraft (Los Angeles: William Andrews Clark Memorial Library, 1980)

POPLE, ANTHONY, 'Systems and Strategies: Functions and Limits of Analysis', in *Theory, Analysis, and Meaning in Music*, ed. by Anthony Pople (Cambridge: Cambridge University Press, 1994), pp. 108–23

POUND, EZRA, 'Janequin, Francesco da Milano', *Townsman*, 1 (January 1938), 18

——*ABC of Reading* (London: Routledge, 1934; repr. London: Faber & Faber, 1951)

—— *Guide to Kulchur* (London: Faber, 1938)

—— *Collected Early Poems* (London: Faber, 1977)

—— *The Cantos*, 4th collected edn (London: Faber, 1987)

——and DOROTHY POUND, *Ezra and Dorothy Pound: Letters in Captivity, 1945–1946*, ed. by Omar Pound and Robert Spoo (New York: Oxford University Press, 1999)

PUTNAM, DANIEL, 'Music and the Metaphor of Touch', *Journal of Aesthetics and Art Criticism*, 44 (1985), 59–66

RAJAN, TILOTTAMA, 'Language, Music, and the Body: Nietzsche and Deconstruction', in *Intersections: Nineteenth-Century Philosophy and Contemporary Theory*, ed. by Tilottama Rajan and David L. Clark (Albany: State University of New York Press, 1995), pp. 147–69

REED, ARDEN, 'The Debt of Disinterest: Kant's Critique of Music', *Modern Language Notes*, 95 (1980), 563–84

RICHARDSON, SAMUEL, *Clarissa or, the History of a Young Lady: Comprehending the Most Important Concerns of Private Life … Published by the Editor of Pamela*, ed. by Angus Ross (Harmondsworth: Penguin Books, 1985)

—— *The History of Sir Charles Grandison … by the Editor of Pamela and Clarissa* (1753–54), ed. by Jocelyn Harris (Oxford: Oxford University Press, 1985)

ROBERTSON, THOMAS, *An Inquiry into the Fine Arts* (London, 1784)

ROSSETTI, DANTE GABRIEL, 'During Music', in *The Works of Dante Gabriel Rossetti: Edited with Preface and Notes by William M. Rossetti*, rev. and enlarged edn (London: Ellis, 1911), p. 195

ROUSSEAU, JEAN-JACQUES, *A Discourse to which a Prize was Adjudged … on this Question Proposed by that Academy: Whether the Re-establishment of Arts and Sciences has Contributed to Purify our Morals [First Discourse]*, trans. by R. Wynne (London, 1750)

——*Œuvres complètes*, ed. by Bernard Gagnebin and Marcel Raymond, (Paris: Gallimard, La Pléiade, 1959–), I: *Les Confessions* (1959); V: *Écrits sur la musique, la langue, et le théâtre* (1995)

——*Émile, ou de l'éducation* (Paris: Garnier Frères, 1964)

——*Essai sur l'origine des langues* (1781) (Bordeaux: Ducros, 1968)

——*On the Origin of Language: Jean-Jacques Rousseau, 'Essay on the Origin of Languages'; Johann Gottfried Herder, 'Essay on the Origin of Language'*, trans. by John H. Moran and Alexander Gode (New York: Ungar, 1966; repr. Chicago, University of Chicago Press, 1986)

—— *Collected Writings of Rousseau* (Hanover, NH: University Press of New England, 1990–), I: *Rousseau, Judge of Jean-Jacques: Dialogues*, ed. by Roger D. Masters and Christopher Kelly, trans. by Judith R. Bush (1990); VII: *Essay on the Origin of Languages and Writings Related to Music*, ed. and trans. by John T. Scott (1998)

ROWLAND, DAVID, and ROBERT SAMUELS, 'Unit 15: Gender Studies II: Schumann Song Cycles and their Singers', in *Motive, Gender and Large-Scale Form, c. 1840–1900*, Studies in Music, 1750–2000: Interpretation and Analysis, 4 (Milton Keynes: Open University, 2001), pp. 1–36

RUZICKA, PETER, 'Befragung des Materials. Gustav Mahler aus der Sicht aktueller Kompositions-ästhetik', in *Erfundene und Gefundene Musik. Analysen, Portraits und Reflexionen*, ed. by Thomas Schäfer (Hofheim: Wolke, 1998), pp. 27–38

SACHS, KURT-JÜRGN, 'Counterpoint, §§1–11', in *The New Grove Dictionary of Music and Musicians*, ed. by Stanley Sadie and John Tyrrell, 29 vols (London: Macmillan, 2001), VI, 551–61

SAMSON, JIM, ed., *The Cambridge Companion to Chopin* (Cambridge: Cambridge University Press, 1992)

SCHAFER, R. MURRAY, ed., *Ezra Pound and Music: The Complete Criticism* (London: Faber, 1978)

SCHER, STEVEN PAUL, ed., *Music and Text: Critical Inquiries* (Cambridge: Cambridge University Press, 1992)

SCHLEGEL, AUGUST WILHELM VON, *Lectures on Dramatic Art and Literature*, trans. by John Black (1811), repr. in *Four Centuries of Shakespeare Criticism*, ed. by Frank Kermode (New York: Avon, 1965)

SCHOPENHAUER, ARTHUR, *Die Welt als Wille und Vorstellung*, 2 vols (Munich: Piper, 1911)

SCRUTON, ROGER, 'Understanding Music', in *The Aesthetic Understanding* (Manchester: Carcanet, 1983), pp. 77–100

—— 'Analytical Philosophy and the Meaning of Music', *Journal of Aesthetics and Art Criticism*, 46 (1987), 169–76

—— *The Aesthetics of Music* (Oxford: Oxford University Press, 1997)

SEAVER, RICHARD, ed., *I Can't Go On, I'll Go On: A Samuel Beckett Reader* (New York: Grove Weidenfeld, 1976)

SEKORA, JOHN, *Luxury: The Concept in Western Thought, Eden to Smollett* (Baltimore, MD: Johns Hopkins University Press, 1977)

SHAFFER, L. HENRY, 'Cognition and Effect in Musical Performance', *Contemporary Music Review*, 4 (1989), 381–89

SHAKESPEARE, WILLIAM, *The Two Noble Kinsmen*, in *The Riverside Shakespeare*, ed. by G. Blakemore Evans (Boston: Houghton Mifflin, 1974), pp. 1639–82

—— *The Winter's Tale*, in *The Riverside Shakespeare*, ed. by G. Blakemore Evans (Boston: Houghton Mifflin, 1974), pp. 1564–1605

—— *The Sonnets & A Lover's Complaint* (Harmondsworth: Penguin, 1986)

SHARP, WILLIAM, 'During Music', in *Earth's Voices, Transcripts from Nature, Sospitra, and Other Poems* (London: Elliot Stock, 1884), pp. 114–15

SHATTUCK, ROGER, *The Banquet Years: The Origins of the Avant-Garde in France, 1885 to World War I*, rev. edn (New York: Vintage, 1968)

SHAW, ROBERT, 'The Text of Britten's War Requiem', in *Five Centuries of Choral Music: Essays*, ed. by Gordon Paine (Stuyvesant, NY: Pendragon, 1988), pp. 357–83

SHOWALTER, ELAINE, 'Tradition and the Female Talent: *The Awakening* as a Solitary Talent', in *New Essays on The Awakening*, ed. by Wendy Martin (Cambridge: Cambridge University Press, 1988), pp. 33–57

—— *Sexual Anarchy: Gender and Culture at the Fin de Siècle* (New York: Viking, 1990)

SILKIN, JON, *Out of Battle: The Poetry of the Great War* (London: Oxford University Press, 1972)

SILVERMAN, HUGH, ed., *Lyotard: Philosophy, Politics, and the Sublime* (New York: Routledge, 2002)

SMALL, CHRISTOPHER, *Musicking: The Meanings of Performing and Listening* (Hanover, NH: University Press of New England, 1998)

SMEND, F., 'Die Johannes-Passion von Bach. Auf ihren Bau untersucht', *Bach-Jahrbuch*, 23 (1926), 105–28

SMITH, ADAM, *An Inquiry into the Nature and Causes of the Wealth of Nations* (1776), cd. by Edwin Cannan, 2 vols (London: Methuen, 1961)

SMITH, F. JOSEPH, *The Experiencing of Musical Sound: Prelude to a Phenomenology of Music* (New York: Gordon & Breach, 1979)

SMOLLETT, TOBIAS, *The Expedition of Humphry Clinker*, ed. by Lewis M. Knapp, rev. by Paul-Gabriel Boucé (Oxford: Oxford University Press, 1984)

SOKOLOWSKI, ROBERT, 'The Issue of Presence', *Journal of Philosophy*, 77 (1980), 631–43

SOLIE, RUTH, 'Whose Life? The Gendered Self in Schumann's *Frauenliebe* Songs', in *Music and Text: Critical Inquiries* (see Scher, above), pp. 219–40

SOLOMON, MAYNARD, *Beethoven* (New York: Schirmer, 1977)

—— *Beethoven Studies* (Cambridge, MA: Harvard University Press, 1988)

SPONHEUER, BERND, 'Dissonante Stimmigkeit. Eine rezeptionsgeschichtliche Studie zum dritten Satz der Mahlerschen Ersten', in *Gustav Mahler*, ed. by Hermann Danuser (Darmstadt: Wissenschaftliche Buchgesellschaft, 1992), pp. 165–71

SPRINKER, MICHAEL, 'Poetics and Music: Hopkins and Nietzsche', *Comparative Literature*, 37 (1985), 334–56

STAËL, GERMAINE DE, *Corinne, ou l'Italie* (1807), ed. by Simone Balayé (Paris: Gallimard, 1985); Eng. trans. by Avriel H. Goldberger (New Brunswick, NJ: Rutgers University Press, 1987)

—— *De la littérature*, ed. by Gérard Gengembre and Jean Goldzink (Paris: Flammarion, 1991)

—— *Lettres sur les ouvrages et le caractère de J.-J. Rousseau*, in *Madame de Staël: Œuvres de jeunesse*, ed. by Simone Balayé and John Isbell (Paris: Desjonquères, 1997)

STAROBINSKI, JEAN, *Jean-Jacques Rousseau. La Transparence et l'obstacle suivi de sept essais sur Rousseau* (Paris: Gallimard, 1971); Eng. trans. by Arthur Goldhammer (Chicago: Chicago University Press, 1988)

—— 'Critique et principe d'autorité (Madame de Staël et Rousseau)', in *Le Préromantisme. Hypothèque ou hypothèse?*, ed. by Paul Viallaneix (Paris: Klincksieck, 1975)

—— Introduction to Jean-Jacques Rousseau, *Essai sur l'origine des langues*, in *Œuvres complètes*, v (see Rousseau, above)

STARRETT, SHARI NELLER, 'Nietzsche on Music: Womb/Birth Allegories and Analogies', *International Studies in Philosophy*, 28.3 (1996), 33–38

STEINER, WENDY, ed., *The Sign in Music and Literature* (Austin: University of Texas Press, 1981)

STRAVINSKY, IGOR, *Igor Stravinsky: An Autobiography* (1936), with an introduction by Eric Walter White (London: Calder and Boyars, 1975)

STRINDBERG, AUGUST, *The Chamber Plays*, trans. by Evert Spinchorn, Seabury Quinn, Jr, and Kenneth Petersen (New York: Dutton, 1962)

STRONG, TRACY B., 'Nietzsche and the Song in the Self', *New Nietzsche Studies*, 1 (1996), 1–14

SUBOTNIK, ROSE ROSENGARD, REVIEW OF *Musical Elaborations* by Edward Said, *Journal of the American Musicological Society*, 46 (1993), 476–85

TATLOW, RUTH, 'Number Symbolism', in *J. S. Bach*, ed. by Malcolm Boyd (Oxford: Oxford University Press, 1999), pp. 320–21

TAUSSIG, MICHAEL, '"Dying is an Art, Like Everything Else"', *Critical Inquiry*, 28 (2001), 305–16

TENENBAUM, SUSAN, 'Liberal Heroines: Mme de Staël on the "Woman Question" and the Modern State', *Annales Benjamin Constant*, 5 (1985), 37–52

TERRAS, VICTOR, *A Karamazov Companion: Commentary on the Genesis, Language and Style of Dostoevsky's Novel* (Madison: University of Wisconsin Press, 1981)

TERRELL, CARROLL F., *A Companion to the Cantos of Ezra Pound* (Berkeley: University of California Press, 1984)

THOMPSON, DIANE OENNING, *Dostoevsky and the Poetics of Memory* (Cambridge: Cambridge University Press, 1991)

TIFFANY, DANIEL, 'Lyric Substance: On Riddles, Materialism, and Poetic Obscurity', *Critical Inquiry*, 28 (2001), 72–99

TODD, NEILL, 'A Model of Expressive Timing in Tonal Music', *Music Perception*, 3 (1985), 33–58

TROUILLE, MARY, 'A Bold New Vision of Woman: Staël and Wollstonecraft Respond to Rousseau', *Studies on Voltaire and the Eighteenth Century*, 292 (1991), 293–324

TURRELL, MARTIN, *Baudelaire: A Study of his Poetry* (New York: New Directions, 1954)

URMSON, J. O., 'The Ethics of Musical Performance', in *The Interpretation of Music: Philosophical Essays*, ed. by Michael Krausz (Oxford: Clarendon Press, 1993), pp. 157–64

VALLOIS, MARIE-CLAIRE, *Fictions féminines: Mme de Staël et les voix de la Sibylle* (Saratoga, CA: Anma Libri, 1987)

VOGÜÉ, E.-M. DE, *Le Roman russe* (Paris: Plon-Nourrit, 1886)

WADE, THOMAS, 'Written after Hearing Great Music', in *The Poems and Plays of Thomas Wade*, ed. by John L. McLean (Troy, NY: Whitston, 1997), p. 368

WAGNER, RICHARD, *Wagner on Music and Drama*, ed. by Albert Goldman and Evert Sprinchorn, trans. by H. Ashton Ellis (London: Gollancz, 1970)

WAITE, EDWARD, 'House Fantastic', in *The Collected Poems of Arthur Edward Waite* (London: William Rider, 1904), p. 112

WALDER, DENNIS, ed., *The Nineteenth Century Novel: Identites* (New York: Routledge, 2001)

WALLACE, ROBERT K., *Emily Bronte and Beethoven: Romantic Equilibrium in Fiction and Music* (Athens, GA, and London: University of Georgia Press, 1986)

WARMINSKI, ANDRZEJ, 'Introduction: Allegories of Reference', in Paul de Man, *Aesthetic Ideology* (Minneapolis: University of Minnesota Press, 1996), pp. 1–33

WATT, WILLIAM, 'Stanzas on Hearing a Young Lady Perform on the Piano Forte', in *Poems, on Sacred and Other Subjects, Humorous and Sentimental* (Glasgow: William Eadie, 1860), p. 254

WELIVER, PHYLLIS, *Woman Musicians in Victorian Fiction, 1860–1900: Representations of Music, Science and Gender in the Leisured Home* (Aldershot: Ashgate, 2000)

WHEELER, KATHLEEN, ed., *German Aesthetic and Literary Criticism: The Romantic Ironists and Goethe* (Cambridge: Cambridge University Press, 1984)

WITTGENSTEIN, LUDWIG, *Philosophical Investigations* (1953), trans. by G. E. M. Anscombe (Oxford: Basil Blackwell, 1972)

WORDSWORTH, WILLIAM, *The Oxford Authors: William Wordsworth*, ed. by Stephen Gill (Oxford: Oxford University Press, 1984)

WRATISLAW, THEODORE, 'Le Piano que baise', in *Caprices* (London: Gay and Bird, 1893), p. 26

YOUNG, JULIAN, *Nietzsche's Philosophy of Art* (Cambridge: Cambridge University Press, 1992)

ŽIŽEK, SLAVOJ, *The Abyss of Freedom*; with F. W. Schelling, *Ages of the World*, trans. by Judith Norman (Ann Arbor: University of Michigan Press, 1997)

INDEX